MW00748240

INTERNATIONAL DEVELOPMENT IN FOCUS

Achieving the Demographic Dividend in the Arab Republic of Egypt

Choice, Not Destiny

SAMEH EL-SAHARTY, HEBA NASSAR, SHERINE SHAWKY, AMR ELSHALAKANI,
MARIAM M. HAMZA, YI ZHANG, AND NAHLA ZEITOUN, EDITORS

Contents

Tables

Foreword

There is a strong link between demographics and economic growth, as demonstrated by the demographic dividend—the economic benefits accruing when a country undergoes a rapid decline in mortality, and then fertility, with a consequent demographic transition. As countries achieve lower fertility and fewer children per household, a growing working-age population will increase productivity and per capita income, leading to accumulated savings, investments, and economic growth.

The Arab Republic of Egypt was well along the path to achieving its demographic dividend at the turn of this century, but that progress has temporarily stalled. Fortunately, the country has the opportunity to regain the dividend in the coming decade, and this report—a collaborative venture between a team of Egyptian and World Bank experts from different disciplines—suggests the way forward.

The report reviews the trends in determinants of the rising total fertility rate (TFR), the factors that may have led to the reversal in fertility decline, the government's initial response and plans, and the sectoral and social drivers that may have contributed to this reversal. An important contribution of this report is an assessment of the economic impact of the demographic changes, including estimates of savings forgone as a result of increased fertility and the potential future gains from an accelerated fertility decline. Finally, on the basis of available global evidence, the report proposes six policy and strategic priorities, complemented by four policy imperatives.

The six priorities include increasing the contraceptive prevalence rate, which is a key strategy for helping to lower the TFR and no doubt the most important of the six; reducing school dropouts; increasing female labor force participation; delaying early marriage; leveraging social protection programs; and improving governance of the population program.

Concomitant policies include ensuring broad-based socioeconomic development, including creating productive jobs; investing in and leveraging human capital; enhancing financial inclusion and entrepreneurship, especially for women; and sustaining macroeconomic stability and ensuring policy predictability.

We believe that this report will be an important contribution to the population agenda in Egypt and will contribute to the government's ongoing efforts and plans to address the country's population challenges. Egypt certainly has the political will, resources, and capacity to achieve its demographic dividend.

Marina Wes
Regional Director,
Arab Republic of Egypt, Republic
of Yemen, and Djibouti
The World Bank

Keiko Miwa
Director for Human Development,
Middle East and North Africa Region
The World Bank

Acknowledgments

This report is a product of the Human Development Practice Group in the Middle East and North Africa (MENA) department at the World Bank Group.

The report was prepared under the direction of Marina Wes (Country Director, Arab Republic of Egypt, Republic of Yemen, and Djibouti), Keiko Miwa, (Regional Director, Human Development, MENA), and Rekha Menon (Practice Manager; Health, Nutrition and Population; MENA).

The report was prepared by a team led by Sameh El-Saharty (Lead Health Specialist) and composed of Amr Elshalakani (Senior Health Specialist and Co-Team Leader) and the following chapter co-authors: Heba Nassar (Health Economics Consultant, chapter 5); Sherine Shawky (Public Health Consultant, chapters 2 and 3); Abdo S. Yazbeck (Health Economics Advisor, chapters 1 and 6); Yi Zhang (Health Economist, chapters 1 and 5); Mariam M. Hamza (Health Economist, Introduction and chapter 5); and Seemeen Saadat (Reproductive Health Consultant, Introduction and chapters 2 and 4). Contributions to chapters 4 and 7 were made by Nahla Zeitoun (Senior Social Protection Specialist), Bridget Crumpton (Senior Education Specialist), Cornelia Jesse (Senior Education Specialist), Amira Kazem (Senior Operations Officer), and Souraya El-Assiouty (Social Protection Consultant).

The report benefited from useful and constructive comments from the following peer reviewers: Sameera Al-Tuwaijri (Global Lead, Population and Development), Syud Amer Hasan (Senior Economist), and Rifat Hasan (Senior Health Specialist).

The team would like to express its gratitude to the different ministries and organizations that reviewed the report and provided detailed comments, including the Ministry of Health and Population, the Ministry of Planning and Economic Development, the Ministry of Social Solidarity, the National Council for Women, the National Population Council, and the Cairo Demographic Center. Specifically, the team would like to thank H. E. Dr. Tarek Tawfik, Deputy Minister of Health and Population for Population; H. E. Dr. Ahmed Kamaly, Deputy Minister, Ministry of Planning and Economic Development; and Dr. Amira Tawadros, Director of Cairo Demographic Center, for their technical comments that have greatly enriched the final report.

The team is grateful for the upstream comments received during the report preparation from Daniel Lederman (Deputy Chief Economist) and Marcio Cruz (Senior Economist), on the macroeconomic analysis; and Emi Suzuki (Demographer) and Toshiko Kaneda (Senior Research Associate, Population Reference Bureau), on the demographic projections; and from Maria Laura Sanchez Puerta (Program Leader, Human Development). The report was edited by Jonathan Aspin (Consultant) and Seemeen Saadat (Consultant). Mariam W. Guirguis (Operations Analyst), Iman Sadek (Team Assistant), Juliana Williams (Team Assistant), and Hanzada Aboudoh (Senior Executive Assistant) provided administrative support. Maissa Abdalla (External Communications Officer) managed the launch, media relations, and dissemination of the report.

The report was partially funded by the World Bank Global Financing Facility.

Executive Summary

IT'S NOT TOO LATE FOR THE ARAB REPUBLIC OF EGYPT TO CLAIM ITS DEMOGRAPHIC DIVIDEND

Egypt exhibited a strong track record of managing population growth in the two decades through 2008. Replicating that record is vital for Egypt to achieve its demographic dividend, defined as the "economic benefit to a country that can happen within a window of 15 to 20 years when it undergoes a demographic transition due to a rapid decline in mortality followed by a rapid decline in fertility" (Hasan et al. 2019, 1).

Key investments in family planning (FP) and reproductive health, and in women's empowerment, contributed to an impressive decline in the country's total fertility rate (TFR), from 4.5 to 3.0 births per woman between 1988 and 2008 (MOHP, El-Zanaty and Associates, and ICF International 2015). However, between 2008 and 2014, the TFR began climbing—reaching 3.5 births per woman in 2014. This reversal was not only alarming but has been seen in only a handful of countries worldwide.

The reversal saw the annual population growth rate increase and led to changes in demographic and socioeconomic indicators. By 2014, a "youth boom" had been recorded, with 33.2 percent of the population under the age of 14 years, whereas 5.1 percent of the population was age 60 and above. This reversal led to an increase in the dependency ratio (youth and old-age) from 59.6 to 61.8 percent between 2010 and 2014, thus delaying the demographic dividend. This report therefore aims to support evidence-based policy dialogue on achieving the demographic dividend in the context of recent population changes in Egypt.

TRENDS IN DETERMINANTS OF THE RISING TFR

Contrary to generally observed fertility behavior worldwide, Egypt's increase in fertility was led by more-educated women in urban areas, and the urban population generally led the reversal in the fertility decline after 1992. Between 2008 and 2014, though, rural fertility also began to increase. Fertility was highest among younger women, with a 26 percent increase in fertility between 2008 and 2014 among women ages 20–24 years. From 2003, fertility among the highest wealth quintile rose steadily, though between 2008 and 2014 fertility increased across all wealth quintiles, with the sharpest increase in the middle quintile.

After 2005, the greatest increase in desired fertility was among urban, educated women, with women in the middle wealth quintile having the fastest rate of increase in desired fertility. The median age at first marriage saw a decline for women with secondary education and may have declined slightly for those with tertiary education, while it continued to rise for other cohorts.

In keeping with these trends, the overall contraceptive prevalence rate (CPR) has stagnated since 2003, and in fact fell considerably in the youngest age groups. Reflecting the desire for a larger number of children, the CPR between 2008 and 2014 also declined most for women with one or two children. The CPR either stagnated or fell in both rural and urban areas.

A STRATEGY AND PLAN TO REVERSE THE RISING TFR

The Egypt National Population Strategy 2015–2030 (ENPS 2015–2030) and its associated first five-year Egypt Population Implementation Plan 2015–2020 (EPIP 2015–2020) came as critical responses to the rising TFR.

ENPS 2015–2030 identified the key population challenges as the post-January 2011 decline in public resources for FP; a decline in FP social marketing and media campaigns; rising poverty; the increasing influence of the "conservative wave" that opposes women's empowerment, including fertility choices; and continuing geographic disparities in population and development indicators. It noted the need for multisectoral collaboration and investment to address the underlying causes of rising fertility and identified the National Population Council (NPC) as the responsible agency for ensuring collaboration across different ministries.[1]

EPIP 2015–2020 set as its priority the reduction of the population growth rate. Largely following the above strategy, it set targets for health and other sectors. These were not achieved, however, for reasons including fragmented governance, poor accountability, wavering political commitment, and rapid turnover in the leadership of the NPC; a 50 percent shortfall in funding; a failure to expand geographic coverage of services (reflecting shortfalls in funding, in doctors in primary health care units (PHCUs), and in mobile clinic visits); and weak data analysis.

DEMOGRAPHIC CHANGES BETWEEN 2015 AND 2020

To analyze the impact of the strategy and plan, a diagnostic was carried out using data from the Central Agency for Public Mobilization and Statistics (CAPMAS); however, except for population size, CAPMAS has no indicators on demographic changes. The analysis therefore used proxy indicators for the TFR, including the crude birth rate (CBR) and general fertility rate (GFR), alongside the data on population size. The analysis was conducted at national and subnational levels and revealed that the national figures masked wide geographic disparities.

The years from 2015 to 2019 saw declines in the national GFR and CBR. The GFR declined from 123 to 97 children per 1,000 women; the CBR declined from 30.2 to 23.4 live births per 1,000 population. However, because of the population momentum (the increase of the population driven by the young age structure), the population reached 98.9 million on January 1, 2020—higher than the strategy's target of 94 million for 2020.

In education, the school dropout rate for students ages 4–18 years was 2.6 percent in 2006 (CAPMAS 2006). Data for 2018/19 from the Ministry of Education and Technical Education indicate a national dropout rate of 0.25 percent at primary level and 2.0 percent at secondary level (MOETE 2020), pointing to marginal progress. Similarly, little progress was made on illiteracy, which stood at 25.8 percent according to the 2017 census (CAPMAS 2017). Female unemployment, however, turned in a small improvement, declining from 24.2 percent in 2015 to 21.4 percent in 2018.

For a more geographically nuanced perspective, analysis at the governorate level was conducted using the following five social indicators and drawing heavily on CAPMAS (2020) for the source data:

- *Live births.* The CBR was higher in urban than rural areas, but the pace of its decline between 2016 and 2019 was faster in rural areas (27.2 percent) than in urban areas (8.5 percent). Governorates have four "demographic profiles" based on their progress in controlling live births: those with a *high* likelihood and *high* concentration of live births (and so should be prioritized for interventions); those with a *high* likelihood and *low* concentration; those with *low* likelihood and *high* concentration; and those with a *low* likelihood and *low* concentration.

- *Marriage contracts.* The national average marriage contract rate declined slightly, from 10.3 to 9.1 contracts per 1,000 population between 2016 and 2018. Delaying marriages *can* help delay childbearing but did not in fact achieve this in all governorates. In some, with a relatively low rate of marriage, childbearing is higher once married, and these governorates therefore have a strong need for FP interventions.

- *School dropouts.* According to the 2017 census (CAPMAS 2017), school dropouts, especially among adolescent girls, are often linked to early childbearing and high fertility. Several governorates exhibited high rates of school dropouts and high rates of live births.

- *Female unemployment.* The potential for higher fertility increases when unemployment, particularly among women, lowers the cost of childbearing, which was evident in seven governorates that also exhibited high rates of school dropouts.

- *Illiteracy.* With 25.8 percent of the population unable to read or write according to the 2017 census, illiteracy remains a challenge. Its rate exceeded the national average in nine governorates, of which eight exhibited increased likelihood and/or concentration of live births.

The link between high rates of live births, school dropouts, and female unemployment appeared strong in several governorates, and there was an association between high rates of live births, marriage contracts, and illiteracy. These findings underscore the need for a fundamental shift in how Egypt addresses high fertility and population issues, and they emphasize the importance of developing geographically tailored interventions.

SECTORAL AND SOCIAL DRIVERS OF FERTILITY

Health

EPIP 2015–2020 supported scaling up availability of FP services in PHCUs across the country; expanding FP services in remote and underserved areas through mobile clinics; and building capacity and enhancing quality, including provider training, among other initiatives. Outstanding challenges include the shortage of funding and lack of donor support for FP, an inadequate number of PHCUs providing FP services, and PHCUs still suffering from a shortage, particularly, female physicians.

Primary and secondary education

In 2019/20, school enrollment was 100 percent at the primary level; the net enrollment rate was 97.6 percent at the lower-secondary level and 76.6 percent at the upper-secondary level (MOETE 2020). Remaining issues include a sharp fall in enrollment at the upper-secondary level as of 2018 (El-Laithy 2021); failure to translate girls' outperformance at the end of secondary exams into labor market participation or into a decrease in fertility, poor quality of education; a mismatch between what is taught and labor-market needs; and little teaching on population issues and reproductive health.

Tertiary education

Enrollment climbed from 2.7 million to 3.2 million in 2015–20, and female enrollment in public universities accounts for 55 percent of the total (CAPMAS 2019; World Bank 2021). Still, Egypt needs to tackle limited funding and teaching capacity, which have given rise to overcrowding in public universities; the increase in the number of graduates, which has been faster than the growth of the labor market, affecting women's marriage and childbearing behavior; and the concentration of female enrollment at diploma or bachelor level and on humanities and social sciences.

Labor force participation

Women's employment fell from 22 percent in 2006 to a mere 17 percent in 2018, and joblessness among women increased from 25.8 percent to 27.8 percent between 2012 and 2018. A large portion of Egyptian youth are not in education, employment, or training (Amer and Atallah 2019). Between 1998 and 2018, the rate of women laborers with an intermediate education plummeted from over 40 percent to 20 percent. Women face a host of challenges in getting jobs: the decline in public sector jobs, the main employer for women with higher education; low quality of vacancies in the private sector; difficulties in managing the "double burden"—responsibilities at home and at work; and scarcity of access to childcare.

Poverty and social protection

Poverty exacerbates to increased fertility. About 3.2 percent of Egyptians live on less than the international poverty line of US$1.90 (2011 PPP US$) per day; and only 4.1 percent of Egyptians are considered multidimensionally poor, which reflects Egypt's strong performance on dimensions such as consumption, schooling, and access to basic utilities. Yet, the share of the poor measured using the national poverty lines rose from 25.2 percent in 2010 to an estimated 29.7 percent in 2019/20 (CAPMAS 2020).

In 2014, among the lowest two wealth quintiles, the fertility rate was 3.6 children per woman, higher than the national average of 3.5; the age at marriage was the lowest among all wealth quintiles (18.9 and 19.6 years, respectively); and contraceptive use was lower than the national average, at 55.9 and 55.7 percent, respectively (MOHP, El-Zanaty and Associates, and ICF International 2015). Different social reasons may explain these patterns. The poorest families consider children as a source of income, and having more children guarantees income—which could also lead to high rates of school dropouts—and a source of safety nets for parents in old age. With limited income, families face the burden of paying the direct and indirect expenses for FP services (if available); and with high illiteracy rates, mass communication campaign messages may not be that effective.

Gender and social norms

Gender and social norms affect fertility through at least four pathways. First, *early marriage* is still common practice in Egypt despite laws banning child marriage, with an estimated 6 percent and 27 percent of married females ages 15–17 years and 18–19 years, respectively. Second is *norms* that support the idea that having a big family strengthens solidarity (*ezwah*). And some families prefer boys, which may lead them to keep having children until a boy is born. Third, *cultural and religious attitudes* have become more conservative, reflecting the rise of the religious wave over the past decade or so. More pronounced among poor, uneducated, and rural residents, they have also crept into the lives and lifestyles of wealthier, educated, and urban residents (World Bank 2018). Such views on FP may well increase fertility rates, as some conservative groups oppose the use of contraceptives. Finally, *gender gaps* in access to education and employment, due to preferential treatment of sons, help perpetuate women's cycle of poverty and lack of opportunity.

These sectoral and social factors drive demographic changes, which in turn have a huge economic impact.

THE ECONOMIC IMPACT

Retrospective projections of forgone savings and opportunity cost

Demographic changes can affect economic prosperity through changes in the dependency ratio and working-age share of the population (the percentage of population ages 15–64 years in the total population). An increase in the relative number of people in the economy who are able to work will increase income, assuming jobs are available. The literature has shown that the economic impact associated with the demographic dividend is highly significant in terms of magnitude and duration, as seen in, for example, the panel data analysis of the fixed-effects model used to estimate the relationship between population age structures and gross domestic product (GDP) and gross domestic savings (Cruz and Ahmed 2018).

On the basis of its TFR, Egypt was considered an early-dividend country when fertility began to increase, shortening the window for demographic gains. The working-age share of the population increased between 1990 and 2010, but it then started to decline because of higher fertility and population momentum, from nearly 63 percent in 2010 to 61 percent in 2020.

A hypothetical scenario of a continued fertility decline was constructed to forecast various demographic indicators if the fertility decline had continued after 2000. Its results suggest that if, after 2000, the TFR had continued to decline at its earlier-trend rate of 1970–2000, by 2020 it would have fallen to 1.96 births per woman instead of rising to 3.26 births per woman; the population would have been 92.6 million, not 101.7 million; the dependency ratio would have fallen to 50 percent, not risen to 64 percent; and the working-age share of the population would have seen a continued increase past 2011.

Those forecast population data were then used to assess, in real retrospective projections, the forgone savings in public expenditure and welfare opportunity costs of Egypt's population growth over 2005–20 and of the reversal of the fertility decline. The real *forgone savings* (that is, inflation-adjusted) between 2007/08 and 2019/20 in public expenditure on health, housing, and education is estimated at a total of LE 93.46 billion: LE 27.48 billion for health; LE 18.79 billion for housing; and LE 47.19 billion for education. In terms of *welfare opportunity costs*, the analysis showed that a continued decline in fertility would have made GDP per capita grow 4.4 percentage points faster, for an LE 149.8 billion increase in 2019 GDP.

Applying the econometric model used by Cruz and Ahmed (2018) to Egypt indicates that if fertility had continued to decline, per capita GDP in 2019 would have been LE 2,000 higher and aggregate GDP about LE 150 billion higher. Applying the same analysis on gross domestic savings shows that its share of the GDP would have increased to 21.0 percent instead of 13.9 percent, which would be associated with greater investment and economic growth.

Egypt has therefore already forgone large economic gains by failing to claim its demographic dividend. But what would its economic gains be by 2030 if it could start to "bend the fertility curve"?

Prospective estimates

Using the same two-pronged approach used in the retrospective analysis, *prospective* estimates of potential savings in public expenditure and gains in national income from 2020 to 2030 under two hypothetical scenarios were made against a default projection (based on the United Nations medium-fertility variant population projection), which has a TFR of 2.9. The first assumes a moderate decline to a TFR of 2.5, and the second assumes an accelerated decline to a TFR of 2.1 births per woman—that is, the replacement level of fertility—by 2030. All other conditions are held constant. Cumulative potential savings under the moderate and accelerated scenarios, respectively, would amount to LE 4.25 billion and LE 8.79 billion for health, LE 4.76 billion and LE 9.83 billion for housing, and LE 3.60 billion and LE 7.69 billion for education.

Projected GDP under the two scenarios would be lower than that under the default scenario for the first few years, but after 2024 the trend reverses, with the potential cumulative gain in GDP between 2020 and 2030 reaching LE 569.02 billion.

The potential economic benefits from fertility decline are therefore huge, but reaping them requires policies and strategies based on the best available evidence (with the caveat that no two countries are the same, nor are the areas within a country like Egypt).

BEST GLOBAL PRACTICES AND EVIDENCE FOR LOWERING FERTILITY

FP, including reproductive health care, stands out as one of the most cost-effective development interventions to support fertility decline, with every US$1 invested in meeting unmet need for contraceptives yielding an average of US$120 in accrued annual benefits over the long term (FP2020 n.d.). Postpartum FP services, particularly facility based, have the highest impact among all FP service delivery approaches (HIPs 2017). Investing in training community health workers and expanding mobile outreach services would increase contraceptive use in communities where access is otherwise difficult.

Reducing costs of FP services can also further their uptake. For example, evidence from Latin America showed that the CPR was 16.5 percentage points higher among insured women than uninsured women (Fagan et al. 2017). Exposure to mass media programs can also increase modern contraceptive use in a variety of settings, and when coupled with interpersonal communication channels, had high impact with an odds ratio of 1.51 (Weinberger et al. 2019). Global experience also shows that the most successful interventions are those that address both demand for and supply of FP services, as well as the underlying drivers of fertility, especially education. Specifically, evidence has shown that promoting girls' secondary education supports fertility reduction by delaying the age of marriage and enabling young women to make informed decisions about FP. In Brazil, for example, improvements in schooling of girls accounted for about 70 percent of the fertility decline observed in the country during the 1960s and 1970s (Lam and Duryea 1999).

Certainly, evidence from Egypt's own experience between 1980 and 2008 showcases successful reduction in fertility through investment in FP, an expanded contraceptive method mix, incentives to enhance performance of FP providers, and mass-mass media campaigns that engage religious leaders.

SIX POLICY AND STRATEGIC PRIORITIES

The demographic dividend can be achieved in two phases. The first appears as the growing labor force supports fewer children, that is, the dependency ratio falls. The second arises when production is increased and savings build up, leading to increasing investment in human and physical capital (Birdsall, Kelley, and Sinding 2004). The bonus from the first is transitory, while the second produces lasting benefits in the form of greater productivity growth and sustainable development.

The demographic dividend represents an opportunity for—not a guarantee of—greater prosperity and improved living standards (World Bank and IMF 2016). Yet Egypt's population is expected to grow as a result of population momentum, to 159.9 million by 2050 (United Nations World Population Prospects database). However, with an accelerated fertility decline, 2050's population can be pegged at a lower 141.0 million. The actual outcome, of course, will largely depend on how the government implements policies to slow population growth and benefit from the youth bulge, complemented with socioeconomic development interventions that affect people's decisions on the number of children to have. Six policy and strategic priorities are pivotal:

- **Increasing the CPR** through expanding the capacity of the Ministry of Health and Population (MOHP) to provide FP services with a focus on developing human resources, building capacity, and expanding coverage; reintroducing the postpartum contraception program at general and district hospitals; expanding FP services in the public sector to all hospitals and clinics of the Health Insurance Organization; engaging nongovernmental organizations and the private sector more fully; improving the supply chain and quality of contraceptive methods and expanding the method mix; and investing in demand generation.
- **Reducing school dropouts** and increasing girls' enrollment by expanding the secondary-school base, promoting community schools, and ensuring that schools are safe and safely accessible; discouraging dropping out using measures to incentivize education and tracking attendance with systems that flag students at risk of dropping out; empowering girls through creating girls' clubs, teaching life skills, and ensuring availability of feminine hygiene products; giving greater priority to education on sexual and reproductive health; and promoting distance learning approaches.
- **Increasing the female labor force participation rate** and improving women's employability by reducing the skills mismatch between their education and labor market needs; providing support services such as career counseling; creating an enabling and conducive environment for female employment; improving access to affordable childcare; combating all forms of violence and enforcing the legislation on violence against women and girls and sexual harassment; and addressing social norms, attitudes, and gender stereotypes.
- **Delaying early marriage** through empowering girls; engaging parents and communities; improving formal schooling and education opportunities for girls; providing incentives and economic support such as cash transfers; and enacting supportive laws and policies.
- **Leveraging social protection programs** through capitalizing on the cash transfer Takaful and Karama program (TKP) to expand its reach for promoting girls' education and women's access to health, especially FP services; leveraging the existing TKP infrastructure (including the Grievance Redress Mechanism) and social accountability tools and mechanisms (Social Accountability Committees, among others) to address broader issues such as harassment or lack of childcare for female employees; and expanding on-the-job training and adult literacy programs (El-Laithy 2021).
- **Improving governance of the population program** through establishing a strong, independent, and stable institutional framework; providing legal and regulatory support; developing geographically differentiated subnational implementation plans; and developing a national dashboard to monitor progress on the population program.

Ensuring a broad-based socioeconomic development policy

These six priorities need policy support to ensure sustained, inclusive growth characterized by strong leadership and governance; macroeconomic stability (so that markets work); a market orientation to guide structural change; an outward orientation to achieve scale and impose discipline; and a future orientation to boost savings and meet investment needs (Commission on Growth and Development 2008). For Egypt, this translates into the following four policy imperatives:

- **Creating productive jobs** through ensuring an economic transformation to increase productivity within sectors as well as reallocating labor (among other factors of production) toward more productive sectors (McMillan et al. 2017); getting the enabling environment right; for the private sector, reducing barriers to competition; and ensuring that both the supply and demand sides (including reducing informality) are well aligned to absorb the labor force across different income levels (Troiano 2015). Such measures are needed to overcome the feeble labor-productivity growth of the last 15 years or so.
- **Investing in and leveraging human capital** through investing in early childhood development, education, and vocational and technical training; expanding vocational and on-the-job training; enhancing labor market mobility; and investing more in human development.
- **Enhancing financial inclusion and entrepreneurship, especially for women,** through ensuring a conducive legal, regulatory, and business enabling environment, and bringing more women into the formal financial system.
- **Sustaining macroeconomic stability and ensuring policy predictability** through laying the foundation for the second phase of the demographic dividend, notably through consolidating the country's public finances; enhancing government fiscal and debt management and transparency; and improving the business environment, including cutting red tape, especially that related to taxes and customs.

The way forward and a time frame

A time frame with immediate (within 1 year), short to medium (1–3 years), and long-term (2–5 years) activities aims to ensure optimal sequencing of implementation; harmonization and complementarity across priorities; and expectation-setting about the implementation timeline and expected results from each intervention (table ES.1). Successful and timely implementation will allow Egypt to fully claim its long-delayed demographic dividend. The president's "Decent Life Initiative," launched in January 2019, and the "National Project for the Development of the Egyptian Family," launched in February 2022, can be used as the platform to implement many of the proposed policies and strategies.

TABLE ES.1 Proposed time frame for the policy and strategic priorities

	IMMEDIATE (WITHIN 1 YEAR)	SHORT-MEDIUM (1–3 YEARS)	LONG-TERM (2–5 YEARS)
Increasing the contraceptive prevalence rate (CPR)	• Meeting unmet need • Reintroducing the postpartum contraception program • Improving the supply chain and quality of methods • Expanding the capacity of the Ministry of Health and Population (MOHP) to provide family planning (FP) services • Generating demand for FP use	• Expanding FP services in the public sector • Reducing contraceptive discontinuation • Engaging nonpublic-sector providers • Expanding the method mix in the public and private sectors	
Reducing school dropouts	• Reducing girls' dropouts • Prioritizing education on sexual and reproductive health (SRH)	• Increasing girls' enrollment, particularly at secondary level	• Creating an enabling environment to incentivize girls' retention in education

continued

TABLE ES.1, *continued*

	IMMEDIATE (WITHIN 1 YEAR)	SHORT-MEDIUM (1–3 YEARS)	LONG-TERM (2–5 YEARS)
Increasing female labor force participation	• Providing support services that facilitate female employment	• Combating violence against women and girls • Creating an enabling and conducive environment for female employment • Addressing impediments in the private sector	• Addressing the social norms and values system • Boosting women's participation in promising new sectors
Delaying age of marriage	• Enforcing laws and policies • Engaging parents and communities	• Improving formal schooling and education opportunities for girls	
Leveraging social protection programs	• Boosting the "Two Is Enough" program	• Expanding coverage of the Takaful and Karama program (TKP)	• Leveraging the TKP to address broader issues (such as gender violence)
Improving governance of the population program	• Establishing a strong institutional framework • Developing differentiated subnational implementation plans	• Developing a national dashboard for the population program • Providing legal and regulatory support	
Ensuring a broad-based socioeconomic development policy			
Creating productive jobs	• Identifying sectors for potential value-added growth • Easing regulations to access loans from commercial banks • Removing barriers to female labor force participation	• Reallocating labor toward more productive sectors • Reducing barriers to competition • Reducing the cost of establishing formal enterprises	• Increasing productivity within sectors • Encouraging job creation and formal hiring by private firms
Investing in and leveraging human capital	• Reskilling and upskilling the labor force to address the skills mismatch • Investing in technical and vocational education and training • Promoting healthy lifestyles	• Investing in early child development • Adopting quality standards in production and service delivery	• Enhancing labor market mobility
Enhancing financial inclusion and entrepreneurship	• Enhancing women's financial literacy and changing their attitudes toward banking	• Easing regulations to access loans from commercial banks • Encouraging financial institutions to produce gender-specific products and encouraging women to use them	• Ensuring nondiscrimination in access to credit
Sustaining macroeconomic stability and ensuring policy predictability	• Resuming fiscal consolidation plans • Maintaining a market-determined and competitive exchange rate • Achieving low and stable inflation	• Improving the investment climate for domestic and foreign investment in higher-value sectors • Enhancing government fiscal and debt management and transparency	• Incentivizing domestic savings • Facilitating access to land

Source: Original illustration for this publication.

NOTE

1. The NPC was later upgraded to a Ministry of State for Population. It then reverted to the NPC, and the Ministry of Health became the Ministry of Health and Population (MOHP).

REFERENCES

Amer, Mona, and Marian Atallah. 2019. "The School to Work Transition and Youth Economic Vulnerability in Egypt." ERF Working Paper 1353, Economic Research Forum, Cairo. https://erf.org.eg/publications/the-school-to-work-transition-and-youth-economic-vulnerability-in-egypt1/.

Birdsall, Nancy, Allen C. Kelley, and Steven W. Sinding. 2004. *Population Matters: Demographic Change, Economic Growth, and Poverty in the Developing World.* Open WorldCat. New York: Oxford University Press. https://www.worldcat.org/title/population-matters -demographic-change-economic-growth-and-poverty-in-the-developing-world/oclc /57368185.

CAPMAS (Central Agency for Public Mobilization and Statistics). 2006. "Egypt, Arab Rep.—Population and Housing Census 2006." Cairo: CAPMAS. http://www.capmas.gov.eg/.

CAPMAS (Central Agency for Public Mobilization and Statistics). 2017. "Egypt Population, Housing, and Establishments Census 2017." Cairo: CAPMAS. http://www.enow.gov.eg /Report/EgyptCensus2017.pdf.

CAPMAS (Central Agency for Public Mobilization and Statistics). 2019. "Statistical Yearbook." December. Cairo: CAPMAS. http://www.capmas.gov.eg/.

CAPMAS (Central Agency for Public Mobilization and Statistics). 2020. *Egypt in Figures 2020.* March. https://www.capmas.gov.eg/Pages/StaticPages.aspx?page_id=5035.

Commission on Growth and Development. 2008. *The Growth Report: Strategies for Sustained Growth and Inclusive Development.* Washington, DC: World Bank.

Cruz, Marcio, and S. Amer Ahmed. 2018. "On the Impact of Demographic Change on Economic Growth and Poverty." *World Development* 105: 95–106. https://ideas.repec.org/a/eee/wdevel /v105y2018icp95-106.html.

El-Laithy, Heba. 2021. "Inequality of Education Opportunities in Egypt: Impact Evaluation." Egyptian Center for Economic Studies (ECES). http://www.eces.org.eg/PublicationsDetail s?Lang=EN&C=12&T=1&ID=1287&Inequality-of-Education-Opportunities-in-Egypt: -Impact-Evaluation.

Fagan, T., A. Dutta, J. Rosen, A. Olivetti, and K. Klein. 2017. "Family Planning in the Context of Latin America's Universal Health Coverage Agenda." *Global Health: Science and Practice* 5 (3): 382–98. https://doi.org/10.9745/GHSP-D-17-00057.

FP2020. n.d. "Family Planning's Return on Investment." Fact Sheet. Washington, DC: Family Planning 2020. https://www.familyplanning2020.org/sites/default/files/Data-Hub/ROI /FP2020_ROI_OnePager_FINAL.pdf.

Hasan, Rifat, Corrina Moucheraud, Hadia Samaha, Sara Troiano, S. Ahmed, Israel Osorio-Rodarte, Emi Suzuki, et al. 2019. "Demographic Dividend in DRC: Catalyzing Economic Growth through Demographic Opportunities." Washington, DC: World Bank Group.

HIPs (High Impact Practices in Family Planning). 2017. "Immediate Postpartum Family Planning: A Key Component of Childbirth Care." Washington, DC: USAID. https://www .fphighimpactpractices.org/briefs/immediate-postpartum-family-planning/.

Lam, David, and Suzanne Duryea. 1999. "Effects of Schooling on Fertility, Labor Supply, and Investments in Children, with Evidence from Brazil." *Journal of Human Resources* 34 (1): 160. https://doi.org/10.2307/146306.

McMillan, Margaret, John Page, David Booth, and Dirk Willem te Velde. 2017. "Supporting Economic Transformation: An Approach Paper." Overseas Development Institute. https:// odi.org/en/publications/supporting-economic-transformation-an-approach-paper/.

MOETE (Ministry of Education and Technical Education). 2020. "Statistical Yearbook 2019/2020." Cairo: MOETE. http://emis.gov.eg/Site%20Content/book/019-020/main _book2020.html. In Arabic.

MOHP (Ministry of Health and Population), El-Zanaty and Associates, and ICF International. 2015. *Egypt Demographic and Health Survey 2014.* Cairo and Rockville, MD: MOHP and ICF International. https://dhsprogram.com/pubs/pdf/FR302/FR302.pdf.

Troiano, S. 2015. "Population Dynamics and the Implications for Economic Growth, Poverty and Inequality—What Is Relevant for Southern Africa." Washington, DC: World Bank.

Weinberger, Michelle, Jessica Williamson, John Stover, and Emily Sonneveldt. 2019. "Using Evidence to Drive Impact: Developing the FP Goals Impact Matrix." *Studies in Family Planning* 50 (4): 289–316. https://doi.org/10.1111/sifp.12104.

World Bank. 2018. "Women Economic Empowerment Study." Washington, DC: World Bank Group. http://documents.worldbank.org/curated/en/861491551113547855/Women -Economic-Empowerment-Study.

World Bank. 2020. *Poverty & Equity Brief: Arab Republic of Egypt.* April. https://databank
.worldbank.org/data/download/poverty/33EF03BB-9722-4AE2-ABC7-AA2972D68AFE
/Global_POVEQ_EGY.pdf.

World Bank. 2021. World Development Indicators (database). http://www.data.worldbank.org.

World Bank and IMF (International Monetary Fund). 2016. *Global Monitoring Report 2015/2016:
Development Goals in an Era of Demographic Change.* Washington, DC: World Bank.
doi:10.1596/978-1-4648-0669-8.

About the Editors

Sameh El-Saharty is Lead Health Specialist at the World Bank. Since joining it in 1998, he has been responsible for leading policy dialog and strategy development as well as preparing and managing programs and projects in more than 30 countries in Africa, Asia, and the Middle East, as well as in the United States. His work has recently focused on human capital formation in the Gulf Cooperation Council countries, as well as noncommunicable diseases, population policy, health financing, health policy reform, service delivery, and implementation science. Before joining the World Bank, he held several positions with the World Health Organization (WHO), the United States Agency for International Development, the United Nations Population Fund, and Harvard University. He was also an adjunct assistant professor of international health at Georgetown University. He has authored more than 50 publications on diverse health and human development topics. He is a member of distinguished boards including the Dean's Leadership Council of Harvard Chan School of Public Health and Chair of the Advisory Committee of the Middle East and North Africa (MENA) Health Policy Forum. He is a medical doctor graduated from Cairo University and holds a master's degree in public health and epidemiology from the military medical academy in the Arab Republic of Egypt and a master's degree in international health policy and management from Harvard University.

CONTRIBUTING EDITORS

Amr Elshalakani is a Senior Health Specialist at the World Bank. He is working on Arab Republic of Egypt, Iraq, and Republic of Yemen health projects related to health care quality, viral hepatitis, coronavirus (COVID-19) response and vaccination, universal health insurance, community health workers, and social inclusion and safety nets. Before that, he served as Manager of the Technical Office for the Minister of Health and Population, Egypt. He worked in the implementation team for the pilot study of the Egyptian Social Health Insurance program at Suez, then as a personal assistant to the Heads of the Curative Care Sector, Ministry of Health and Population, and of the Egyptian Health Insurance

Organization. He served as a member in various national committees, including that responsible for drafting the Social Health Insurance law, that for overseeing the feasibility and registration of new immuno-modularity and rheumatologic treatments, and that for drafting the Medical Cadre law. He obtained his Medical degree from Cairo University, and completed a five-year residency program in obstetrics and gynecology to pass his Gynecology and Obstetrics Board Certification exams; he also completed his MBA at ESLSCA Business School in Paris, France. He has a degree in health care quality management from the American University in Cairo and a health economics diploma from the Arab Academy for Science and Technology.

Mariam Hamza is a Consultant in the Global Health, Nutrition, and Population Practice of the World Bank. She joined the Middle East and North Africa Region in 2018. She is a Ph.D. candidate at American University in Washington, DC, with a concentration in development economics. Her research interests revolve around human resources for health and human capital. She is interested in merging quantitative, robust, econometrics methods with qualitative methods, including ethnographic ones, to produce the most policy-relevant research. She is working with several governments on issues related to health system performance, health system financing, and human resources for health. Before coming to the United States and joining the World Bank, Hamza completed her bachelor's degree in economics, with minors in anthropology and business administration from the American University in Cairo in 2016. She received her master's degree in applied economics from American University in Washington, DC, in 2019.

Heba Nassar is Professor of Economics and Director of the *Academic Journal of the Faculty of Economics and Political Science (Review of Economics and Political Science)* and Vice Chair for the *Journal of Humanities and Social Science*, Cairo University. She was Vice President of Cairo University, Chair of the Economic Department, Vice Dean of the Faculty of Economics and Political Science, and Director of the Center for Economic and Financial Research and Studies. She is also a Board Member of the National Health Insurance Organization and the Women Arab Alliance as well as several committees under the Higher Council of Universities, the National Council for Women and the Organization of Drugs, and the UN Working Group on Global Compact for Universities. She is also a Founding Member of the Middle East and North Africa Health Policy Forum and Policy Affiliate to the Economic Research Forum. From 1994 through 2019, she directed several research projects at the Social Research Center of the American University in Cairo in cooperation with international and national organizations and was the economic consultant for the Economic Committee of the Parliament. Nassar has authored several publications and journal articles on migration, small business, microfinance, social protection, population, economic participation of women, the labor market, and human resource development.

Sherine Shawky is Senior Researcher at the Social Research Center (SRC) of the American University in Cairo. Since joining the SRC in 2004, she has been responsible for leading health research, writing reports, and capacity building, as well as monitoring and evaluating programs in the Arab Republic of Egypt, the Eastern Mediterranean, and Arab countries. Her work has recently focused on social determinants of health, health equity, and the development of health indicators and equity measures in Arab countries, as well as capacity building. Before joining SRC, she held several positions, including Expert in Rwanda as part of the Egyptian Rwandan Cooperation Program, Researcher in a EUROCAT project in the School of Public Health of the Catholic University of Louvain, and Associate Professor at the Faculty of Medicine and Health Sciences in King Abdul Aziz University in Jeddah. She has authored more than 50 publications. Shawki is a Commissioner at the Rockefeller-Boston University high-level Commission on Health Determinants, Data, and Decision-making; and member of the World Health Organization Regional Office for the Eastern Mediterranean (WHO EMRO) regional Evidence-Informed Policy Network. She is a consultant for the World Bank, WHO, United Nations Development Programme (UNDP), United Nations Population Fund, FHI 360, Population Council, and Qatar Ministry of Public Health. She is a medical doctor graduated from Ain Shams University and holds a doctorate in public health from the Catholic University of Louvain in Belgium.

Nahla Zeitoun has been Senior Social Protection Specialist at the World Bank, Arab Republic of Egypt, since January 2016. Her duties include strategic leadership of the Social Protection team, facilitating policy dialogue, and designing projects. She is the Task Team Leader for the largest cash transfer operation in the Middle East and North Africa (MENA). She is also the MENA Gender Focal Point leading key policy analytics in the area of women's economic empowerment/equality. She is also MENA focal point for disability and social care. Before joining the World Bank, she served for 18 years at United Nations Development Programme (UNDP) Egypt, and her last position was Assistant Resident Representative and Poverty Reduction Team Leader. At UNDP, she led the poverty portfolio and oversaw the production of key flagship publications—the 2008 and 2010 "Egypt Human Development Report" (HDR), the 2007 and 2015/2016 "Business Solutions for HDR," and the 2010 and 2015 "Millennium Development Goals Report." Zeitoun was honored with Egypt's 2020 "Top 50 Most Influential Women" award. She is a Sasakawa Fellow of the Young Leaders Scholarship Award 2002–2005, and she was a recipient of the Eisenhower Fellowship—Women's Leadership Program in October 2020.

Yi Zhang is a Health Economist at the World Bank. Since joining the Bank as a young professional, he has been working in countries in South Asia, the Middle East and North Africa, and Sub-Saharan Africa, where he supports various teams in advanced analytics, health insurance and health finance, digital health, health economics and noncommunicable diseases, and coronavirus (COVID-19) emergency response. Zhang holds a doctoral degree in health informatics, and his dissertation focused on analytics and technology for health insurance risk assessment, population health management, and physician profiling. He also holds a bachelor's degree in biochemistry from the University of Minnesota. Before joining the Bank, he worked in a large health insurance company for provider finance and network innovation, and in an international management consulting firm for transaction advisory services (mergers and acquisitions) and advanced analytics in the health care sector.

Abbreviations

CAPMAS	Central Agency for Public Mobilization and Statistics
CBR	crude birth rate
C-section	cesarean section delivery
CCO	Curative Care Organization
CHW	community health worker
CPR	contraceptive prevalence rate
EDHS	Egypt Demographic and Health Survey
ENPS 2015–2030	Egypt National Population Strategy 2015–2030
EPIP 2015–2020	Egypt First Five-Year Population Implementation Plan 2015–2020 (also called Egypt National Population Strategy First Five-Year Implementation Plan 2015–2020)
FP	family planning
GFR	general fertility rate
HIO	Health Insurance Organization
ILO	International Labour Organization
IUD	intrauterine device
LE	Egyptian pound
LFPR	labor force participation rate
M&E	monitoring and evaluation
MOETE	Ministry of Education and Technical Education
MOHP	Ministry of Health and Population
MOP	Ministry of Population
MOYS	Ministry of Youth and Sports
NCW	National Council for Women
NPC	National Population Council
PHCU	primary health care unit
PPFP	postpartum family planning
RH	reproductive health
rID%	relative index of dissimilarity expressed in percent
SRH	sexual and reproductive health
TKP	Takaful and Karama program

TFR	total fertility rate
UNFPA	United Nations Population Fund
USAID	United States Agency for International Development

In this document, all dollar amounts are U.S. dollars, unless otherwise indicated.

Glossary of Terms

Adult mortality rate: The adult mortality rate is the probability of dying between the ages of 15 and 60—that is, the probability of a 15-year-old dying before reaching age 60—if subject to age-specific mortality rates of the specified year between those ages.

Contraceptive prevalence rate (CPR): The CPR is defined as the percentage of married women of reproductive age who are using any contraceptive method. The unmet need for family planning is defined as the percentage of married women of reproductive ages (15–49 years) who want to stop or delay childbearing and are at risk of pregnancy but are not using any method of contraception among all married women in the same age group. The proportion of use of modern methods is defined as the number of women who use modern contraceptive methods, such as intrauterine devices and injectables, among all women who use any contraceptive method.

Crude birth rate (CBR): The CBR is the total number of live births per 1,000 population in the middle of the year. It does not take into account the gender differences or the age distribution in the population.

Dependency ratio: The dependency ratio is the ratio of dependents—people younger than 15 or older than 64—to the working-age population—those ages 15–64. Data are shown as the proportion of dependents per 100 working-age population.

General fertility rate (GFR): The GFR is the number of births in a year for every 1,000 women of reproductive age (15–44 years). It does not, however, differentiate between married and unmarried women and does not take into account the fertility rate in different age groups.

Total fertility rate (TFR): The TFR is the mean number of children a woman would have by age 50 if she survived to age 50 and were subject, throughout her life, to the age-specific fertility rates observed in a given year. The total fertility rate is expressed as the number of children per woman.

Working-age population: The working-age population is commonly defined as persons ages 15 years and older, but this varies from country to country. In addition to using a minimum age threshold, certain countries also apply a maximum age limit. For calculating dependency ratios, it is the share of the population ages 15–64 years.

Introduction

**SEEMEEN SAADAT, SAMEH EL-SAHARTY,
AND MARIAM M. HAMZA**

There is a strong, well-documented link between demographics and economic growth. Countries that can successfully bring down their total fertility rates when these are high have the potential to boost their economic growth through lessening the burden of care per capita on the working-age population. In other words, lower fertility and fewer children per household mean that more can be invested in the health, education, and skills development of these children—that is, greater human capital formation. In parallel, households can accumulate savings, which can boost economic growth through investments back into the economy (Bloom, Canning, and Malaney 2000; Lee and Mason 2006; World Bank and IMF 2016).

THE DEMOGRAPHIC DIVIDEND: TWO PHASES OF THE DEMOGRAPHIC TRANSITION

Introduced in the late 1990s, the concept of a "demographic dividend" has been used to describe the interplay between changes in population structure and fast economic growth, most notably in the context of East Asian economies (Bloom, Canning, and Malaney 2000; Bloom and Williamson 1998; Canning, Raja, and Yazbeck 2015).

Put simply, a demographic dividend is the share of economic growth attributable to changes in an economy's age structure. It is the "economic benefit to a country that can happen within a window of 15 to 20 years when it undergoes a demographic transition due to a rapid decline in mortality followed by a rapid decline in fertility. This leads to smaller, healthier families, and a youth cohort that can be educated and empowered to enter the labor market and match a dynamic labor demand" (Hasan et al. 2019, 1).

As fertility rates decline and countries undergo the demographic transition, they have the opportunity to pass through two phases of the demographic dividend (Lee and Mason 2006; World Bank and IMF 2016). The first phase of the dividend is a direct and immediate consequence of the growth of the size of the labor force relative to the cohort of children—that is, when the dependency ratio falls and the share of the working-age population rises as more people are able to work at the most productive stages of their lives. For the first phase to materialize, three things need to happen. First is a decline in fertility, usually due to health improvements that lead to greater child survival and families' desire to have fewer children. This decline in birth rates contributes to one large cohort of children followed by subsequently smaller cohorts, resulting in the "youth bulge."[1] When the first cohort reaches working age (that is, 15–64 years of age), the dependency ratio begins to fall.

The second requirement is twofold: (a) greater investment in the health and education of the subsequent smaller cohorts of children as more resources are available per child, contributing to their human capital accumulation (Kalemli-Ozcan, Ryder, and Weil 2000; Schultz 2005), and (b) women's increased capacity to participate in the labor force due to lower fertility (Bloom et al. 2009).

The third requirement is investment in the economic environment, such that the bulge cohort can find well-paying jobs, rather than be unemployed or forced into low-productivity work. However, essential to this first phase is "the youth bulge," which is only possible with the decline in fertility.

The second phase of the demographic dividend may arise if changes in age structure create space for higher savings and lead to increasing investments in human and physical capital, which can further enhance labor productivity (Birdsall, Kelley, and Sinding 2004). The declining dependency ratio resulting from falling fertility is a necessary condition for countries to achieve the additional benefits of increased savings, investments, and per capita gross domestic product (GDP).

The bonus from the first phase is transitory; the second phase produces lasting benefits in the form of greater productivity growth and sustainable development (figure I.1). The two phases thus represent an opportunity—not a guarantee—of greater prosperity and improved living standards. These outcomes are not automatic—they depend on well thought out and implemented policies (World Bank and IMF 2016). A key point underlying the demographic dividend is that the population *structure* (and the dependency ratio) is far more important than the population *size*.

The Global Monitoring Report (GMR) 2015/16 (World Bank and IMF 2016) uses two criteria drawn from the demographic dividend framework—the total fertility rate (TFR) and growth in the share of the working-age population—to identify countries' stage of demographic transition and their potential for achieving the demographic dividend: pre-, early-, late-, or post-dividend. At a TFR of 3.1 births per woman, the Arab Republic of Egypt is an early-dividend country.[2] As figure I.1 shows, it is at a very early stage of the first phase.

FIGURE I.1

First and second phases of the demographic dividend

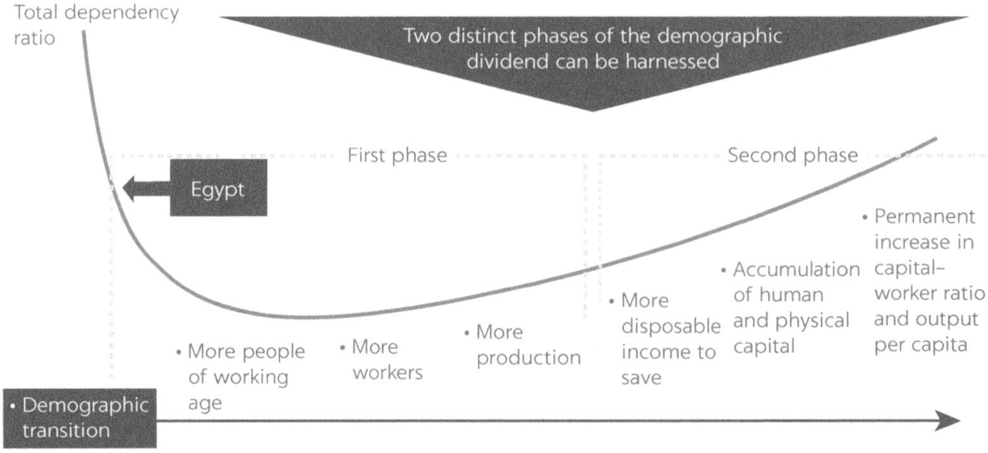

Source: Adapted from World Bank and IMF 2016.

DEMOGRAPHIC DIVIDEND AND ECONOMIC GROWTH

Cruz and Ahmed (2018) further corroborate the theory of demographic change and economic growth using the global share of the working-age population in 1950–2050 to explain the changes driving the phases of the demographic dividend (figure I.2). Panel a of figure I.2 shows a theoretical model, where the support ratio (working-age population divided by the non-working-age population)

FIGURE I.2

Demographic dividend and the working-age share of the population, 1950–2050

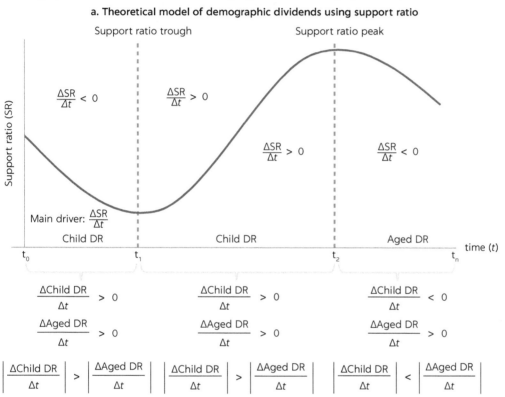

a. Theoretical model of demographic dividends using support ratio

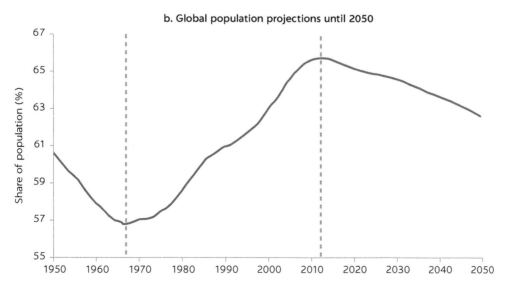

b. Global population projections until 2050

Source: Cruz and Ahmed 2018.
Note: DR = dependency ratio.

is graphed over time: it declines because of increased fertility, then increases with reduced fertility and children entering their productive ages (phases 1 and 2 of the demographic dividend). The final stage is when the large working-age population starts to grow older and leaves the workforce, thus reducing the support ratio. This progression is corroborated by graphing the working-age share (ages 15–64 years) of the population (figure I.2, panel b).

The economic impact associated with the demographic dividend is highly significant in terms of magnitude and duration. Mason and Kinugasa (2008) estimated that for some countries in East Asia, the contribution of the first phase of the demographic dividend explains between 9.2 and 15.5 percent of their per capita economic growth over 1960–2000. The first phase could persist for decades. As fertility rates decline, child dependency ratios fall and the share of the working-age population rises and remains high for a few generations, without a significant increase in the old-age (65+ years) dependency ratio, allowing more people to work, be economically active, and generate income.

FERTILITY AND THE DEMOGRAPHIC DIVIDEND

Fertility is important in achieving the first phase of the demographic dividend and setting the stage for the second phase. "The demographic dividend occurs only when fertility falls and the cohorts that follow are smaller, lowering the youth dependency ratio and allowing larger investment per child. Without a fertility decline, countries will face an ever-growing population base and ever-larger youth cohorts—and children will be further exposed to health risks, malnutrition, and lower public and private educational investments" (Canning, Raja, and Yazbeck 2015, 5–6).

Fertility is influenced by two broad groups of factors or determinants—those that are biological or behavioral and have a direct effect on fertility (or its proximate determinants), such as proportion of marriages (or sexual activity) and contraceptive use; and those that indirectly affect fertility through socioeconomic and cultural factors (that is, the distal determinants), such as education and income. Figure I.3 presents the proximate and distal determinants of fertility.

Given the unique contexts across different countries, different determinants may have a more prominent role than others in affecting fertility. Mohanty and

FIGURE I.3

Distal and proximate determinants of fertility

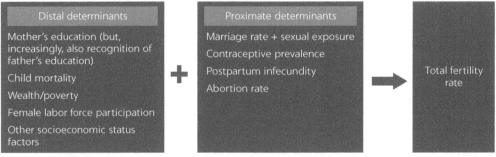

Source: Original figure based on Amin, Casterline, and Spess 2007; Bongaarts 1978, 2015; Bongaarts and Watkins 1996; Cleland and Rodriguez 1988; Davis and Blake 1956; Drèze and Murthi 2001; Mohanty et al. 2016; Stover 1998.

others (2016) find that fertility reduction in one-third of the districts in India is due to decreases in child mortality and more girls' education. Gertler and Molyneaux (1994) attribute 75 percent of fertility decline in Indonesia to contraceptive use, which was due to greater female education and labor force participation during the 1980s. In several countries, a stall in fertility decline was attributed to unmet need and unwanted births, pointing to issues of access to family planning for all women, even though these programs existed in the countries (Bongaarts 2006).

Although fertility decline is an important and necessary condition for achieving the demographic dividend, it has to be accompanied by investments in education and labor market opportunities, especially for women. On the one hand, these investments contribute to fertility decline (as its distal determinants); on the other, they help build up and leverage the human capital of women, which is often untapped or, if leveraged, poorly so. In actively engaging women in the economy, countries can increase their share of the working-age population and potentially enhance their demographic dividend.

EGYPT'S POPULATION CHALLENGE

Egypt's population program began in the early 1970s and was very successful in bringing down the country's fertility rate. Key investments in reproductive health and family planning, as well as women's empowerment, contributed to an impressive decline in the country's TFR, from 4.5 to 3.0, between 1988 and 2008. However, by 2014, the TFR decline had reversed. This reversal was not only alarming, but it has been seen in only a handful of countries worldwide.

Egypt's population will continue to grow in the foreseeable future, given "population momentum"—that is, the increase in population size driven by the youth bulge when it reaches reproductive age and begins childbearing. According to the United Nations (UN) population projections, Egypt's population will grow to 120.8 million in 2030 and will have a TFR of 2.7 if all other factors remain the same. This is destiny.

However, the first phase of the demographic dividend can in fact be realized if the TFR declines from an estimated 3.1 in 2020 to the fertility replacement level of 2.1, which could be achieved by 2030, or shortly thereafter, with a total population of only 117.3 million (as described in the scenario in chapter 5, representing accelerated fertility decline). A TFR decline of one child per decade is possible—Egypt itself achieved it in the 1980s and 1990s, along with other countries such as Algeria, Bangladesh, the Islamic Republic of Iran, the Kyrgyz Republic, Morocco, Oman, Peru, South Africa, Tunisia, Turkmenistan, Uzbekistan, and Vietnam.

The actual outcome will, of course, greatly depend on how the government implements policies both to slow population growth and to benefit from the youth bulge, complemented with social and economic development interventions that influence people's decisions on the number of children they will have and that create productive jobs. This is choice.

OBJECTIVE OF THIS REPORT

This report aims to support evidence-based policy dialogue on achieving the demographic dividend in the context of recent population changes in Egypt.

It provides a quantitative analysis of the fertility changes and a qualitative description of their sectoral and social drivers, an estimation of the economic impact, and the policies and strategies primarily for achieving the first phase of the demographic dividend, as a precondition for achieving the second phase.

Chapter 1 focuses on the demographic changes that took place in Egypt, particularly between 2000 and 2014, and examines the trends in the drivers of fertility that contributed to the fertility increase. Chapter 2 discusses the government of Egypt's policy response to the fertility increase—specifically the Egypt National Population Strategy 2015–2030 (ENPS 2015–2030) and its accompanying first five-year plan, the Egypt Population Implementation Plan 2015–2020 (EPIP 2015–2020)—as well as an assessment of the institutional and implementation capacity. Chapter 3 examines the changes that took place in fertility and other cross-sectoral areas targeted by EPIP 2015–2020 during its implementation period. It also examines the gaps and the reasons for them. Chapter 4 dives deeper into the sectoral and social drivers that may explain the fertility changes and the remaining challenges. It focuses on health, education, female labor force participation, poverty and social protection, and gender and social norms. Chapter 5 estimates the economic losses from the rise in fertility between 2008 and 2020, using the concepts of forgone savings and economic opportunity costs, and estimates the potential savings and income due to a fertility decline between 2020 and 2030. Chapter 6 brings in global experiences and best practices to provide guidance on how countries have addressed fertility in different contexts. Chapter 7 focuses on key policy directions and strategic priorities for Egypt. Multiple data tables are in the appendixes.

NOTES

1. A *youth bulge* is defined as a high proportion (40 percent or more) of the population 15–29 years old compared with the adult population above age 15 (May 2012, 265).
2. An early-dividend country has a TFR below 4 births per woman and above the replacement level of 2.1 births per woman, as classified in World Bank and IMF (2016).

REFERENCES

Amin, S., J. B. Casterline, and L. Spess. 2007. "Poverty and Fertility: Evidence and Agenda." Working Paper 4, Population Council, New York.

Birdsall, Nancy, Allen C. Kelley, and Steven W. Sinding. 2004. *Population Matters: Demographic Change, Economic Growth, and Poverty in the Developing World. Open WorldCat.* New York: Oxford University Press. https://www.worldcat.org/title/population-matters-demographic -change-economic-growth-and-poverty-in-the-developing-world/oclc/57368185.

Bloom, David E., David Canning, Günther Fink, and Jocelyn E. Finlay. 2009. "Fertility, Female Labor Force Participation, and the Demographic Dividend." *Journal of Economic Growth* 14 (2): 79–101. https://doi.org/10.1007/s10887-009-9039-9.

Bloom, David E., David Canning, and Pia N. Malaney. 2000. "Population Dynamics and Economic Growth in Asia." *Population and Development Review* 26: 257–90. https://www .jstor.org/stable/3115219?refreqid=excelsior%3Ae6df768aef06bae79147ff1be2f38b0a&seq =1#metadata_info_tab_contents.

Bloom, David E., and Jeffrey G. Williamson. 1998. "Demographic Transitions and Economic Miracles in Emerging Asia." *The World Bank Economic Review* 12 (3): 419–55. https://www.jstor.org/stable/3990182?seq=1#metadata_info_tab_contents.

Bongaarts, John. 1978. "A Framework for Analyzing the Proximate Determinants of Fertility." *Population and Development Review* 4: 105–32. doi:10.2307/1972149.

Bongaarts, John. 2006. "The Causes of Stalling Fertility Transitions." *Studies in Family Planning* 37 (1): 1–16. https://doi.org/10.1111/j.1728-4465.2006.00079.x.

Bongaarts, John. 2015. "Modeling the Fertility Impact of the Proximate Determinants: Time for a Tune-Up." *Demographic Research* 33 (September): 535–60. https://doi.org/10.4054/demres.2015.33.19.

Bongaarts, John, and Susan Cotts Watkins. 1996. "Social Interaction and Contemporary Fertility Transitions." *Population and Development Review* 22 (4): 639–82. doi:10.2307/ 2137804.

Canning, David, Sangeeta Raja, and Abdo S. Yazbeck. 2015. "Africa's Demographic Transition." Washington, DC: World Bank. https://openknowledge.worldbank.org/handle/10986/22036.

Cleland, John, and Germán Rodríguez. 1988. "The Effect of Parental Education on Marital Fertility in Developing Countries." *Population Studies* 42 (3): 419–42.

Cruz, Marcio, and S. Amer Ahmed. 2018. "On the Impact of Demographic Change on Economic Growth and Poverty." *World Development* 105: 95–106. https://ideas.repec.org/a/eee/wdevel/v105y2018icp95-106.html.

Davis, Kingsley, and Judith Blake. 1956. "Social Structure and Fertility: An Analytic Framework." *Economic Development and Cultural Change* 4 (3): 211–35.

Drèze, Jean, and Mamta Murthi. 2001. "Fertility, Education and Development: Evidence from India." *Population and Development Review* 27 (1): 33–63. doi:10.1111/j.1728- 4457.2001.00033.x.

Gertler, Paul J., and John W. Molyneaux. 1994. "How Economic Development and Family Planning Programs Combined to Reduce Indonesian Fertility." *Demography* 31 (1): 33. https://doi.org/10.2307/2061907.

Hasan, Rifat, Corrina Moucheraud, Hadia Samaha, Sara Troiano, S. Ahmed, Israel Osorio-Rodarte, Emi Suzuki, et al. 2019. "Demographic Dividend in DRC: Catalyzing Economic Growth through Demographic Opportunities." Washington, DC: World Bank.

Kalemli-Ozcan, Sebnem, Harl E. Ryder, and David N. Weil. 2000. "Mortality Decline, Human Capital Investment, and Economic Growth." *Journal of Development Economics* 62 (1): 1–23. https://doi.org/10.1016/s0304-3878(00)00073-0.

Lee, Ronald, and Andrew Mason. 2006. "What Is the Demographic Dividend?" *Finance and Development* 43 (3). https://www.imf.org/external/pubs/ft/fandd/2006/09/basics.htm.

Mason, Andrew, and Tomoko Kinugasa. 2008. "East Asian Economic Development: Two Demographic Dividends." *Journal of Asian Economics* 19 (5–6): 389–99. https://doi.org/10.1016/j.asieco.2008.09.006.

May, John F. 2012. *World Population Policies: Their Origin, Evolution, and Impact*. Dordrecht, Netherlands; New York: Springer.

Mohanty, Sanjay K., Günther Fink, Rajesh K. Chauhan, and David Canning. 2016. "Distal Determinants of Fertility Decline: Evidence from 640 Indian Districts." *Demographic Research* 34: 373–406. https://www.jstor.org/stable/26332039?seq=4#metadata_info_tab_contents.

Schultz, T. Paul. 2005. "Productive Benefits of Health: Evidence from Low-Income Countries." In *Health and Economic Growth: Findings and Policy Implications*, edited by Guillem Lopez-Casasnovas, Berta Riveras, and Luis Currais. Cambridge, MA: MIT Press.

Stover, John. 1998. "Revising the Proximate Determinants of Fertility Framework: What Have We Learned in the Past 20 Years?" *Studies in Family Planning* 29 (3): 255. https://doi.org/10.2307/172272.

World Bank and IMF (International Monetary Fund). 2016. *Global Monitoring Report 2015/2016: Development Goals in an Era of Demographic Change*. Washington, DC: World Bank. https://openknowledge.worldbank.org/handle/10986/22547.

Additional reading

Bongaarts, John, W. Parker Mauldin, and James F. Phillips. 1990. "The Demographic Impact of Family Planning Programs." *Studies in Family Planning* 21 (6): 299. https://doi .org/10.2307/1966918.

World Bank. 2010. *Reproductive Health Action Plan 2010–2015*. Washington, DC: World Bank.

1 Analysis of Demographic Trends and Changes, 1988–2014

YI ZHANG, ABDO S. YAZBECK, AND SAMEH EL-SAHARTY

The Arab Republic of Egypt used to have a strong track record in managing its population growth. The investment in family planning and women's empowerment contributed to an impressive decline in births per woman, which went from 4.5 in 1988 to 3.0 in 2008 (MOHP, El-Zanaty and Associates, and ICF International 2015). Then the trend reversed and the number of births per woman climbed to 3.5 in 2014—a switch seen in only a handful of countries globally. Focusing on fertility, this chapter presents data on demographic trends and changes during this time and analyzes the reasons for these changes.

EGYPT'S ATYPICAL DEMOGRAPHIC TRENDS

Between 1988 and 2004, Egypt made considerable improvements in its population and demographic trends, but the next decade saw a reversal. The total fertility rate (TFR) declined sharply, from 4.5 births per woman in 1988 to 3.5 births per woman in 2000. After that, however, the TFR was either stagnant or rising (CSDH 2008). A demographic plateau was seen, with the TFR oscillating between 3.0 and 3.3 births per woman in the first decade of the new millennium, followed by an increase to 3.5 births per woman in 2014 (World Bank 2020). According to data from the Central Agency for Public Mobilization and Statistics (CAPMAS), the birth rate reached its highest level in 2014: 31.3 per 1,000 inhabitants (CAPMAS 2017b).

Mortality rates decreased across all age groups. The infant mortality rate declined from 33 per 1,000 live births during 2000–04, to 22 per 1,000 live births in 2010–14; and the under-five mortality rate declined from 39 to 27 per 1,000 live births over the same period (MOHP, El-Zanaty and Associates, and ICF International 2015). The adult female mortality rate (ages 15–60 years) fell from 122.2 to 113.1 per 1,000 adult females, and the adult male mortality rate decreased from 198.3 to 189.9 per 1,000 adult males during the same period.

Overall, the annual population growth rate increased from 2.0 percent to 2.3 percent during 2010–14, in absolute terms rising from 1.4 million in 2010 to 1.9 million in 2014 (World Bank 2020). The population density climbed from 83.1 people per square kilometer in 2010 to 90.8 in 2014.

These demographic trends were reflected in the age structure of the population and in development efforts. In 2014, a clear "youth boom" was noted, with

33.2 percent of the population under 14 years of age and 5.1 percent of the population 60 years old or above. The dependency ratio increased from 59.6 percent in 2010 to 61.8 percent in 2014. The increase in the elderly population led to a decrease in the labor force participation rate from 49.4 percent in 2010 to 48.1 percent in 2014 (World Bank 2020), with a corresponding increase in the unemployment rate from 8.8 percent to 13.1 percent. This affected women's economic participation in particular, with a nearly stagnant female labor force participation rate (ranging from 23.0 percent to 23.7 percent of the total labor force) and adolescent childbearing rising from 53.2 percent in 2010 to 55.0 percent in 2014 (CAPMAS 2017a).

Geographically, birth rates exceeded the national average in 11 governorates—seven in Upper Egypt (excluding Giza and Aswan), and in Beheira, Ismailia, Matrouh, and South Sinai—while birth rates were lower than the national average in the other governorates (CAPMAS 2017b).

Despite the increase in the contraceptive prevalence rate of modern methods among women 15–49 years, from 53.9 percent in 2000 to 56.9 percent in 2014, geographic disparities were evident in family planning (FP) outcomes. The contraceptive prevalence rate was below the national average in all governorates of Upper Egypt (except Giza) and the frontier governorates. Unmet need for FP in Upper Egypt reached 12.3 percent among married women ages 15–49 and increased to 16.0 percent in 2014, compared with 10.4 percent and 11.1 percent in Lower Egypt and urban governorates, respectively (MOHP, El-Zanaty and Associates, and ICF International 2015). Data also show that about one-third of married women ages 15–49 discontinued use during the first year for various reasons, including poor quality of service (CAPMAS 2017a, 2017b).

FERTILITY TRENDS

After years of decline, Egypt's fertility rate—going against global trends—picked up after 2008. It had declined steadily from 4.5 in 1988 to 3.0 in 2008, but then increased to 3.5 in 2014 (figure 1.1). Egypt's Demographic and Health Surveys (EDHSs) (box 1.1) reflect the three years preceding each survey. It is plausible

FIGURE 1.1

Total fertility rate for women ages 15–49, Egypt, 1988–2014

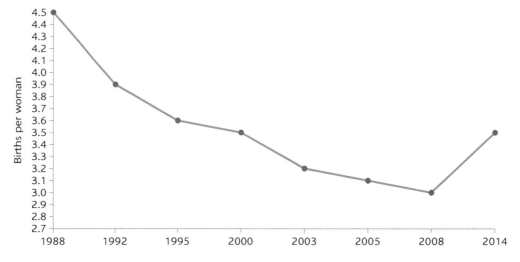

Sources: MOHP, El-Zanaty and Associates, and ICF International 2015.
Note: The Egypt Demographic and Health Survey was not conducted in 2011.

Box 1.1

Fertility change in Egypt

This chapter exploits the wealth of household data on fertility in Egypt generated by Demographic and Health Surveys (EDHSs), which started in 1988 and provide an in-depth understanding of the uptick in fertility between 2008 and 2014 that motivated this report. EDHSs are extremely important because they are large, nationally representative samples of randomly selected households—and thus offer an unbiased picture of important variables like fertility and determinants of fertility, such as education and relative wealth—and because they facilitate analysis by geographic location, including urban and rural areas. (Data based on administrative reports have been

shown globally to be influenced by internal pressures to report relative to specific targets.)

A further reason that the EDHS data help the analysis is consistency over time. Identical questions about fertility and the distal and proximate determinants of fertility have been asked in every survey over the 26-year period. This information can help to develop a nuanced view of the dynamics of fertility over time, and it can provide important hints for the range, appropriateness, and potential effectiveness of policy responses (see chapter 7). This view is crucial for a country that has shown so many unusual fertility trends.

FIGURE 1.2

Total fertility rate, Egypt, 1999–2014

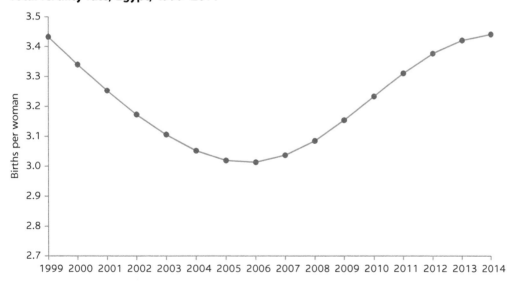

Source: World Bank data, Health, Nutrition, and Population statistics, https://datatopics.worldbank.org/health/.

that the uptick in fertility started before 2008 (discussed below); that the TFR stagnated between 2005 and 2006; and that the steady increase in fertility really started in 2007 (figure 1.2). A steady fertility decline is usually highly predictable in middle-income countries, with the main variability being in the rate of fertility decline, not the direction of change. The predictability is because fertility changes very slowly and requires substantial and difficult shifts, such as changes in educational stocks, women's empowerment, cultural beliefs, and sustained health sector responses targeted at the supply of services, as well as behavior change programs.

Global data over 60 years of national birth rates show that national fertility-rate reversals are atypical. A reversal of fertility decline was observed in a few

FIGURE 1.3

Crude birth rates, six countries in Middle East and North Africa, 2000–18

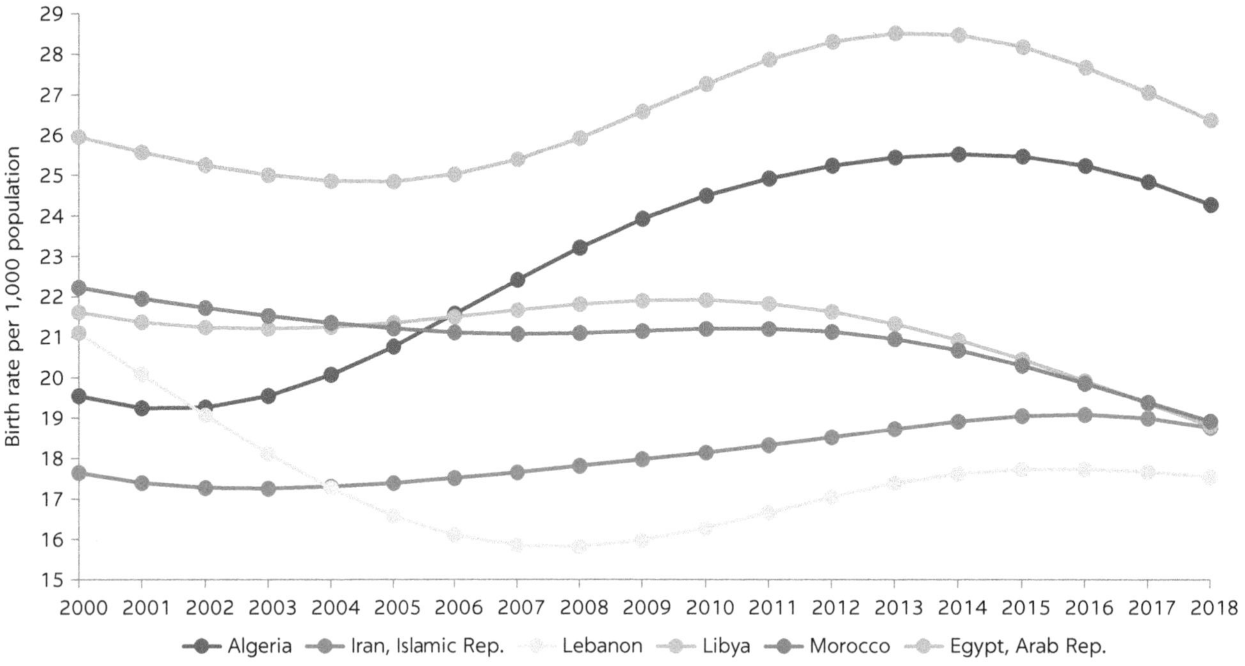

Source: World Bank data, Health, Nutrition, and Population statistics, https://datatopics.worldbank.org/health/.

countries only as demonstrated by the trends in crude birth rates. The list of countries and periods with crude birth rate reversals *may* point to potential regional drivers for the fertility reversal observed in Egypt. Those countries and periods are Algeria, 2002–14; Islamic Republic of Iran, 2004–16; Lebanon, 2009–15; Libya, 2004–10; and Morocco, 2008–11 (figure 1.3). Identifying these regional drivers is beyond the scope of this study, however. For Egypt, the following sections delve deeper into the country's unusual fertility trends, as analyzed by education level, urban–rural split, and wealth quintile. Elements in these trends—demand for children, median age at first marriage, and use of contraceptive methods—are then reviewed, leading to the conclusion that people's desire for children may well be the main reason for the fertility-rate reversal.

Egypt's increase in fertility was led by more educated women. This is going against one of the most enduring relationships in demography, which is between fertility rates and women's education level. In countries with multiple EDHSs, secondary or higher education is almost always strongly associated with lower fertility. This relationship is consistent with economic theory about educated women entering the paid labor market and social theory about female empowerment. This was also evident in Egypt between 1988 and 1995, when women with no education or only primary education displayed higher fertility than women who had completed secondary education or higher. Also, the rate of fertility decline for the two groups was roughly similar over the period. However, from 1995, the fertility gap between the more and less educated women began to narrow. Initially this was driven by a surprising and hard-to-explain sharp increase in fertility for the *more* educated group—contrary to global trends. At the same time, the rate of fertility decline for the less educated group slowed, which led to a convergence in fertility for the two groups in Egypt (figure 1.4).

FIGURE 1.4

Total fertility rate by education level for women ages 15–49, Egypt, 1988–2014

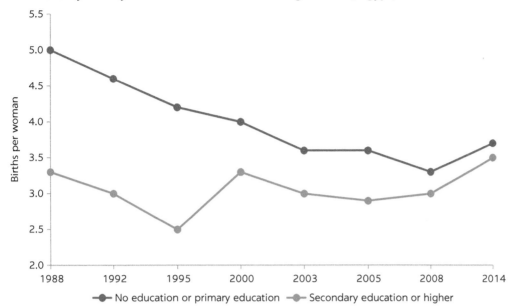

Source: Egypt Demographic and Health Surveys, 1988-2014.

FIGURE 1.5

Age-specific fertility rate for 20–24 and 25–29 age groups, Egypt, 1988–2014

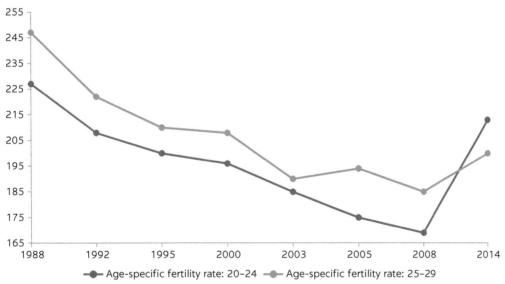

Source: Egypt Demographic and Health Surveys, 1988-2014.

Egypt's increase in fertility was highest among younger women. Fertility rates increased across all age groups except women ages 40–49. The increase was highest among women in the 20–24 age group; fertility rose by 26 percent in this age group between the 2008 and 2014 EDHS (figure 1.5).

Egypt's urban population led the reversal in the fertility decline after 1992. A second enduring fertility relationship is the timing and rate of decline in fertility between urban and rural populations. Globally, the fertility-rate decline starts in

FIGURE 1.6

Total, urban, and rural fertility rates for women ages 15–49, Egypt, 1988–2014

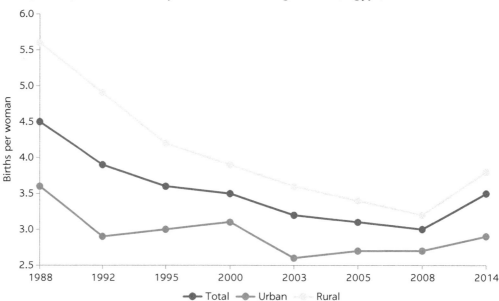

Source: Egypt Demographic and Health Surveys, 1988–2014.

urban settings before rural populations join and drive the overall decline, consistent with economic and social theories of female labor markets and gender empowerment. Once again, however, Egypt shows a different trend after 1992 (figure 1.6).

Egypt's deviation from the global trend for urban and rural populations starts even earlier than that for fertility rates by education level. The fertility rate of the urban population shows a small uptick from 1992, then a flattening, which was masked by the overall declining trend of fertility until 2008. (Because Egypt is more rural than urban, the rural numbers drive the national numbers.) Fertility rates in urban Egypt are in fact identical in 1992 and 2014. For the rural figures, there appear to be two inflection points, 1995 and 2008. Between 1988 and 1995, rural fertility rates decline faster than those of the urban population. The rate of decline in fertility slows between 1995 and 2008. The rural reversal in fertility rates starts in 2008, again driving national figures upward. It is tempting to focus only on the post-2008 numbers since that is when the national figures increase, but Egypt's urban fertility rate change and (mostly) stagnation after 1992 should be considered for partially understanding the fertility-reversal narrative.

Examining urban, rural, and subnational regional characteristics together highlights the following trends and shifts (figure 1.7):

- In urban areas, the fertility rate pickup occurred in two stages. In the first, TFR for urban Upper Egypt and urban governorates started to increase beginning in 1992, which lasted until 1995 and 2000, respectively. This was followed by an increase in urban Lower Egypt in 1995–2000. In the second stage, all urban areas (urban Lower Egypt, urban Upper Egypt, and urban governorates) saw fertility rate increases in 2003, a trend that lasted until 2005 (and until 2008 for urban governorates), with the largest increase in urban Upper Egypt.
- In rural areas, the fertility pickup started in rural Upper Egypt and rural Lower Egypt in 2008. Before then, a significant downtrend was observed, with a rapid decrease in 1988–95. The largest decline was in rural Upper Egypt.

FIGURE 1.7

Total fertility rate by subnational groupings for women ages 15–49, Egypt, 1988–2014

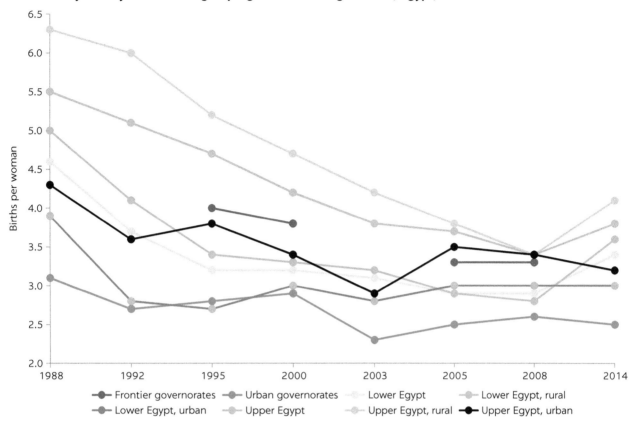

Source: Egypt Demographic and Health Surveys, 1988–2014.
Note: No data are available for frontier governorates after 2008.

- In Upper Egypt, rural areas showed a continuous decrease in fertility from 1988 to 2008; urban areas showed decreasing trends in 1988–92, 1995–2003, and 2005–14. After 2008, urban areas showed a downtrend but rural areas showed an uptrend.
- Upper Egypt and Lower Egypt started uptrends in 2008. Urban governorates started uptrends in 2003, then declined since 2008.

Egypt's fertility rebound was led by the wealthier populations. A third enduring fertility relationship in the global literature that is consistent with economic and social theory on fertility decline relates to fertility and wealth. Among higher educated women and in urban settings globally, data typically show that fertility decline is led by wealthier groups, while lower wealth groups maintain stubbornly high fertility rates.

The Egyptian story, however, once again shows a different trajectory in several ways. Between 2003 and 2008, the only wealth quintile showing an increase in fertility is the highest wealth group, when—again going against most global trends—the fertility rate for the poorest wealth quintile shows the fastest decline. (The wealth variables are available in EDHSs only from 2003.) Even harder to understand or to try to explain is what happens between 2008 and 2014, when the highest and lowest wealth quintiles show a slight increase in fertility, while the second, third (especially), and fourth quintiles show sharp increases. The 2014 comparison of fertility rates by wealth quintile no longer

FIGURE 1.8

Total fertility rate by wealth quintile for women ages 15–49, Egypt, 2003–14

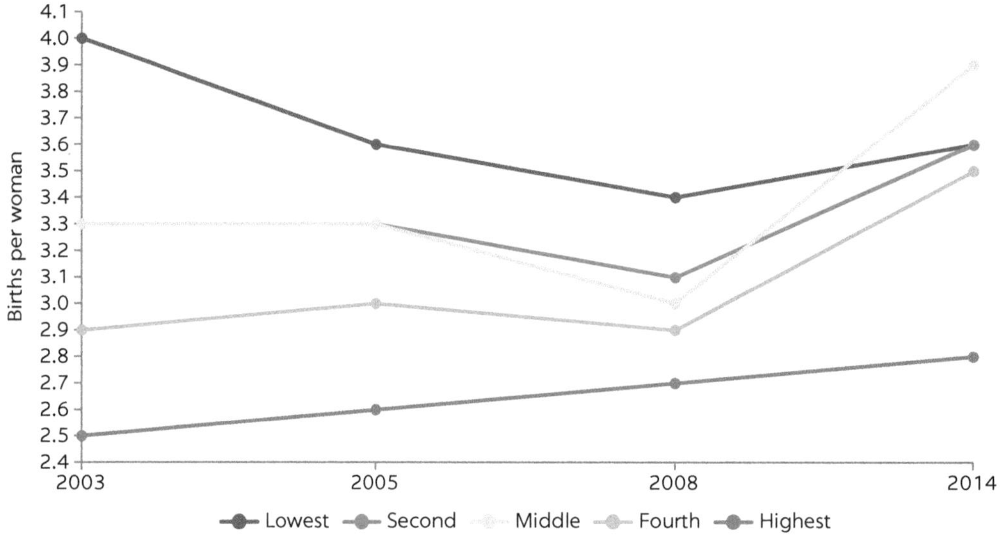

Source: Egypt Demographic and Health Surveys, 2003–14.

shows the expected gradient and instead shows a clear gap between the wealthiest quintile and the other four, and the middle wealth quintile exhibits the highest fertility rate. (figure 1.8).

DEMAND FOR CHILDREN

The increase in demand for children was led by educated urban and wealthier women after 2005. A change in fertility rate over time is usually the result in the population's change in desire for children, and this is likely the case in Egypt. Yet globally, the change in how many children on average a population *wants* is not always the only factor (though it is the dominant driver of the actual fertility rate), as families may want fewer children but do not have access to reliable contraception. In Egypt, after demand for children decreased from 3.0 in 1988 to 2.3 in 2005, it reverted back to 3.0 in 2014.

Figure 1.9 shows several trends consistent with the unexpected changes in actual rates observed in figure 1.6. The first and most obvious one is in 1992 for the urban population sample, where the desired family size increases. This is consistent with the changes in the actual fertility rate observed in the urban population in figure 1.6. Another surprising trend is how the change in the desired family size in the rural population at first lags the urban population, then shadows it. A final unexpected observation is that the desired family size in the urban population appears to be slightly lower for 1988, the first data point, than for 2014, the last data point. Some of the similarity may be the result of rapid urbanization, but this stark finding is not typical globally, where urban demand for children usually continues to decline.

Figure 1.10 similarly shows patterns for the impact of education on demand for children in Egypt. This finding, too, is aligned with the finding on actual fertility rates (see figure 1.4) and is inconsistent with global evidence. The change in direction in the desire for children begins in 1995 and is dominated by the

FIGURE 1.9

Desired fertility rate by urban and rural residence, Egypt, 1988–2014

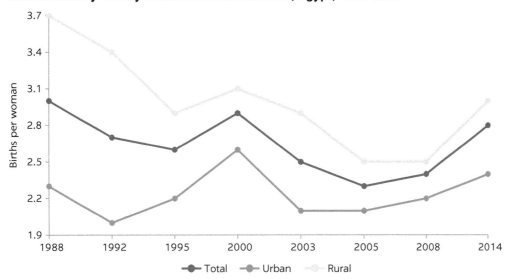

Source: Egypt Demographic and Health Surveys, 1988–2014.

FIGURE 1.10

Desired fertility rate by education, Egypt, 1988–2014

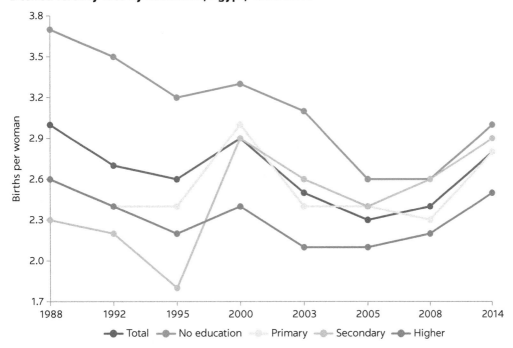

Source: Egypt Demographic and Health Surveys, 1988–2014.

population of women with primary and secondary education. For women with no education, the desired number of children showed little change between 1995 and 2003, then decreased from 2003 to 2005, then started to increase in 2008.

Desired fertility also increased after 2005 across all wealth quintiles, particularly among the middle (third) and second-highest wealth quintiles (figure 1.11). This followed a decline between 2003 and 2005 that was observed across all wealth quintiles, consistent with global trends.

FIGURE 1.11
Total desired fertility rate by wealth quintile, Egypt, 2003–14

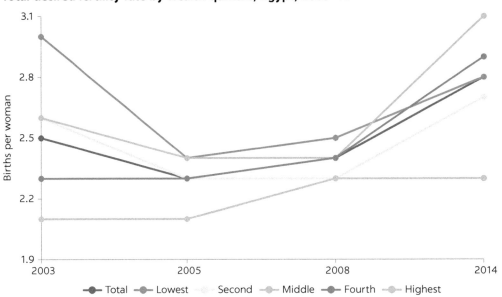

Source: Egypt Demographic and Health Surveys, 2003–14.

The data in the above three figures are highly suggestive of important shifts in the population's desire for children, which appears to be driving fertility change in Egypt. That the changes took place in different locations (beginning with urban areas); among women with different education levels (beginning with higher education); and across different wealth groups (beginning with the middle wealth quintile) provides important hints as to what was happening in Egypt at the time to produce these changes. These trends are also consistent with the increase in the ideal number of children reported since 2003 (with more people responding that the ideal number of children should be three or four). It is therefore plausible to conclude that the demand for children is likely the main reason for the change in fertility rate, which should also provide important input on how to prioritize population policy.

MEDIAN AGE AT FIRST MARRIAGE

Between 1988 and 2014, the median age at first marriage for women ages 25–49 years increased nationally from 18.5 to 20.8 years. The increase was driven mainly by women with no education, as those with primary or higher education showed little increase (figure 1.12). Conversely, there was a distinct decline in the age at first marriage for women with secondary education. The reasons for this are unclear, especially since secondary education is often viewed as a protective factor against early marriage, but lack of job opportunities for females may have played a role. It is likely that the national average age at marriage would have been higher if not for this downward trend among women with secondary education.

At the same time, the median age at first marriage increased more among rural than urban women—3.0 years versus 2.4 years, respectively (figure 1.13).

FIGURE 1.12

Median age at first marriage for women ages 25–49 by education, Egypt, 1988–2014

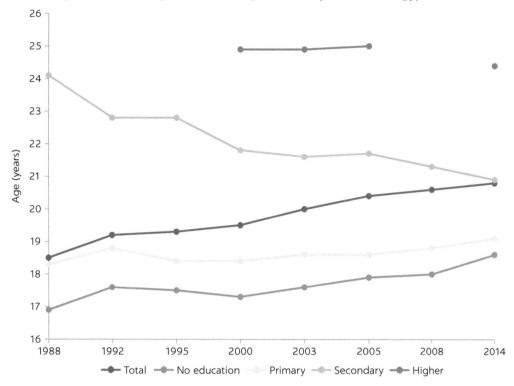

Source: Egypt Demographic and Health Surveys, 1988–2014.

FIGURE 1.13

Median age at first marriage for women ages 25–49 by urban and rural residence, Egypt, 1988–2014

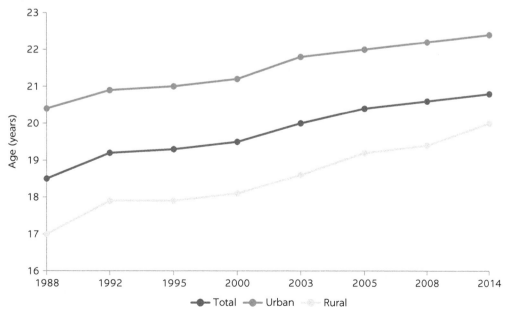

Source: Egypt Demographic and Health Surveys, 1988–2014.

FIGURE 1.14

Median age at first marriage for women ages 25-49 by wealth quintile, Egypt, 2003-2014

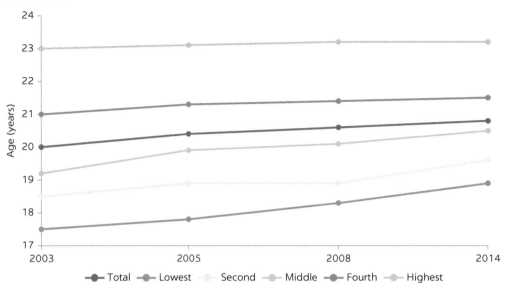

Source: Egypt Demographic and Health Surveys, 2003-14.

The median age at first marriage also increased across all wealth quintiles, with the highest increase among the lowest wealth quintile (figure 1.14).

USE OF CONTRACEPTIVE METHODS

From 1988 until 2003, the contraceptive prevalence rate (using any method) increased nationally and across all age groups in Egypt; but between 2003 and 2008, the trend stagnated nationally with fluctuations across all age groups. After 2008, this rate declined nationally and across all age groups, except for women married or in a union who are ages 45–49. More specifically, since 2003, this rate significantly decreased among women ages 15–19 (by 19.3 percent), 20–24 (by 11.9 percent), and 30–34 (by 6.7 percent); it increased only among women ages 45–49, by 15 percent, while plateauing among other age groups (figure 1.15).

Similarly, the use of any contraceptive method increased across all regions until 2003, then the rate started to decline, first in urban governorates and urban Lower Egypt, followed by rural Lower Egypt in 2005, and Upper Egypt (rural and urban areas) in 2008. Since 2008, the rate decreased in all regions, except for rural Lower Egypt and urban governorates; Upper Egypt and urban Lower Egypt showed the largest decline, while it remained flattish for rural Lower Egypt (figure 1.16).

Use of any contraceptive method declined after 2008 across all women with living children. Between 1988 and 2003, use of any contraceptive method increased across all women with living children, then it slightly declined in 2005 before it increased slightly in 2008. After that, the use declined across all groups, particularly among those with one or two children (figure 1.17).

FIGURE 1.15

Percentage of women married or in a union currently using any method of contraception by age group, Egypt, 1988–2014

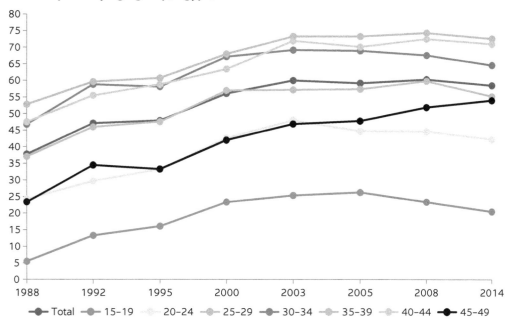

Source: Egypt Demographic and Health Surveys, 1988–2014.

FIGURE 1.16

Percentage of women married or in a union currently using any method of contraception by region, Egypt, 1988–2014

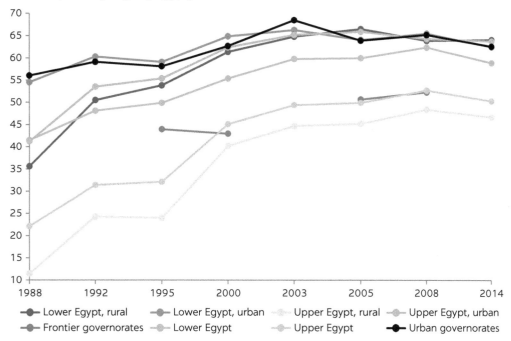

Source: Egypt Demographic and Health Surveys, 1988–2014.

FIGURE 1.17

Percentage of women married or in a union currently using any method of contraception by number of living children, Egypt, 1988–2014

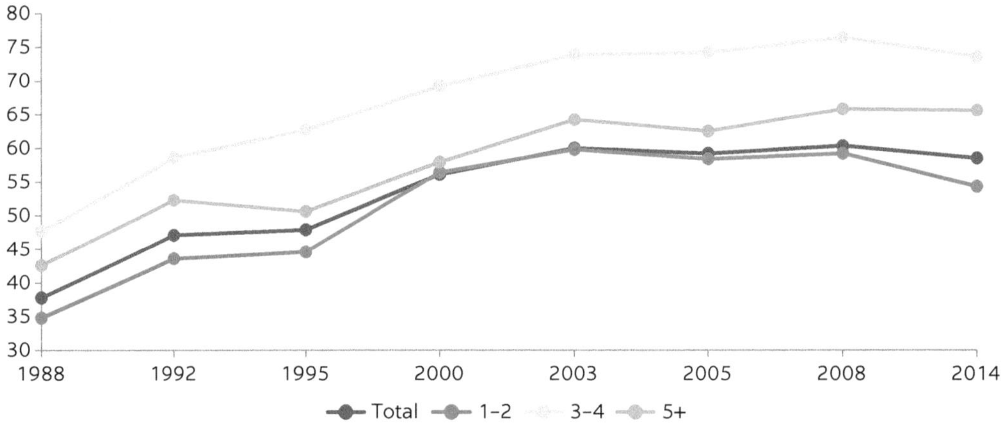

Source: Egypt Demographic and Health Surveys, 1988–2014.
Note: The share of women with no living children was less than 1 percent except for 1995, when it was 1.2 percent. In 2014, it was 0.1 percent.

POSSIBLE DRIVERS OF OBSERVED CHANGES IN FERTILITY

There are two possible sets of drivers behind the observed changes in fertility in Egypt: those directly related to fertility and family planning services (which come under the purview of proximate determinants) and those related to socio-economic factors (distal determinants). For the proximate determinants, Egypt's fertility increase is driven by the following: decreased exposure to family planning and reproductive health messages in the media and to less availability of information and counseling on family planning and reproductive health; limited contraceptive method mix and a shift in the methods women choose, from intra-uterine devices (IUDs) to oral contraceptives; discontinuation of methods because of mismanagement of side effects; a trend toward earlier marriage, having the first child sooner, and having shorter birth intervals; fewer young women using contraception; and a steady decline in the age at marriage among educated, young women in urban areas—that is, they were marrying younger even as the overall age at marriage increased (JSI 2020; MOHP, El-Zanaty and Associates, and ICF International 2015; Radovich et al. 2018).

Simultaneously, the change in the overall economic and labor market situation in Egypt has also likely had an effect on women's lives and fertility behavior (JSI 2020). Although the male labor force participation rate is close to 100 percent, that of women is very low, at under 24 percent in 2014 (CAPMAS 2017a), and is estimated to have declined since then (World Bank 2020). In parallel, unemployment has been high for some time and even increased slightly, reaching 25 percent for women and 9 percent for men in 2014 (Goujon and Al Zalak 2018). The lack of job opportunities in the formal sector, unfavorable working environments for women (for instance, maternity policies, lack of flexible hours), and the disproportionate burden of household responsibilities are some of the contributing factors, which also contribute to women leaving the labor market to instead invest their time and effort in marriage and childbearing (Assaad, Krafft, and Selwaness 2017; Constant et al. 2020; Girgis and Adel 2021; also see chapter 4).

CONCLUSIONS

Egypt experienced an alarming trajectory in its demographic indicators between 2008 and 2014 and slipped off the path to reducing its fertility—an important driver for achieving its population goals. After declining from 4.5 births per woman in 1988 to 3.0 births per woman in 2008, Egypt's TFR then climbed to 3.5 births per woman in 2014. This increase in fertility was led mainly by wealthier and more educated women in urban areas—going against three global trends. The population's desire for more children appears to be the driving force behind the fertility change in Egypt, rather than a lack of availability of contraceptives. In fact, the overall rate of use of any contraceptive method has remained stagnant since 2003. On the other hand, the median age at first marriage for women increased nationally, driven mainly by women with no education and by rural women. These changes raised concerns about the consequences for development and economic growth in the country, to which the government responded.

REFERENCES

Assaad, Ragui, Caroline Krafft, and Irene Selwaness. 2017. "The Impact of Marriage on Women's Employment in the Middle East and North Africa." ERF Working Paper 1086, Economic Research Forum, Cairo.

CAPMAS (Central Agency for Public Mobilization and Statistics). 2017a. "Egypt Population, Housing, and Establishments Census 2017." Central Agency for Public Mobilization and Statistics. https://www.capmas.gov.eg/party/party.html.

CAPMAS (Central Agency for Public Mobilization and Statistics). 2017b. "Statistical Yearbook 2017" (issue no.108). Cairo: CAPMAS. http://www.capmas.gov.eg/.

Constant, Louay, Ifeanyi Edochie, Peter Glick, Jeffrey Martini, and Chandra Garber. 2020. "Barriers to Employment That Women Face in Egypt." Santa Monica, CA: RAND Corporation. https://www.rand.org/content/dam/rand/pubs/research_reports/RR2800/RR2868/RAND_RR2868.pdf.

CSDH (Commission on Social Determinants of Health). 2008. *Closing the Gap in a Generation: Health Equity through Action on the Social Determinants of Health.* Final Report of the Commission on Social Determinants of Health. Geneva: World Health Organization. https://www.who.int/social_determinants/final_report/csdh_finalreport_2008.pdf.

Girgis, Hanan, and Noha Adel. 2021. "Childcare Services and Its Impact on Women Economic Participation." Baseera, National Council for Women, and World Bank Group, Cairo. http://en.enow.gov.eg/Report/144.pdf.

Goujon, Anne, and Zakarya Al Zalak. 2018. "Why Has Fertility Been Increasing in Egypt?" *Population & Societies* 555 (1): 1-4. https://doi.org/10.3917/popsoc.551.0001.

JSI (John Snow Inc.). 2020. "Population and Family Planning in Egypt." Cairo: John Snow Inc./USAID. https://www.jsi.com/resource/population-family-planning-in-egypt/.

MOHP (Ministry of Health and Population), El-Zanaty and Associates, and ICF International. 2015. *Egypt Demographic and Health Survey 2014.* Cairo and Rockville, MD: MOHP and ICF International.

Radovich, Emma, Atef el-Shitany, Hania Sholkamy, and Lenka Benova. 2018. "Rising Up: Fertility Trends in Egypt before and after the Revolution." PLoS ONE 13 (1): e0190148. https://doi.org/10.1371/journal.pone.0190148.

World Bank. 2020. World Development Indicators (database). Washington, DC: World Bank. https://databank.worldbank.org/source/world-development-indicators.

Egypt Demographic and Health Surveys, 1988–2014, by Year

EI-Zanaty, Fatma H., Hussein A. A. Sayed, Hassan H. M. Zaky, and Ann A. Way. 1993. *Egypt Demographic and Health Survey 1992.* Calverton, MD: National Population Council and Macro International Inc. https://dhsprogram.com/pubs/pdf/FR48/FR48.pdf.

EI-Zanaty, Fatma, Enas M. Hussein, Gihan A. Shawky, Ann A. Way, and Sunita Kishor. 1996. *Egypt Demographic and Health Survey 1995.* Calverton, MD: National Population Council and Macro International Inc. https://dhsprogram.com/pubs/pdf/FR71/FR71.pdf.

El-Zanaty, Fatma, and Ann Way. 2001. *Egypt Demographic and Health Survey 2000.* Calverton, MD: Ministry of Health and Population, National Population Council, and ORC Macro. https://dhsprogram.com/pubs/pdf/FR117/FR117.pdf.

El-Zanaty, Fatma, and Ann Way. 2004. *Egypt Interim Demographic and Health Survey 2003.* Cairo: Ministry of Health and Population, National Population Council, El-Zanaty and Associates, and ORC Macro. http://dhsprogram.com/pubs/pdf/FR149/FR149.pdf.

El-Zanaty, Fatma, and Ann Way. 2006. *Egypt Demographic and Health Survey 2005.* Cairo: Ministry of Health and Population, National Population Council, El-Zanaty and Associates, and ORC Macro. https://www.dhsprogram.com/pubs/pdf/FR176/FR176.pdf.

El-Zanaty, Fatma, and Ann Way. 2009. *Egypt Demographic and Health Survey 2008.* Cairo: Ministry of Health, El-Zanaty and Associates, and Macro International. http://dhsprogram.com/pubs/pdf/FR220/FR220.pdf.

MOHP (Ministry of Health and Population), El-Zanaty and Associates, and ICF International. 2015. *Egypt Demographic and Health Survey 2014.* Cairo and Rockville, MD: MOHP and ICF International. https://dhsprogram.com/pubs/pdf/FR302/FR302.pdf.

Sayed, Hussein Abdel-Aziz, Magu+ed I. Osman, Fatma El-Zanaty, and Ann A. Way. 1989. *Egypt Demographic and Health Survey 1988.* Cairo: National Population Council and Institute for Resource Development/Macro Systems. http://dhsprogram.com/pubs/pdf/FR14/FR14.pdf.

2 A National Strategy and Plan to Address Demographic Changes

SHERINE SHAWKY AND SAMEH EL-SAHARTY

Cognizant of the challenges facing the Arab Republic of Egypt that were caused by the fertility reversal and population growth, the government launched a new strategy to bend the population growth curve in November 2014—the Egypt National Population Strategy 2015–2030 (ENPS 2015–2030). Accompanying it was the First Five-Year Population Implementation Plan 2015–2020 (EPIP 2015–2020). This chapter examines the policy change and the steps the government has taken since 2015 to enact those changes.

EGYPT NATIONAL POPULATION STRATEGY 2015–30

ENPS 2015–2030 cross-references Article 41 of the Egypt's 2014 Constitution, which states that "the State shall implement a population program aimed at striking a balance between population growth and available resources; and shall maximize investments in human resources and improve their characteristics with the goal of achieving [the country's] sustainable development" (unofficial translation). The 2014 Constitution also explicitly provides, for the first time, a list of rights that, if assured, would make a leap in the quality of life of the population, while also providing a precedence for a legal framework for addressing population issues.

ENPS 2015–2030 made it clear that there are two main population challenges facing the country: the reversal of the steady state of fertility decline, and the persistence of geographic disparities in population and development indicators.

Aligned with Egypt's aspirations, ENPS 2015–2030 was built on political commitment and multisectoral collaboration. It was founded on human rights, social justice, government accountability, and respect for citizens, and it defined clear goals and axes for intervention. It entrusted the Ministry of Population (MOP)[1] and the Ministry of Health, with primary responsibility for managing the population program. A summary of ENPS 2015–2030 is given in figure 2.1.

FIGURE 2.1

Summary of ENPS 2015–2030

Source: Original figure based on Egypt National Population Strategy 2015–2030 (in Arabic).
Note: ENPS = Egypt National Population Strategy; NGOs = nongovernmental organizations.

Finally, ENPS 2015–2030 defined a monitoring and evaluation (M&E) plan with a set of strategic objectives. It identified seven strategic indicators and proposed estimates for three scenarios (table 2.1) based on data from the 2014 Demographic and Health Survey (MOHP, El-Zanaty and Associates, and ICF International 2015a). The strategy indicated that the baseline population size was 118.9 million and the target population in 2030 was 110.9 million.

TABLE 2.1 **ENPS 2015–2030 estimates under three scenarios**

	SCENARIO		
INDICATOR	CONTINUING CURRENT FERTILITY RATE	REACHING THE TARGET	REACHING THE REPLACEMENT RATE
Total fertility rate	3.5	2.4	2.1
Population size (millions)	118.9	110.9	108.7
Number of births (millions)	2.9	2.0	1.7
Contraceptive prevalence rate (%)	60.2	71.6	74.7
Contraceptive discontinuation rate within a year (%)	25.9	18.0	15.0
Proportion of unmet need for family planning (%)	9.2	6.0	5.0
Proportion of use of modern methods (%)	75.0	85.0	90.0

Source: ENPS 2015–2030, 36 (in Arabic).

FIRST FIVE-YEAR POPULATION IMPLEMENTATION PLAN 2015–2020

The general structure of EPIP 2015–2020 is based on transforming the main directions and principles established in ENPS 2015–2030. EPIP 2015–2020 adheres to the objectives, principles, and axes of ENPS 2015–2030, with slight modifications as key channels for achieving the goals of the strategy. EPIP 2015–2020 stresses reduction in the population growth rate as its first goal. Figure 2.2 provides a summary of EPIP 2015–2020 and table 2.2 illustrates its five axes and the objectives.

EPIP 2015–2020 also developed an M&E plan to monitor progress against the strategic objectives set out in ENPS 2015–2030, including the use of data produced by the Central Agency for Mobilization and Statistics (CAPMAS) whenever they become available.

The progress made under each of the five axes of EPIP 2015–2020, between 2015 and 2018, is summarized below and discussed in more detail in appendix A.

Axis I: Family planning and reproductive health

Since the implementation of EPIP 2015–2020, numerous achievements have been realized to improve use of family planning (FP) services. The number of FP services in primary health care units (PHCUs) increased by 94.4 percent; while FP services provided through mobile clinic visits reached 90 percent of the planned target. Provision of FP services through "medical caravans"—a group of several mobile clinics and teams that visited remote locations periodically—reached 67.5 percent of the target value. Thirty-two clinics were either opened or reactivated to provide FP and reproductive health (RH) services, including 19 in university hospitals, 4 clinics in police hospitals, and 9 outlets in health insurance hospitals. In addition, 64 new clinics operated by nongovernmental organizations (NGOs) were opened to provide FP services.

The National Population Council (NPC) and the Ministry of Health and Population (MOHP) conducted numerous awareness campaigns and training sessions. The MOHP also supplied 152 stores in 15 governorates with necessary equipment and FP methods. Funding for the purchase of FP methods was made

FIGURE 2.2
Summary of EPIP 2015–2020

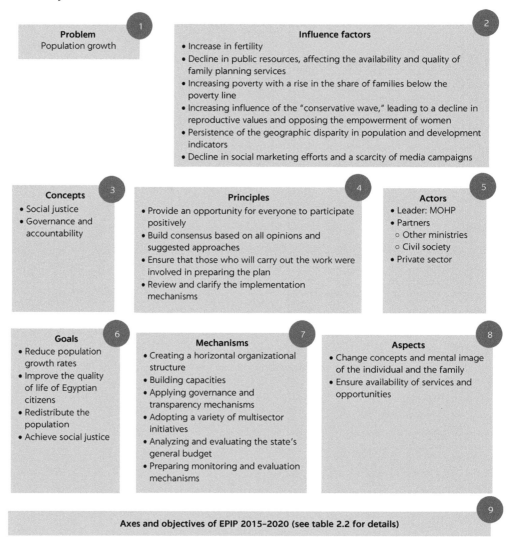

1 Problem
Population growth

2 Influence factors
- Increase in fertility
- Decline in public resources, affecting the availability and quality of family planning services
- Increasing poverty with a rise in the share of families below the poverty line
- Increasing influence of the "conservative wave," leading to a decline in reproductive values and opposing the empowerment of women
- Persistence of the geographic disparity in population and development indicators
- Decline in social marketing efforts and a scarcity of media campaigns

3 Concepts
- Social justice
- Governance and accountability

4 Principles
- Provide an opportunity for everyone to participate positively
- Build consensus based on all opinions and suggested approaches
- Ensure that those who will carry out the work were involved in preparing the plan
- Review and clarify the implementation mechanisms

5 Actors
- Leader: MOHP
- Partners
  - Other ministries
  - Civil society
- Private sector

6 Goals
- Reduce population growth rates
- Improve the quality of life of Egyptian citizens
- Redistribute the population
- Achieve social justice

7 Mechanisms
- Creating a horizontal organizational structure
- Building capacities
- Applying governance and transparency mechanisms
- Adopting a variety of multisector initiatives
- Analyzing and evaluating the state's general budget
- Preparing monitoring and evaluation mechanisms

8 Aspects
- Change concepts and mental image of the individual and the family
- Ensure availability of services and opportunities

9 Axes and objectives of EPIP 2015–2020 (see table 2.2 for details)

Source: Original figure based on EPIP 2015–2020 (in Arabic).
Note: EPIP = Egypt First Five-Year Population Implementation Plan 2015–2020; MOHP = Ministry of Health and Population.

available through the national general budget, with financial support (particularly for long-acting IUD and hypodermic capsules) through development partners, that is, United Nations Population Fund (UNFPA) and the World Bank. More recently, with support from the World Bank, the government of Egypt has launched the "Continue, We Want You" initiative to address the shortage of physicians by rehiring retired doctors (ages 60–65 years) to provide FP services in the governorates of Upper Egypt.

Despite this progress, the FP program suffered from three major challenges. First, this axis was assigned only a very small share of the national budget, accounting for only 2.2 percent of the total budget for all activities and 6.2 percent of the total budget for priority activities. Second, the persistent shortage of doctors and the weak integration of FP services as part of comprehensive reproductive health services in health care units and mobile clinics were another major obstacle for providing FP services. Third, partnerships with NGOs

TABLE 2.2 **Axes and objectives of EPIP 2015–2020**

AXIS	OBJECTIVE
Axis I: Family Planning and Reproductive Health	1- Raise the rate of use of family planning methods from 58.5 percent to 64.0 percent within five years. 2- Amend laws and regulations in line with constitutional rights and Egypt's ratified international obligations. 3- Commit to apply the referral system between levels of care to the required standards in 100 percent of primary care units. 4- Provide safe maternity services and breastfeeding awareness for priority areas, especially rural and disadvantaged areas. 5- Offer support services for HIV/AIDS patients at all levels of health care. 6- Provide high-quality basic health care services.
Axis II: Adolescent and Youth Health	1- Develop the skills of adolescents and youth. 2- Reduce the unemployment rate among youth by 5 percent within five years by 1 percent annually. 3- Reduce the rate of children at risk by 2 percent annually. 4- Reduce the employment rate of children working in the labor market from 9 percent to 4 percent within five years. 5- Increase the share of valid concepts of reproductive and sexual health among adolescents and youth (18–35 years) by 10 percent annually for five years. 6- Increase the youth participation rate, by 10 percent annually, in setting policies and making decisions related to population policies in their societies, and monitor their implementation. 7- Establish mechanisms for youth participation in addressing social issues, and increase volunteerism rates by 15 percent annually.
Axis III: Education	1- Integrate population issues into the education process in its different types. 2- Increase the enrollment rate from 93.4 percent to 100 percent. 3- Reduce the percentage of dropouts from education to zero, and provide them with a second chance of high-quality education. 4- Reduce the illiteracy rate from 21.7 percent to 7.0 percent. 5- Upgrade technical education and link it to the needs of society and the labor market. 6- Build the capabilities of Islamic and Christian religious leaders, enabling them to develop religious discourse and advance population issues.
Axis IV: Communication and Social Media	1- Increase the share of media materials that include population issues by the various media. 2- Increase public mobilization to support population issues.
Axis V: Empowerment of Women	1- Increase the share of women's participation in the labor force from 23 percent to 35 percent. 2- Raise the share of females in senior leadership and management positions in the government sector from 11 percent to 20 percent. 3- Include equal opportunity units in ministries from the administrative structure and increase their number from 26 to 32 units. 4- Increase the share of women business owners from 2 percent to 10 percent. 5- Reduce the unemployment rate of women in rural areas from 20.2 percent to 15.0 percent. 6- Increase the share of lending to women, especially for female breadwinners, from 40 percent to 70 percent. 7- Increase the participation of women in political life—the House of Representatives—from 12 percent to 25 percent, and raise the share of women's participation in local councils from 25 percent to 40 percent, or executive councils in the governorates from 10 percent to 25 percent. 8- Raise the share of women in boards of directors of NGOs to 25 percent. 9- Reduce exposure to violence, which includes two subgoals. 10- Reduce early marriage by 50 percent within five years.
Additional Axes	1- Redevelop slums. 2- Increase job opportunities and reduce the unemployment rate. 3- Increase access of people with special needs, in the age group 18–60 years, to health, social, and economic services, especially females. 4- Reduce the rate of female circumcision in new generations by 10 percent.

Source: Based on EPIP 2015–2020 (in Arabic).

appeared weak, and the private sector was largely absent. These challenges were reflected in the delays in launching or achieving many activities.

The absence of data on FP indicators at the national and program levels rendered it impossible to measure progress toward planned targets under this axis. However, using the crude birth rate (CBR) as a proxy indicator for FP services, there is a demonstrated failure in coverage of all geographic areas, most notably the rural areas of Alexandria, Giza, Sohag, and Qena; and the urban areas of Dakahlia, Sharqia, Gharbia, Beheira, Beni Suef, Menia, Assiut, and Aswan, where live births are high and concentrated.

Axis II: Adolescent and youth health

The financial resources for this axis were either unavailable or insufficient to conduct or sustain planned activities. Thus, most adolescent and youth health activities were conducted and implemented outside the EPIP 2015–2020 framework as part of the goals of other ministries and civil society organizations, often resulting in overlapping and fragmented actions. In addition, data were not available for any of the outcome indicators under this axis.

Axis III: Education

Egypt's education sector has witnessed significant achievements in the past few years on enrollment and gender parity. Enrollment in primary school rose from 9.5 million in 2005 to 12.2 million in 2017, and at the secondary level from 6.7 million in 2009 to 8.9 million in 2015, reaching 100 percent at the primary level, 85 percent at the lower-secondary level, but only 28 percent at the upper-secondary level. A major achievement is that Egypt has attained overall gender parity, with slightly higher enrollment of girls recorded at all levels of education. The most notable development in recent years has been the adoption of a sectorwide reform to modernize the education system and prioritize learning.

However, financial resources were not available for many activities under this axis. Thus, most education activities fell outside the scope of EPIP 2015–2020 and focused on the goals of the Ministry of Education and Technical Education (MOETE). Population issues were not among its priorities.

Moreover, progress on most activities could not be monitored because data were either unavailable or data sharing across programs is not acceptable to most institutions with data. Despite the lack of data, it is apparent that little if any progress has been made on the targets under this axis. This includes class density, secondary-education enrollment, school dropout rate, number of community schools and classes, and the illiteracy rate. In addition, many geographic inequalities were common; adult illiteracy was higher among females, and while achievements have been made in increasing girls' enrollment, male secondary enrollment is now lagging.

Axis IV: Communication and social media

As above, financial resources were unavailable for many activities. Most activities were not conducted under the EPIP 2015–2020 framework. Activities were fragmented and overlapping, and the messages were not specific to population growth or FP. There were no available data on the indicators, making it hard to monitor progress toward targets.

Axis V: Empowerment of women

As with other axes, activities and outcomes are impossible to monitor because of a lack of information at the program and national levels. From the very limited data available, it is evident that women's share in the labor force is consistently lower than that of men (24.5 percent versus 72 percent in 2018), and female unemployment is high (21.4 percent) and concentrated in 15 governorates. Further, early marriages do take place for both females and males, notably in rural areas. Data show that 5.7 percent of females and 0.2 percent of males in 15–17 age group are married (CAPMAS 2017).

CHALLENGES FACING THE IMPLEMENTATION OF ENPS 2015–2030 AND EPIP 2015–2020

An overall look at ENPS 2015–2030 and EPIP 2015–2020 demonstrates several key challenges, including in political commitment, governance, financing, and target groups.

Changing governance and leadership of the program. The strategy and plan were driven by political commitment—one that required integrating the population component into economic and social development plans under the leadership of the relatively new Ministry of Population (MOP). However, this did not materialize because of the changes to the MOP, its span of control, and leadership. Specifically, the strategy was expected to be implemented by the MOP, which had been created by raising the status of the NPC. However, the MOP was later downgraded back to the NPC under the Ministry of Health, which then became the Ministry of Health and Population (MOHP). Although initially a post was created for a deputy minister for population, it was later can-celled. Moreover, there was a rapid turnover of the leadership of the NPC, which affected its stability, its coordination and management role, and its capacity to monitor the implementation of the strategy (UNFPA 2020). These factors have led to inconsistent decision-making and plans that are not related to the popula-tion issues and goals (Dawood and Abdel Latif 2019). This lack of coordination also led to two new population strategies being launched—the July 24, 2017, "Disciplined Population Strategy" and the February 18, 2020, updated "Population Awareness Strategy"—without any analysis or evaluation of the progress on EPIP 2015–2020.

Inadequate role of the private sector and civil society. ENPS 2015–2030 and EPIP 2015–2020 adopt a multisectoral framework and theory of change, but this approach is missing in practice. The channels of communication and bonds between the various stakeholders remain weak. The public sector plays a domi-nant role in the implementation of the population strategy and is suspicious of civil society and the private sector, which has led to mistrust between these stakeholders. Further, the difference in technological resources and skilled human resources between the private and public sectors has broadened the chasm between the two sides. Moreover, civil society members feel insecure because they are largely dependent on grants that are not always available, and the private sector is absent from the scene.

Target population. ENPS 2015–2030 and EPIP 2015–2020 assume that, following historical and global trends, those with highest fertility and most in need of FP are rural residents, the poor, and those with little or no education.

However, recent data trends for Egypt suggest quite the opposite: with the socio-economic and political changes in Egypt, the rise in fertility has been driven by the educated, rich, and urban residents (chapter 1). Hence, the strategy and plan are not geared toward the population that is driving fertility.

Limited capacity for financial analysis. Estimation of the costs of population and FP services and the capacity to do financial modeling are lacking. Budget preparation for EPIP 2015–2020 reflected weak budgeting and auditing skills. The three scenarios used to estimate the cost of programs were not realistic and did not give reasonable weights to the five axes or the various activities. The result was insufficient or unavailable financial resources for most of the activities.

Lack of attention to men. Men's reproductive health and their role in decisions about childbearing and contraception are well recognized (Duvander et al. 2020; Inhorn and Wentzell 2011; Shawky, Soliman, and Sawires 2009; Testa, Cavalli, and Rosina 2014). Yet that role was neglected in ENPS 2015–2030, with all the axes focusing on women. Men's central role in reproduction was not clearly addressed, and there were no programs to engage them in solving the population challenge.

Data limitations contributing to inaccurate target setting. ENPS 2015–2030 based its strategic objectives and targets, along with the M&E plan and proposed estimates for three population scenarios, on data from the 2014 Demographic and Health Survey (MOHP, El-Zanaty and Associates, and ICF International 2015a). However, the data on population were updated in the 2017 census (CAPMAS 2017), indicating that the population had reached 104.2 million (including the international diaspora) by 2017. This was considerably different from the population baseline and projected estimates for the strategy, rendering its population projections inaccurate.

M&E challenges. The EPIP 2015–2020 M&E plan examines progress at three levels: initial results, intermediate results, and the final impact or outcomes. Baseline and 2020 targets in the M&E framework were based on the 2014 Demographic and Health Survey, but these data do not align with the 2017 census data, where comparable indicators are available (CAPMAS 2018, 2020). Further, the strategy and plan only identify national targets, which do not respond to the differences in population outcomes and uneven distribution of challenges among population subgroups and across Egypt's governorates.

Barriers to data sharing contributing to weak M&E. Although data are gathered by various programs and departments, and program or project managers may have precise documentation of activities completed and the associated expenditure, this information is not shared among institutions or even departments within the same sector. Moreover, the collected information is only on paper, and the capacity for electronic documentation is still lagging. Finally, these are data used only to verify service implementation and budgetary compliance. The M&E of programs stops at the level of outputs and does not evaluate outcomes and impact. This limitation may be caused by any number of factors, including a lack of statistical capacity, of knowledge about the importance of evaluations, of interest, or of sufficient financial resources.

Diluted focus of the implementation plan. EPIP 2015–2020 has widened the scope of its activities and identified four additional objectives for achieving results: slum redevelopment; increased job opportunities and reduced unemployment; increased access to health, social, and economic services for people ages 18–60 years with disabilities, especially females; and reduced percentage of female circumcision in new generations by 10 percent by enforcing the law criminalizing the act and activating related ministerial decisions. Although these are important areas of work, their inclusion broadens the scope of EPIP 2015–2020, thus straining its already weak management and coordination and diluting its capacity to deliver results.

At the same time, FP programs suffer from other implementation challenges.

Missed opportunities in integrating FP services. FP activities oscillated between being provided as stand-alone vertical services or being horizontally integrated within the continuum of sexual and reproductive health (SRH) services. Vertical FP activities were only partially implemented because of insufficient financial resources. Coverage of FP services in integrated SRH programs was fragmented. There was a missed opportunity to incorporate these services and/or information about FP at critical points of the reproductive cycle, including puberty, premarital counseling, pregnancy, and the postnatal period (Shawky, Rashad, and Khadr 2019). Premarital counseling is not fully implemented, and reproductive health and FP counseling has disappeared from ill-health screenings. Antenatal care focuses only on the medical checkup, with no counseling on FP. Demand for postnatal care is very low, and for those who still access it, the focus is on medical care for the mother and child (MOHP, El-Zanaty and Associates, and ICF International 2015a, 2015b; Rashad, Shawky, and Khadr 2019; Shawky, Rashad, and Khadr 2019).

Inconsistencies in the modes of FP service delivery. The provision of FP services was covered through fixed or static clinics and mobile delivery. Because of insufficient funding, mobile clinics were unable to cover all the target areas and populations. Their unreliable schedules, lack of continuity of care, and lack of privacy were cited in anecdotal evidence suggesting that clients did not favor them (Rabie et al. 2013). Women were also reluctant to seek services for fear of being noticed and stigmatized for using FP services.

Shortage of health care professionals in the public sector. This has been a point of concern for FP services, irrespective of mode of delivery. Some of the ways that health care providers seek to overcome the low salaries and poor working conditions in the public sector include raising rates and holding dual jobs, migrating to cities, and moving to the private sector. These patterns have depleted the public health workforce and affected the availability and quality of these services (WHO 2014).

CONCLUSION

ENPS 2015–2030 and EPIP 2015–2020 came as critical responses to the alarming demographic trend in the country. However, their goals, objectives, and axes, though appearing comprehensive, suffer from several pitfalls, including (a) fragmented governance and poor accountability, with wavering political commitment to maintain the Ministry of Population and rapid turnover in the leadership of the NPC; (b) insufficient financial resources, with a funding gap of around 50 percent, and weak financial and budgeting skills, which especially affected axis I, a core part of the strategy and plan; (c) limited reach, with a failure to expand geographic coverage of services due in part to low budget allocation and in part to lower capacity, resulting from a shortage of doctors in health care units and fewer mobile clinic visits than planned; (d) lack of attention to the evidence on the changing sociodemographic context, that is, the emerging sources of higher fertility (including among urban residents, the rich, and the educated) and a focus only on the poorest villages; (e) failure to engage men as partners in reproductive health and fertility decisions, especially given their strong influence on women's decisions about childbearing and contraception; (f) weak M&E, with a plan based on estimates for baselines and targets that did not reflect reality, as well as reliance on overall averages with no disaggregation or equity lens; and (g) lack of coordination and oversight of activities related to the social determinants of fertility under axes II–V, which were implemented outside the EPIP 2015–2020 framework of activities, and which could not be monitored because of a paucity of data at program and national levels.

The next chapter drills down further into the strategic objectives related to the first goal in EPIP 2015–2020—to reduce the rate of population growth—going beyond overall averages to illustrate trends and patterns by geographic disaggregation.

NOTE

1. ENPS 2015–2030 was prepared under the auspices of the Ministry of Population (MOP) with the mandate of addressing Egypt's population challenges. However, the MOP was later downgraded to the National Population Council under the Ministry of Health, which then became the Ministry of Health and Population (MOHP).

REFERENCES

CAPMAS (Central Agency for Public Mobilization and Statistics). 2017. "Egypt Population, Housing, and Establishments Census 2017." Cairo: CAPMAS. https://www.capmas.gov.eg/party/party.html.

CAPMAS (Central Agency for Public Mobilization and Statistics). 2018. "Egypt in Figures 2018." March 2018. Cairo: CAPMAS. https://www.sis.gov.eg/UP/Egypt%20in%20Figures%202018/egypt-in-numbers2018.pdf.

CAPMAS (Central Agency for Public Mobilization and Statistics). 2020. "Statistical Yearbook." December 2020. Cairo: CAPMAS. http://www.capmas.gov.eg/.

Dawood, Ahmed, and Abla Abdel Latif. 2019. "Population Policy in Egypt: An Analysis of the Constituents for Success and the Optimal Institutional Form, a Comparative Study." Working Paper 203, Egyptian Center for Economic Studies, Cairo. http://www.eces.org.eg/cms/NewsUploads/Pdf/2019_12_8-15_45_41Working%20Paper%20203.pdf. In Arabic.

Duvander, Ann-Zofie, Susanne Fahlén, Maria Brandén, and Sofi Ohlsson-Wijk. 2020. "Who Makes the Decision to Have Children? Couples' Childbearing Intentions and Actual Childbearing." *Advances in Life Course Research* 43 (March): 100286. https://doi.org/10.1016/j.alcr.2019.04.016.

Inhorn, Marcia C., and Emily A. Wentzell. 2011. "Embodying Emergent Masculinities: Men Engaging with Reproductive and Sexual Health Technologies in the Middle East and Mexico." *American Ethnologist* 38 (4): 801–15. Retrieved October 6, 2020, from http://www.jstor.org/stable/41410434.

MOHP (Ministry of Health and Population), El-Zanaty and Associates, and ICF International. 2015a. Egypt Demographic and Health Survey, 2014. Cairo: MOHP. https://dhsprogram.com/publications/publication-fr302-dhs-final-reports.cfm.

MOHP (Ministry of Health and Population), El-Zanaty and Associates, and ICF International. 2015b. "Egypt Health Issues Survey 2015." Cairo and Rockville, MD: MOHP and ICF International. https://dhsprogram.com/pubs/pdf/FR313/FR313.pdf.

Rabie, Tamer, Zuzana Boehmova, Loraine Hawkins, Nahla Abdel Tawab, Sally Saher, and Atef El Shitany. 2013. "Transforming Family Planning Outlook and Practice in Egypt: A Rights-Based Approach." Washington, DC: World Bank. http://documents1.worldbank .org/curated/en/351971468026087900/pdf/905960WP0Box3800July0160FINAL0PROOF .pdf.

Rashad, Hoda, Sherine Shawky, and Zeinab Khadr. 2019. "Reproductive Health Equity in the Arab Region: Fairness and Social Success. Regional Study." Cairo: The Social Research Center, The American University in Cairo, the United Nations Population Fund/Arab States Regional Office. http://schools.aucegypt.edu/research/src/Documents/SRH-Inequities /Reproductive-Health-Equity-in-the-Arab-Region.pdf.

Shawky, Sherine, Hoda Rashad, and Zeinab Khadr. 2019. "Reproductive Health Inequalities in Egypt: Evidence for Guiding Policies." Cairo: The Social Research Center/The American University in Cairo, the United Nations Population Fund/Arab States Regional Office. https://documents.aucegypt.edu/Docs/src/Reproductive%20Health%20Inequalities%20 in%20Egypt.pdf

Shawky, Sherine, Cherif Soliman, and Sharif Sawires. 2009. "Gender and HIV in the Middle East and North Africa: Lessons for Low Prevalence Scenarios." *Journal of Acquired Immune Deficiency Syndrome* 51 (Suppl 3): S73–74. https://pubmed.ncbi.nlm.nih.gov/19553781/.

Testa, Maria Rita, Laura Cavalli, and Alessandro Rosina. 2014. "The Effect of Couple Disagreement about Child-Timing Intentions: A Parity-Specific Approach." *Population and Development Review* 40 (1): 31–53. https://doi.org/10.1111/j.1728-4457.2014.00649.x.

UNFPA (United Nations Population Fund). 2020. "Review of the Executive Plan 2015–2020 in the Context of the National Population and Development Strategy 2015–2030." Cairo: United Nations Population Fund in collaboration with Egypt National Population Council and the Embassy of Switzerland. https://egypt.unfpa.org/en/publications/review-executive -plan-2015-2020-context-national-population-and-development-strategy.

WHO (World Health Organization). 2014. "Assessing the Regulation of the Private Health Sector in the Eastern Mediterranean Region: Egypt. WHO, Regional Office for the Eastern Mediterranean." https://apps.who.int/iris/bitstream/handle/10665/250541/EMROPUB _2014_EN_1757.pdf?sequence=1&isAllowed=y.

3 Analysis of Demographic Changes from 2015 to 2020

SHERINE SHAWKY AND SAMEH EL-SAHARTY

This chapter focuses on the strategic objectives related to the first goal in First Five-Year Population Implementation Plan (EPIP) 2015–2020—that is, to "reduce the rate of population growth." It aims to illustrate the progress made over the period using available data on fertility. Because the estimates and baseline for the strategic indicators were based on data from the 2014 Egypt Demographic and Health Survey (EDHS), the most recent EDHS, the analysis uses the data provided by the Central Agency for Public Mobilization and Statistics (CAPMAS) in the two periods, 2008–14 and 2015–20, to ensure comparability.

All the strategic indicators for demographic change, except population size, are unavailable in the CAPMAS statistics. The following analysis therefore uses the population size and proxy indicators to monitor progress on fertility. To the extent possible with the available data, the analysis illustrates the progress through overall averages and by geographic disaggregation, including distributional inequalities and their magnitude, using the relative index of dissimilarity expressed as percentages (Ontario Agency for Health Protection and Promotion 2013).

ACHIEVEMENT IN OVERALL AVERAGES

Total fertility rate

The total fertility rate (TFR) is the main indicator used in EPIP 2015–2020 to monitor progress on reducing the population growth. The main source of the baseline indicator is the 2014 EDHS (MOHP, El-Zanaty and Associates, and ICF International 2015). In the absence of more recent EDHS data, and the omission of this indicator in CAPMAS statistics, the general fertility rate (GFR) and the crude birth rate (CBR) can be used as proxy indicators to reflect the trajectory of population growth.

Between 2014 and 2019, the GFR for the Arab Republic of Egypt declined from 123 to 97 children per 1,000 women—a decrease of 21.1 percent. The CBR, according to CAPMAS (2020), was 30.2 live births per 1,000 population in 2015, decreasing to 23.4 per 1,000 population in 2019. After the CBR plateaued between 2010 and 2015, a downward trend in the CBR was seen, with 6.8 fewer births per 1,000 people in 2019 than in 2015 (a 22.5 percent decrease; see figure 3.1).

Population size

EPIP 2015–2020 aimed to reduce the rate of population growth, so that Egypt's population size would increase from 87.0 million in 2015 to 94.0 million in 2020, or 8.0 percent over the course of five years (that is, 1.6 percent annually). According to CAPMAS statistics, however, the population was 89.0 million in 2015/16 and reached 98.9 million on January 1, 2020, for an increase of around 9.9 million (11.1 percent, or 2.8 percent annually).[1] Although the increase in total population size exceeded the target in EPIP 2015–2020, a comparison of the CAPMAS statistics between 2010 and 2019 (figure 3.2) showed a reduction in the *rate* of population growth, from 13.1 percent in 2010–15 to 11.1 percent in 2015–19 (or from 3.3 percent down to 2.8 percent annually).

Family planning

The family planning–related indicators, which include the contraceptive prevalence rate (CPR), the proportion of unmet need for family planning, and the proportion of use of modern methods, are not reported in CAPMAS statistics and therefore are not included in the discussion.

FIGURE 3.1

Crude birth rate, Egypt, 2010–19

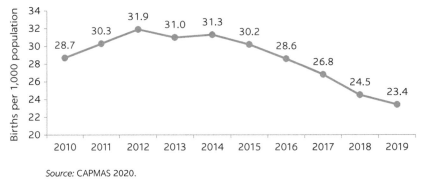

Source: CAPMAS 2020.

FIGURE 3.2

Population size, Egypt, 2010–19

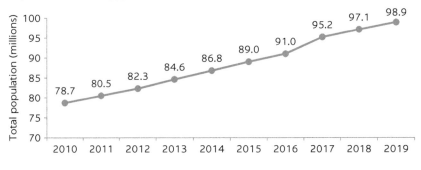

Source: CAPMAS 2020.

TABLE 3.1 **Total number of community schools, classes, and students, 2015/16 and 2019/20**

	2015/16	2019/20
Schools or classes	5,083	4,995
Students	114,939	133,692
Density[a]	23	27

Source: MOETE 2020.

a. Density represents the number of students per school or class.

Education

Objectives for two education-related indicators—the school dropout rate and the illiteracy rate—were laid out under the education axis. Objective 3 on dropouts had a target to reduce the percentage of dropouts from education to zero and to provide them with a quality educational service as a second chance. The baseline for this indicator is derived from the results of the 2006 census, which indicates a dropout rate of 2.6 percent of the population ages 6–18 years. The 2017 census showed a dropout rate of 7.3 percent for children 4 years and above (CAPMAS 2017). Statistics from the Ministry of Education and Technical Education (MOETE) for 2018/19 indicate a dropout rate of 0.25 percent for primary education and 2.0 percent for secondary education, with the dropout rate slightly higher for boys than girls at both levels (MOETE 2020). The age-group definition for this indicator is inconsistent in the various sources, making it difficult to compare. However, there was not much progress on this indicator.

Objective 4 on illiteracy aimed to "reduce the illiteracy rate from 21.7 to 7.0 percent." According to the 2017 census (CAPMAS 2017), the illiteracy rate was 25.8 percent for those ages 10 years and above—that is, no progress was made on this indicator. This outcome may potentially be attributed to the reduction in the number of community schools and classes (table 3.1).

Empowerment of women

Under axis V, on the empowerment of women, objective 5 aimed to "reduce the rate of female unemployment in rural areas from 20.2 percent to 15.0 percent." Data on this geography-specific indicator were unavailable, however, and the national female unemployment rate was used as a proxy. That rate in 2015 was 24.2 percent (and 9.4 percent for males), edging down to 21.4 percent (and 6.8 percent for males) in 2018 (figure 3.3). Thus, while female unemployment declined, the change was small, and considerably less (11.6 percent) than the male rate (27.7 percent).

GEOGRAPHIC DISAGGREGATION

In the absence of the TFR in the CAPMAS statistics, live births are the key proxy indicator that can be used to assess progress on fertility. Live births are in turn affected by other social determinants, which can be assessed using the following proxy indicators: marriage contracts, school dropouts, unemployment, and illiteracy (shown later in table 3.5).

FIGURE 3.3

Trend in unemployment rate by gender, Egypt, 2015–18

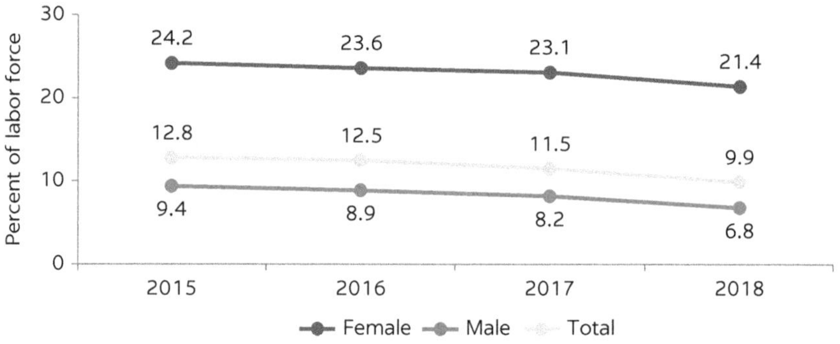

Source: CAPMAS 2020.

This section provides an analysis of all these indicators at the subnational level, with a focus on three dimensions: the likelihood (or risk) of the occurrence of the event, the trend over time, and the geographic disparities *between* governorates or concentration *within* them (appendix B). (In the case of literacy, only likelihood or risk is used in the analysis.)

Live births

Table 3.2 provides the CBR by governorate to assess the likelihood of increased live births (CAPMAS 2020). The national average (rural and urban) CBR declined from 28.6 per 1,000 population in 2016 to 23.4 per 1,000 population in 2019, or by 18.3 percent. In addition, the following trends are observed:

- Ten governorates had a CBR higher than the national average in 2019 and a slower rate of CBR decline: Kafr El-Sheikh, Menia, Assiut, Sohag, Qena, Aswan, Luxor, Red Sea, Matrouh, and South Sinai, with South Sinai showing the highest CBR increase (34.5 percent).
- Beheira, Ismailia, Fayoum, and Beni Suef also showed a CBR higher than the national average in 2019 but had a faster rate of CBR decline than the national average.
- Despite having a CBR lower than the national average in 2019, Cairo and Alexandria had a slower rate of CBR decline.

The CBR was higher in urban than rural areas in both 2016 and 2019, but the pace of CBR decline was faster in rural areas (27.2 percent) than in urban areas (8.5 percent). The data highlight the following trends:

- Kafr El-Sheikh, Assiut, Sohag, and Matrouh showed a CBR higher than the national average in 2019 and a slower rate of CBR decline in both rural and urban areas.
- The following governorates showed a rural CBR higher than the national average in 2019 and a slower rate of rural CBR decline: Giza, Beni Suef, Fayoum, and Qena.
- Menia and Luxor had a higher than average rural CBR in 2019 but showed a faster decline. Also, in 2019, the CBR was greatly above average in rural Alexandria, but the trend could not be calculated, as Alexandria, until 2016, was reported as an urban governorate only.

TABLE 3.2 **Change in crude birth rates by governorate and rural-urban disaggregation, 2016–19**

	2016 (PER 1,000 POPULATION)			2019 (PER 1,000 POPULATION)			CHANGE 2016–2019 (%)		
	RURAL	**URBAN**	**TOTAL**	**RURAL**	**URBAN**	**TOTAL**	**RURAL**	**URBAN**	**TOTAL**
Urban governorates									
Cairo	n.a.	25.4	25.4	n.a.	21.5	21.5	n.a.	−15.4	−15.4
Port Said	n.a.	22.4	22.4	n.a.	16.2	16.2	n.a.	−27.7	−27.7
Suez	n.a.	26.2	26.2	n.a.	19.8	19.8	n.a.	−24.4	−24.4
Lower Egypt									
Alexandria	—	21.8	25.2	137.6	18.5	20.7	—	−15.1	−18.0
Damietta	18.8	39.7	27.0	12.3	31.3	19.9	−34.6	−21.2	−26.2
Dakahlia	15.7	49.2	25.4	10.6	43.3	20.3	−32.5	−12.0	−20.1
Sharqia	24.5	39.2	27.9	15.0	42.4	21.9	−38.8	8.2	−21.5
Qalyoubia	25.0	25.9	25.4	17.3	22.4	19.5	−30.8	−13.5	−23.3
Kafr El-Sheikh	26.7	30.3	27.5	21.9	36.9	25.6	−18.0	21.8	−7.0
Gharbia	17.4	44.0	25.6	10.8	43.5	20.4	−37.9	−1.1	−20.3
Menoufia	22.3	50.3	28.1	16.5	38.0	21.1	−26.0	−24.5	−25.1
Beheira	20.5	65.6	29.7	14.1	62.0	23.5	−31.2	−5.5	−20.8
Ismailia	25.4	37.1	30.8	12.9	37.8	24.2	−49.2	1.9	−21.6
Upper Egypt									
Giza	31.0	26.6	28.4	25.7	20.0	22.3	−17.1	−24.8	−21.6
Beni Suef	27.8	53.9	34.0	20.3	47.1	26.7	−27.0	−12.6	−21.6
Fayoum	30.3	44.9	33.6	22.3	28.4	23.7	−26.4	−36.7	−29.5
Menia	32.7	34.4	33.0	23.8	44.8	27.7	−27.2	30.2	−16.2
Assiut	27.6	46.3	32.6	23.0	47.5	29.5	−16.7	2.6	−9.5
Sohag	31.2	35.0	32.0	27.5	34.9	29.1	−11.9	−0.3	−9.1
Qena	32.0	27.8	31.2	29.3	24.8	28.5	−8.4	−10.8	−8.7
Aswan	35.5	19.3	28.8	5.3	51.6	25.3	−85.1	167.4	−12.2
Luxor	30.8	25.6	28.8	19.7	33.9	25.5	−36.0	32.4	−11.6
Frontier governorates									
Red Sea	2.4	28.3	26.8	1.3	25.3	24.5	−45.8	−10.6	−8.5
El-Wadi El-Gedid	24.7	28.5	26.5	1.8	41.4	20.8	−92.7	45.3	−21.6
Matrouh	47.2	49.2	48.6	38.5	52.4	47.3	−18.4	6.5	−2.7
North Sinai	28.9	24.0	26.0	18.1	18.6	18.4	−37.4	−22.5	−29.1
South Sinai	11.2	27.7	19.7	5.4	44.3	26.5	−51.8	59.9	34.5
National average	26.1	31.9	28.6	19.0	29.2	23.4	−27.2	−8.5	−18.3

Source: Original calculations based on CAPMAS 2020.
Note: CBR = crude birth rate; — = not available; n.a. = not applicable.

- The following governorates showed an urban CBR higher than the national average in 2019 and a slower rate of urban CBR decline: Sharqia, Gharbia, Beheira, Ismailia, Menia, Aswan, Luxor, El-Wadi El-Gedid, and South Sinai.
- Damietta, Dakahlia, Menoufia, and Beni Suef had an urban CBR higher than the national average in 2019 but showed a faster decline than the national average after 2016.

As for the geographic distribution, live births exceeded the population distribution in Beheira, Ismailia, Beni Suef, Fayoum, Menia, Assiut, Sohag, Qena, and Matrouh in 2016 (figure 3.4). But this metric fell within the population distribution in Beheira, Ismailia, and Fayoum in 2019, while the concentration of live births persisted in Beni Suef, Menia, Assiut, Sohag, Qena, and Matrouh in 2019 (figure 3.5). In 2019, the distribution of live births in Kafr El-Sheikh, Aswan, and Luxor exceeded the population distribution. In short, this indicates a persistent concentration in six governorates and an emerging concentration in three governorates of higher than average number of live births. The relative index of dissimilarity (expressed as percentages, or rID%) also increased from 4.6 percent in 2016 to 6.1 percent in 2019, indicating increased geographic disparities in live births between 2016 and 2019.[2]

The concentration of live births in rural areas (figure 3.6) and in urban areas (figure 3.7) shows high disparities in live births (rID% = 14.7 percent and 18.2 percent, respectively). Accordingly, the governorates can be classified into the following:

- Seven governorates where live births are concentrated in rural and urban settings (Kafr El-Sheikh, Beni Suef, Menia, Assiut, Sohag, Luxor, and Matrouh)
- Four governorates where live births are concentrated only in rural settings (Alexandria, Giza, Fayoum, and Qena)
- Seven governorates where live births are concentrated only in urban settings (Dakahlia, Sharqia, Gharbia, Menoufia, Beheira, Ismailia, and Aswan).

Marriage contracts

Table 3.3 shows the marriage contract rate per governorate to assess the likelihood of increased birth rates. The national average marriage contract rate

FIGURE 3.4

Distribution of live births by governorates compared with the population distribution, 2016

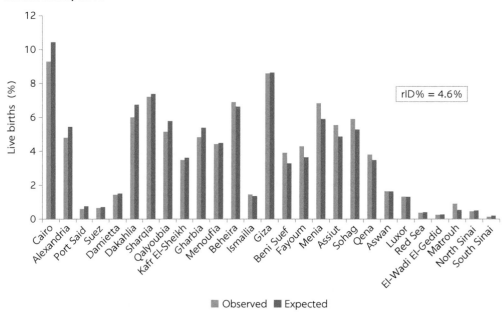

Source: CAPMAS 2020.
Note: rID% = relative index of dissimilarity.

FIGURE 3.5

Distribution of live births by governorates compared with the population distribution, 2019

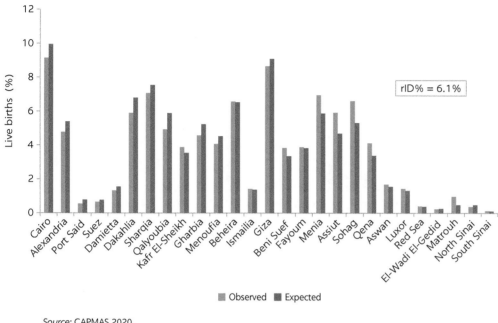

Source: CAPMAS 2020.
Note: rID% = relative index of dissimilarity.

FIGURE 3.6

Distribution of live births in rural settings by governorates compared with the population distribution, 2019

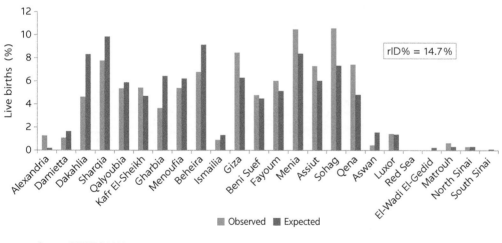

Source: CAPMAS 2020.
Note: rID% = relative index of dissimilarity.

declined from 10.3 per 1,000 population in 2016 to 9.1 per 1,000 population in 2018. At the governorate level, the following were observed:

- Three governorates—Beni Suef, Menia, and Matrouh—exceeded the national average in 2018 and showed an increase over 2016 rates.
- Three governorates—Cairo, Alexandria, and Qena—also exceeded the national average in 2018 but showed a decline from 2016 rates.

FIGURE 3.7

Distribution of live births in urban settings by governorates compared with the population distribution, 2019

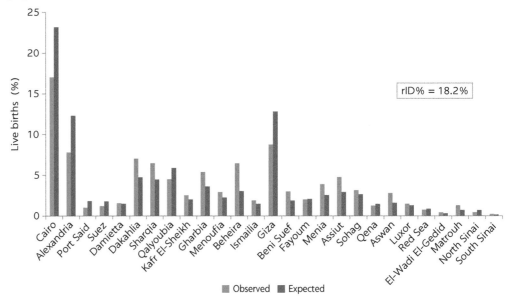

Source: CAPMAS 2020.
Note: rID% = relative index of dissimilarity.

TABLE 3.3 **Change in marriage contract rates by governorate, 2016–18**

GOVERNORATE	2016 (PER 1,000 POPULATION)	2018 (PER 1,000 POPULATION)	CHANGE 2016–18 (%)
Urban governorates			
Cairo	14.0	13.7	−2.1
Port Said	10.2	6.7	−34.3
Suez	10.3	7.4	−28.2
Lower Egypt			
Alexandria	10.5	9.4	−10.5
Damietta	9.2	8.2	−10.9
Dakahlia	10.0	8.7	−13.0
Sharqia	9.7	8.4	−13.4
Qalyoubia	8.2	7.3	−11.0
Kafr El-Sheikh	9.5	8.4	−11.6
Gharbia	10.1	8.4	−16.8
Menoufia	8.2	7.4	−9.8
Beheira	9.5	8.4	−11.6
Ismailia	8.8	7.6	−13.6
Upper Egypt			
Giza	9.7	7.7	−20.6
Beni Suef	9.0	10.0	11.1
Fayoum	10.4	9.1	−12.5

continued

TABLE 3.3, *continued*

GOVERNORATE	2016 (PER 1,000 POPULATION)	2018 (PER 1,000 POPULATION)	CHANGE 2016–18 (%)
Menia	9.7	9.8	1.0
Assiut	10.5	9.0	−14.3
Sohag	10.5	8.6	−18.1
Qena	15.2	12.8	−15.8
Aswan	10.0	8.4	−16.0
Luxor	10.6	8.4	−20.8
Frontier governorates			
Red Sea	6.4	5.8	−9.4
El-Wadi El-Gedid	8.0	7.1	−11.3
Matrouh	9.2	12.4	34.8
North Sinai	9.5	6.3	−33.7
South Sinai	2.2	7.1	222.7
National average	10.3	9.1	−11.7

Source: Original calculations based on CAPMAS 2020.

- South Sinai showed a rate below the national average yet had the highest increase from its 2016 rate.

The trends in these governorates point to challenges in achieving the population growth targets.

The observed marriage contract distribution in 2016 greatly exceeded the population distribution in Cairo and Qena (figure 3.8). In 2018, marriage concentration continued in Cairo and Qena, yet also appeared in Alexandria, Beni Suef, Menia, and Matrouh (figure 3.9). The rID%, though showing moderate disparity, increased from 5.7 percent in 2016 to 7.5 percent in 2018, indicating increasing geographic disparities in marriage contracts.

School dropouts

According to the 2017 census, 13 governorates have a dropout rate higher than the national average (figure 3.10), namely, Alexandria, Damietta, Dakahlia, Gharbia, Menoufia, Beheira, and Ismailia in Lower Egypt; and Sohag, Qena, Aswan, and Luxor in Upper Egypt; and Matrouh and South Sinai in the frontier governorates.

Geographic disparities in school dropouts are high, as reflected in the rID% of 24.2 percent (figure 3.11).

Unemployment

Unemployment stalks both women and men (table 3.4). In six governorates (Cairo, Suez, Damietta, Aswan, Red Sea, and North Sinai), unemployment for both females and males was higher than the national average for each sex. Further, in eight governorates (Dakahlia, Beheira, Ismailia, Giza, Assiut, Qena, Luxor, and Matrouh), female unemployment was higher than the

FIGURE 3.8

Distribution of marriage contracts by governorates compared with the population distribution, 2016

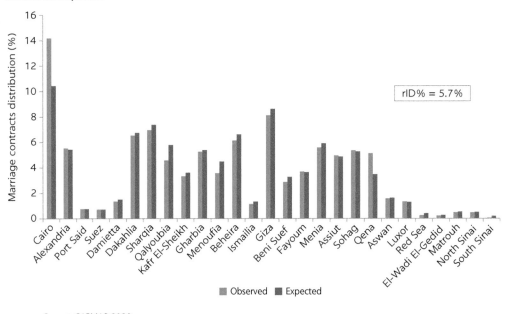

Source: CAPMAS 2020.
Note: rID% = relative index of dissimilarity.

FIGURE 3.9

Distribution of marriage contracts by governorates compared with the population distribution, 2018

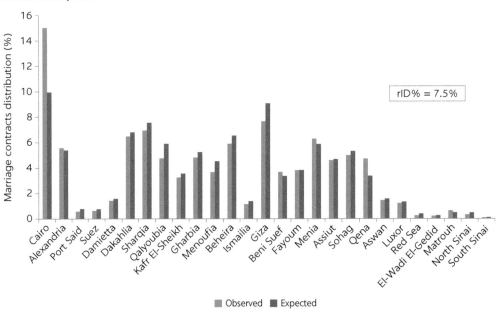

Source: CAPMAS 2020.
Note: rID% = relative index of dissimilarity.

FIGURE 3.10

School dropout rate by governorate, 2017

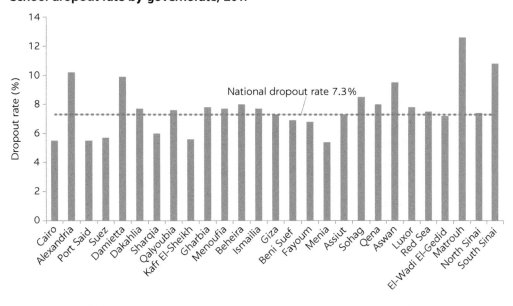

Source: CAPMAS 2017.

FIGURE 3.11

School dropout distribution by governorate, 2017

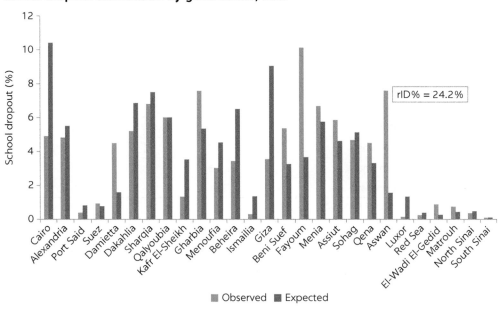

Source: CAPMAS 2017.
Note: rID% = relative index of dissimilarity.

TABLE 3.4 **Unemployment rate by gender and governorate, 2018**

GOVERNORATE	FEMALE (%)	MALE (%)
Urban governorates		
Cairo	24.5	9.4
Port Said	23.9	3.9
Suez	30.5	15.5
Lower Egypt		
Alexandria	19.7	8.7
Damietta	39.7	9.7
Dakahlia	27.4	6.6
Sharqia	19.9	5.3
Qalyoubia	19.3	9.1
Kafr El-Sheikh	7.4	4.3
Gharbia	16.5	8.6
Menoufia	8.2	4.8
Beheira	27.3	5.1
Ismailia	32.1	4.7
Upper Egypt		
Giza	27.6	7.5
Beni Suef	9.0	4.4
Fayoum	7.4	3.4
Menia	14.6	3.8
Assiut	34.1	7.7
Sohag	21.4	4.7
Qena	28.1	3.3
Aswan	49.7	16.8
Luxor	38.0	3.2
Frontier governorates		
Red Sea	50.2	16.1
El-Wadi El-Gedid	5.0	4.1
Matrouh	29.4	5.0
North Sinai	73.6	32.3
South Sinai	11.3	4.7
National average	21.4	6.8

Source: CAPMAS 2020.

national average for females, while in three governorates (Alexandria, Qalyoubia, and Gharbia), male unemployment was higher than the national average for males.

The distributions of female and male unemployment (compared with female and male labor force distributions) confirm that, for both females (figure 3.12) and males (figure 3.13), unemployment is concentrated in governorates where the rates are above the national average. Unemployment is clearly a shared burden for both women and men in many governorates, and efforts to address it are not responding to people's needs (Sanad, Kalil, and Beddah 2019).

FIGURE 3.12

Distribution of female unemployment by governorate, 2018

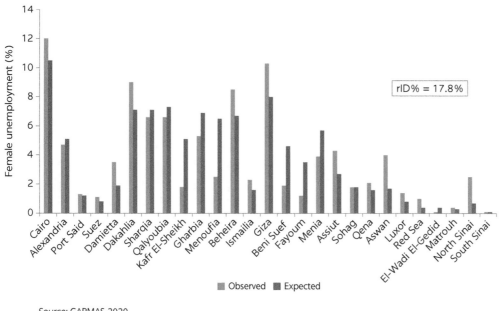

Source: CAPMAS 2020.
Note: rID% = relative index of dissimilarity.

FIGURE 3.13

Distribution of male unemployment by governorate, 2018

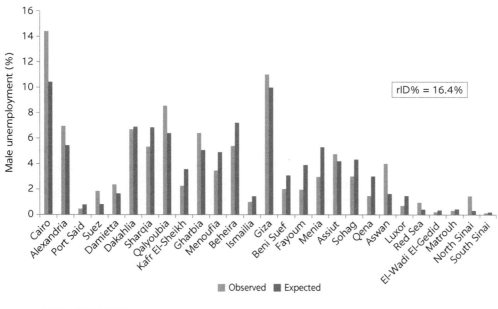

Source: CAPMAS 2020.
Note: rID% = relative index of dissimilarity.

Illiteracy

Illiteracy still appears to be a national challenge, with 25.8 percent of the population unable to read or write. Moreover, the illiteracy rate exceeded the national average in nine governorates: Kafr El-Sheikh, Beheira, Beni Suef, Fayoum, Menia, Assiut, Sohag, Qena, and Matrouh, with the highest illiteracy rate in Menia (figure 3.14).

FIGURE 3.14

Illiteracy rate 10 years and above by governorate, 2017

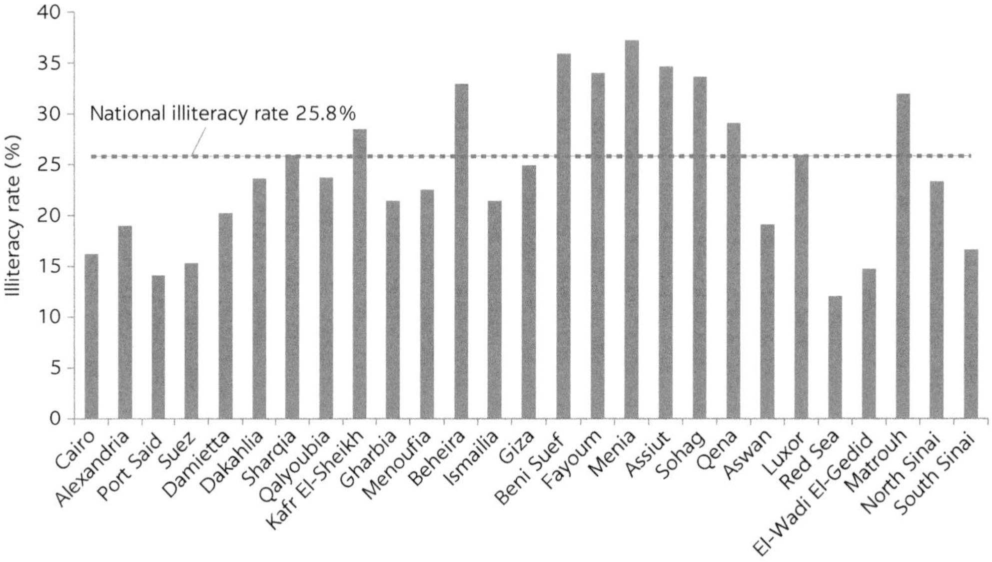

Source: CAPMAS 2017.

GEOGRAPHIC CHALLENGES

Live births

On the basis of the preceding analysis, table 3.5 summarizes the geographic likelihood, trend, and concentration of live births, as well as the likelihood and concentration of their determinants—marriage contracts, school dropouts, unemployment, and illiteracy.

It is evident from table 3.5 that some governorates are progressing in controlling live births while others are lagging. The governorates can be classified as governorates with a high likelihood and high concentration of live births, those where the likelihood of live births is high and concentration is low, those where the likelihood is low and the concentration is high, and those where likelihood and concentration are low.

Governorates with a high likelihood and high concentration of live births should be given a high priority for programmatic and supply-side interventions. These are the rural areas of Alexandria, Giza, Qena, and Sohag, and the urban areas of Dakahlia, Sharqia, Gharbia, Beheira, Beni Suef, Menia, Assiut, and Aswan. Likelihood is also high in urban Sohag, and concentration is high in rural Menia and Assiut. Among these, the most challenging situations seem to be in urban areas of Sharqia, Menia, Assiut, and Aswan, as they show an increasing trend of the live births. The analysis of the other indicators in these governorates reveals the following:

- The likelihood of marriage contracts is high in Beni Suef, Menia, and Qena, with high concentration in Qena.
- The likelihood of school dropouts is high in Alexandria, Qena, Sohag, Dakahlia, Gharbia, Beheira, and Assiut, with high concentration in Aswan, Gharbia, and Qena. Both Assiut and Beni Suef have only high concentrations.

TABLE 3.5 Population challenges at a glance by governorate, Egypt, 2017

GOVERNORATE	LIVE BIRTHS			MARRIAGE CONTRACT		SCHOOL DROPOUT		UNEMPLOYMENT		ILLITERACY
	LIKELIHOOD	TREND	CONC.	LIKELIHOOD	CONC.	LIKELIHOOD	CONC.	LIKELIHOOD	CONC.	LIKELIHOOD
Cairo	U	U	U	G	G	G	G	F/M	F/M	G
Port Said	U	U	U	G	G	G	G	F/M	M	G
Suez	U	U	U	G	G	G	G	F/M	F/M	G
Alexandria	R	R/U	R	G	G	G	G	M	F/M	G
Damietta	R/U	R/U	R/U	G	G	G	G	F/M	F	G
Dakahlia	U	R/U	U	G	G	G	G	F	F	G
Sharqia	U	U	U	G	G	G	G	F/M	F/M	G
Qalyoubia	R/U	R/U	R/U	G	G	G	G	M	M	G
Kafr El-Sheikh	U	U	R/U	G	G	G	G	F/M	F/M	G
Gharbia	U	R/U	U	G	G	G	G	M	M	G
Menoufia	U	R/U	U	G	G	G	G	F/M	F/M	G
Beheira	U	R/U	U	G	G	G	G	F	F	G
Ismailia	U	U	R/U	G	G	G	G	F	F/M	G
Giza	R	R/U	R	G	G	G	G	F	F	G
Beni Suef	U	R/U	U	G	G	G	G	F/M	F/M	G
Fayoum	R/U	R/U	R/U	G	G	G	G	F/M	F/M	G
Menia	U	U	R/U	G	G	G	G	F/M	F/M	G
Assiut	U	U	R/U	G	G	G	G	F	F	G
Sohag	R/U	R/U	R	G	G	G	G	F/M	F/M	G
Qena	R	R/U	R	G	G	G	G	F	F/M	G
Aswan	U	U	U	G	G	G	G	F/M	F/M	G
Luxor	U	U	R/U	G	G	G	G	F	G	G
Red Sea	R/U	R/U	R/U	G	G	G	G	F/M	F/M	G
El-Wadi El-Gedid	U	U	R/U	G	G	G	G	F/M	F/M	G
Matrouh	R/U	U	R/U	G	G	G	G	F	F/M	G
North Sinai	R/U	R/U	R/U	G	G	G	G	F/M	F/M	G
South Sinai	U	U	R/U	G	G	G	G	F/M	F/M	G

Source: Original calculations based on CAPMAS (2020) for live births, marriage contracts, and unemployment; and on CAPMAS (2017) for school dropouts and illiteracy.
Note: Red cells denote high rate (>95%CI above national average) and/or distribution exceeding population distribution by >1%. Green cells denote low rates. High rates highlight the geographic areas at risk because of behaviors or living circumstances. Distribution exceeding population distribution points to the geographic areas where services are not reaching people or are ineffective or irresponsive to people's needs. Conc. = concentration; G = governorate level; U = urban; R = rural; F = female; M = male.

- The likelihood of unemployment among females is high in Giza, Qena, Dakahlia, Beheira, Assiut, and Aswan, and among males in Alexandria, Gharbia, and Aswan, with high concentration in Giza, Dakahlia, Beheira, Assiut, and Aswan among females, and in Gharbia and Aswan among males.
- The likelihood of illiteracy is high in Qena, Sohag, Beheira, Beni Suef, Menia, and Assiut.

Governorates where the likelihood of live births is high and concentration is low are the second-priority governorates. They include urban areas of Kafr El-Sheikh, Ismailia, Luxor, El-Wadi El-Gedid, Matrouh, and South Sinai, and they are all having an increasing trend of live births. Urban areas of Menoufia and rural areas of Matrouh have high likelihood of live births. The high likelihood of marriage contracts is only in Matrouh; but school dropouts have a high likelihood in Menoufia, Ismailia, Luxor, Matrouh, and South Sinai; unemployment among females has a high likelihood in Ismailia, Luxor, and Matrouh; and illiteracy has a high likelihood in Kafr El-Sheikh and Matrouh.

Governorates where likelihood and concentration of live births are low are Cairo, Port Said, Suez, Damietta, Qalyoubia, Fayoum, Red Sea, and North Sinai. These governorates, however, show a high likelihood and concentration of marriage contracts in Cairo; a high likelihood and concentration of school dropouts in Damietta; and only a high concentration in Fayoum of school dropouts. For unemployment, there are high likelihood and concentration rates among both sexes in Cairo and North Sinai, but only among males in Qalyoubia. Also for unemployment, there is only a high likelihood among both sexes in Suez, Damietta, and Red Sea, and only a high concentration among males in Port Said and among females in Damietta. A high illiteracy rate exists only in Fayoum.

As demonstrated, there are considerable variations across governorates in terms of the potential contribution of social determinants to the pattern of live births, which can be further assessed by examining these determinants in more detail to guide the development of potential policies and strategies. In particular, the following trends stand out.

Marriage contracts

Rate of marriage is one of the proximate determinants of fertility, as it is closely associated with childbearing. In Egypt, Beni Suef, Menia, Qena, and Matrouh governorates show high rates of marriage and childbearing, indicating that reducing or delaying age at marriage in these governorates should be a priority that can help in reducing the number of live births. In contrast, Cairo has a high likelihood and concentration of marriage contracts but a low likelihood of live births. Here, the priority should be to reduce the number of live births through family planning programs because interventions to delay age at marriage may not be as effective in reducing the number of live births. In addition, 11 governorates have a low marriage tendency, but the number of live births is high. These governorates are Sharqia, Kafr El-Sheikh, Gharbia, Menoufia, Beheira, Ismailia, Giza, Sohag, Aswan, Luxor, and South Sinai. Delaying age of marriage in these 11 governorates is not an optimal intervention, since the marriage tendency is low; but once married, couples have an increased tendency for childbearing. Thus, strengthening family planning interventions may be the more effective intervention to reduce fertility.

School dropouts

School dropouts, especially among adolescent girls, are often linked to early childbearing and high fertility. Damietta, Gharbia, Qena, and Aswan had a high likelihood and concentration of school dropouts. Nine other governorates showed only a high likelihood of school dropouts, including Alexandria, Dakahlia, Menoufia, Beheira, Ismailia, Sohag, Luxor, Matrouh, and South

Sinai. Except for Damietta, all these governorates had exhibited high rates of live births. This finding suggests a need to prioritize policies that will keep children, particularly girls, in school. Qena and Matrouh also had an increased likelihood and/or concentration of marriage contracts. But surprisingly, the remaining governorates with high levels of school dropouts had low levels of contract marriages. These data should be interpreted cautiously, however, as they may mask the phenomenon of unregistered marriages in some governorates, notably among those below the legal age for marriage. Also, except for Menoufia, Sohag, and South Sinai, all these governorates had high unemployment rates, particularly among females.

Unemployment

The potential for higher fertility increases when unemployment, particularly female unemployment, lowers the cost of childbearing, as data seem to indicate for several governorates in Egypt. There was an increased likelihood and/or concentration of male and/or female unemployment in 10 governorates—Cairo, Damietta, Dakahlia, Qalyoubia, Gharbia, Beheira, Giza, Assiut, Aswan, and North Sinai—with an associated increase in one or more rates of live births in 7 of the 10 governorates: Dakahlia, Gharbia, Beheira, Giza, Assiut, Aswan, and North Sinai. An increased likelihood of unemployment, particularly among females, was evident in seven governorates: Suez, Alexandria, Ismailia, Qena, Luxor, Red Sea, and Matrouh, several of which also had increased rates of live births: Alexandria, Ismailia, Qena, Luxor, and Matrouh. Out of these, 17 governorates also exhibited high rates of school dropouts.

Illiteracy

Illiteracy, particularly female illiteracy, can be associated with early marriage and childbearing, and may have played a role in increased live births in Egypt. The illiteracy rate was high in nine governorates: Kafr El-Sheikh, Beheira, Beni Suef, Fayoum, Menia, Assiut, Sohag, Qena, and Matrouh. Other than Fayoum, all these governorates also exhibit an increased likelihood and/or concentration of live births.

CONCLUSIONS

During the implementation of EPIP 2015–2020, there was a decline in the overall rate of population growth, GFR, and CBR. Despite these positive trends at the national level, considerable challenges persist. First, paucity of data, especially at subnational levels, is a major obstacle for monitoring progress. Although the use of proxy indicators may reveal some insights, it has limitations, especially as overall national averages do not allow for a full understanding of the varied contexts within the country. Their use can also then make it difficult to assess the true impact of Egypt National Population Strategy (ENPS) 2015–2030 and EPIP 2015–2020.

Second, where data are available, evidence points to large variations between and within governorates. In 10 governorates, in both rural and urban areas, current efforts to reduce childbearing appear to have low effectiveness and need to be revisited. In an additional 10 urban areas, the interventions seem to be ineffective.

Moreover, the traditional focus on rural areas and Upper Egypt missed the demographic conditions in urban areas, Lower Egypt, and the frontier governorates.

Third, the nexus between increased live births, school dropouts, and unemployment seems to be the strongest, and there is also an association of increased live births with illiteracy and marriage contracts. However, that association seems different from the earlier trends observed prior to 2014 that showed increased fertility among educated, urban, and wealthier women. A crucial strategy for addressing population growth is therefore to invest in FP services to help people limit the number of children they have.

There is a need for a paradigm shift in how high fertility and population issues are addressed in Egypt—pointing to the importance of developing differentiated subnational strategies and programs that target specific root causes at a local level. These are discussed in detail in chapter 7.

NOTE

1. The discrepancies in the population figures are because EPIP 2015–2020 used the United Nations' estimated population projections while CAPMAS was an actual count of Egyptians in the country at the time of the census.
2. The index of dissimilarity is a demographic measure of the difference in the distribution between two groups. The index score can be interpreted as the percentage of one of the two groups that would have to move in order to produce an even distribution across all areas. A score of zero (0 percent) reflects a perfectly even environment; a score of 1 (100 percent) reflects a completely uneven distribution.

REFERENCES

CAPMAS (Central Agency for Public Mobilization and Statistics). 2017. *Egypt Census 2017*. December. http://www.enow.gov.eg/Report/EgyptCensus2017.pdf.

CAPMAS (Central Agency for Public Mobilization and Statistics). 2020. *Egypt in Figures 2020*. March. https://www.capmas.gov.eg/Pages/StaticPages.aspx?page_id=5035.

MOETE (Ministry of Education and Technical Education). 2020. *Statistical Yearbook 2019/2020*. Cairo: MOETE. http://emis.gov.eg/Site%20Content/book/019-020/main_book2020.html. In Arabic.

MOHP (Ministry of Health and Population), El-Zanaty and Associates, and ICF International. 2015. *Egypt Demographic and Health Survey, 2014*. Cairo: Ministry of Health And Population. https://dhsprogram.com/publications/publication-fr302-dhs-final-reports.cfm.

Ontario Agency for Health Protection and Promotion. 2013. "Summary Measures of Socioeconomic Inequalities in Health." Toronto, Ontario: Queen's Printer for Ontario. https://www.publichealthontario.ca/-/media/documents/S/2013/socioeconomic-inequality-measures.pdf?la=en.

Sanad, Zakaria F., Nora Abd El-Hadi Kalil, and Eman S. El-Rahman Beddah. 2019. "Infertility and Related Risk Factors among Women Attending Rural Family Health Facilities in Menoufia Governorate." *Menoufia Medical Journal* 32 (4): 1365–70. http://www.mmj.eg.net/text.asp?2019/32/4/1365/274250.

Additional reading

WHO (World Health Organization). 2007. "Proposed Operational Approach and Indicators to Measure Social Determinants of Health Equity." Brief Operational Indicators Version 1.5. Briefing note for discussion at the Seventh Meeting of Commissioners, January 17–19, 2007. Department of Equity, Poverty and Social Determinants of Health, World Health Organization, Geneva.

4 Sectoral and Social Drivers of Fertility

NAHLA ZEITOUN, AMR ELSHALAKANI, BRIDGET CRUMPTON,
CORNELIA JESSE, AMIRA KAZEM, SOURAYA EL-ASSIOUTY,
SEEMEEN SAADAT, AND SAMEH EL-SAHARTY

This chapter explores some of the distal and proximate determinants of fertility relevant for the Arab Republic of Egypt, specifically the sectoral and social drivers that influence fertility directly or indirectly, including health, with a focus on contraceptive prevalence, education (particularly for girls), female labor force participation, poverty and social protection, and gender. The chapter highlights the main challenges for Egypt within each sector, the steps that have been taken (or are being taken) to address these issues, and what gaps remain. The chapter also reviews the implications of policies related to women's empowerment that can have a positive influence on women's participation in decision-making on their reproductive health and fertility. And because fertility is one of the main drivers of population growth, how well these issues are addressed will have a lasting impact on Egypt's demographic outcomes.

HEALTH

Child mortality is one of the distal determinants of fertility. As child mortality declines, fertility also declines. Between 1988 and 2008, Egypt's child mortality rate declined from 108 to 33.4 child deaths per 1,000 live births, similar to the declining fertility trend during the same period. Between 2008 and 2014, these two rates were decoupled as child mortality continued its decline, reaching 27 child deaths in 2014, while the fertility rate increased (MOHP, El-Zanaty and Associates, and ICF International 2015).

Contraceptive prevalence is a proximate determinant of fertility. Egypt has made significant strides to improve contraceptive use through its First Five-Year Population Implementation Plan 2015–2020 (appendix A). The plan supported scaling up family planning (FP) services at the primary health care level in urban areas and reaching rural and remote areas, enhancing public awareness and behavior change, and improving the supply chain. FP services were made available in 5,109 of the 5,414 primary health care units (PHCUs) across the country. In addition, the Ministry of Health and Population (MOHP) opened and reactivated 32 FP and reproductive health clinics, including 19 in university hospitals, four in police hospitals, and nine in the Health Insurance Organization (HIO) hospitals and the Curative Care Organization (CCO). The MOHP expanded FP services in remote and deprived areas through mobile clinics, serving more than 3.6 million women. The MOHP shared its updated quality standards guide with the nongovernmental organizations providing FP services and trained their service providers, including doctors and nurses.

The MOHP organized training courses for medical staff, pharmacists, and others in the FP supply chain. Rural female pioneers were trained to conduct home visits. Warehouse officials were also trained on the management of FP methods in terms of needs assessment, storage, and distribution according to the national standards. More recently, the government has launched an initiative with the support of the World Bank to cover the shortage of physicians by contracting with retired doctors (60–65), to provide FP services in selected governorates. The MOHP also held meetings and seminars in health units and public spaces— such as youth centers, government directorates, clubs, public libraries, schools, and universities, while the National Population Council (NPC) organized media seminars. In addition, the MOHP supported 16 million home visits by the female pioneers it trained.

Funds for purchasing FP methods were made available from the state budget and through the financial support of development partners—the United Nations Population Fund and the World Bank—particularly for IUDs and subdermal capsules. Egypt aims to manufacture contraceptives, such as pills and injectables, locally through the Arab Company for Drugs Industries and Medical Appliances.

The MOHP has also helped to shape regulations to support women's empowerment and improved reproductive health. Finally, 700 rural female pioneers were assigned with the support of the World Bank and the Small and Micro Enterprises Authority to reduce the number of families targeted by every worker.

Current challenges

Despite these accomplishments, multiple challenges persist. First, the PHCUs that provide FP services are still insufficient, especially in rural and remote areas. Second, PHCUs suffer from a shortage of physicians, especially female doctors. Although steps have been taken to address these gaps, they have yet to show results. Even though FP services were made available at 94.4 percent of the PHCUs, 1,250 units did not have a physician present, in effect reducing the actual availability of effective FP services to 70 percent. Further, the legal framework and administrative arrangements to allow task-sharing among trained health workers such as nurses to address the shortage in the provision of FP services in remote and hard to reach areas. Third, FP activities oscillated between being conducted independently or as part of the sexual and reproductive health care (SRH) services, and between being offered at mobile or fixed clinics. This lack of stability contributed to fragmented programs and "lost" messaging on FP. FP services also failed to engage men as partners in reducing high fertility. Fourth, inadequate systems of supply and monitoring resulted in stockouts of FP methods in MOHP outlets.

The lack of recent data on fertility and FP services, such as EDHSs and Service Provision Assessments, made it difficult to accurately assess demand and to plan services, and data are not systematically used for planning and policy making. Plans developed by the MOHP were often generic, overstretched, and missed the underlying trends of fertility increase among different populations and regions. Challenges also exist at the policy level. The governance structure of the population program was unstable and fragmented, and the changes in the status of the NPC and rapid leadership turnover weakened the oversight and coordination of the FP program.

Poor engagement with development partners on EPIP 2015–2020 and low budgetary allocation from the government also contributed to setbacks. Partnerships between stakeholders were weak, with each partner working in isolation, and there were no budget-sharing mechanisms. Although EPIP 2015–2020 required multisectoral actions, stakeholders in the nonhealth sectors were not fully engaged with the MOHP. Equally important, all these sectors did not acknowledge their integral role in the mandate, placing the responsibility of achieving population goals squarely on the FP programs. At the same time, the role of the civil society clinics decreased from about 10 percent in 1995 to 0.6 percent in 2004, as they remained financially insecure, mostly depending on grants that were not always available. Further, the role of the private sector was absent from the scene even though it shares almost half of the contraceptive market share.

Some of the contributing factors that may be responsible for these challenges are deeply rooted in the structural causes of increased fertility. These causes have diverse cultural, social, and economic roots. Egypt is a dynamic country in which culture and beliefs hold together the many diversities that affect the principles of fertility and family composition. Factors that play a part in shaping these principles and explain why progress on the population front has stalled include the expansion of slum areas in urban settings and the fact that several rural areas host some of the rich and educated. Another factor is the sexual and reproductive health care needs.

The Egyptian culture does not permit sexual relations outside marriage, so early marriage (under age 18) is relatively high, despite the increase of legal age at first marriage. Although increasing the legal age of marriage is a positive step forward, it should be coupled with increasing awareness about delaying and spacing childbirth.

Other idiosyncrasies in health-seeking behavior patterns also may be contributing to the large number of births in the country. Cesarean deliveries in Egypt are extremely high (51.8 percent) and rising (MOHP, El-Zanaty and Associates, and ICF International 2015), even among poor, uneducated, and rural residents. C-section deliveries negatively affect breastfeeding, which is likely to be interrupted, thus losing a potent, inexpensive, and widely accepted traditional FP method. Demand-side interventions are also needed, especially to tackle norms and change behaviors.

At the same time, any effort needs to be concerted and multisectoral. The NPC and MOHP cannot be solely responsible for fertility outcomes; and actions should not be the result of fragmented sectoral strategies. FP remains the *first* tool to halt the growth in population, but a paradigm shift is needed to reshape the programs addressing the challenge. Multilevel solutions relevant to the real national context should be created to encourage the adoption of smaller families as a lifestyle.

EDUCATION

Egypt's education sector has witnessed significant achievements in the past few years in terms of enrollment and gender parity. Enrollment increased from 8.8 million in 2006/07 to 13.4 million in 2020/21 in primary school, and from 5.9 million in 2006/07 to 10.2 million in 2020/21 at the secondary level (including lower, upper, and technical secondary schools) (MOETE 2021). Net enrollment in those years reached almost 100 percent at the primary level; it was at 97.6 percent at the lower-secondary level but fell to 76.6 percent at the upper-secondary level (MOETE 2020). A major achievement is that Egypt has attained overall gender parity, with high levels of enrollment of girls recorded at all levels of education. A notable development in the last three years has been the adoption of a comprehensive reform to modernize the pre-tertiary education system and prioritize learning beginning with early grades, offering a new curriculum and prescriptive teacher guides.

The government has recently launched initiatives to address the challenges of girls' enrollment, retention, and learning. The initiatives are aimed at equipping girls with the skills and knowledge to have more agency in decisions that affect their fertility, family size, and engagement in the social and employment spheres.

Key strategies include a new education approach (EDU 2.0), which launched in 2018, prioritizing quality and "bringing back learning to the classroom." Over the past two years, key achievements of the Ministry of Education and Technical Education (MOETE) have included (a) advancing the rollout of a new curriculum and teacher training for kindergarten and early grades, with rollout to grade 4 scheduled for 2021/22, and (b) designing and administering a nationwide tablet-based test for secondary education starting in grade 10, which relies less on rote learning and is driven by higher-order thinking skills. However, because of several circumstances (including the COVID-19 pandemic) and delays in the parliamentary approval of the draft law amendments, examinations for grades 10 and 11, as well as the new school leaving examination (grade 12), were paper-based in 2020/21. The anticipated improvements in quality and learning should equip both girls and boys with critical thinking skills and the ability to make better-informed decisions on life choices overall, including fertility.

In 2020, the government launched an investment program to expand the supply of school capacity as part of the wider reform of the education system. The plan is to rehabilitate schools and construct around 39,000 additional classrooms in lagging regions to absorb the annual increase in student numbers and encourage enrollment and retention of groups at risk, including girls. As part of the MOETE's response to COVID-19, the shift to blended learning (digital and TV educational learning resources) is expected to help address the issue of overpopulated classes. In addition, community schools are also being promoted as a viable alternative to public schools in governorates and districts, based on need. Evidence suggests that these community schools and the trend to draw female teachers from the community can be better tailored to the needs of girls and students in underserved areas and build family confidence in school safety for girls.

The introduction of population awareness and reproductive health to the curriculum is another promising initiative. Involving men and boys in reproductive health and FP programs, as well as women and girls, is equally important to have a positive effect on raising awareness and changing behavior (Abdel-Tawab et al. 2020).

Current challenges

Despite this progress, Egypt continues to experience challenges on population growth and the need to keep pace with rising demand for education. It also faces an unusual paradox whereby positive increases in girls' engagement in key education areas that, in the international literature, are typically correlated with lower fertility levels, are not translating into reduced fertility rates. Thus, even such factors as (a) parity of boys and girls at the primary level, (b) a higher transition rate for girls from primary to lower-secondary level (100.6 to 99.2 percent girls to boys;[1] MOETE 2021), (c) representation in upper-secondary net education enrollment at roughly the same level as boys (56.5 percent girls; MOETE 2021), and (d) girls' outperformance in secondary final exams are not leading to a sustained effect on, and decrease of, fertility levels. Although the lower enrollment at upper-secondary levels may affect fertility, an associated challenge is that more educated women in urban areas have higher birth rates, contrary to expectation (as indicated in chapter 2).

One of the immediate impacts of this rising fertility is the rapid growth of the youth population, which in turn increases demand on enrollment, placing a strain on the education system, contributing to classroom overcrowding, and increasing funding needs across the system. Despite the Egyptian government's commitment to building its human capital, education financing has not kept pace with the rising demand and higher enrollment rates. In 2019, Egypt spent 2.3 percent of its GDP on education—a figure that is significantly lower than both the regional average (4.4 percent) and the average for its income group (4.5 percent) (MOF 2021a, 2021b).

Quality of education is another persistent challenge. According to World Bank data, Egypt's learning poverty rate stands at 70 percent, which means that 70 percent of children are unable to read and understand a short, age-appropriate text by age 10. In common with most countries in the Middle East and North Africa (MENA), learning poverty is higher for boys than for girls, and in Egypt it is recorded at 74 percent and 65 percent, respectively. This is the result of two factors: the share of out-of-school children is higher for boys (1.9 percent) than for girls (0.8 percent), and boys are less likely to achieve minimum proficiency at the end of primary school (73.6 percent) than girls (64.6 percent) (World Bank 2019). Expected years of schooling are 11.1, dropping to an average of 6.3 years when this is adjusted for the amount of learning per year (learning-adjusted years of schooling). Learning poverty in Egypt is 6.3 percentage points lower than the average for the MENA region, 14.5 percentage points lower than the average for lower-middle-income countries, and 41 percentage points lower than the average for upper-middle-income countries (World Bank 2020).

These two main challenges—enrollment rates, particularly at the upper-secondary level, and school dropouts—are critical for fertility outcomes. Although the government is committed to "education for all," it remains a challenge to keep pace with the rising demand for enrollment, expand the education system, and construct classrooms to absorb population growth. According to the Minister of Planning and Economic Cooperation, Hala al-Said, student numbers are set to double by 2052 at the current levels of population growth: "The number of students in Egypt will become 44 million in 2052 up from 22 million in 2021, if the same rate of population growth continues. That would require the increase of the current capacity of classrooms and teachers by four times" (El Tawil 2021). While girls' enrollment is higher than boys at all levels of education, a persistent challenge is to increase the level of girls' enrollment and retention at the upper-secondary level (El-Laithy 2021). These averages mask regional variations. For example, girls in Upper Egypt are among groups that are least likely to transition to secondary education. Catch-up and distance education opportunities are also lagging and contribute to persistent high levels of illiteracy.

While dropout levels are declining, challenges persist. According to the 2017 census, the dropout rate was 7.3 percent among students 4 years of age and above. According to the MOETE (2020) statistics for 2019/20, the dropout rates were 0.25 percent for primary and 1.73 percent for lower secondary school levels, with slightly more girls than boys dropping out (2.1 percent for girls versus 1.4 percent for boys). Children from poor families are most at risk, and regional disparities are significant. According to a recent study, the dropout rate at the upper-secondary level may be much higher, at 15.0 percent (17.3 percent girls and 12.6 percent boys; El-Laithy 2021).

Some of the contributing factors that may be responsible for these challenges are at the sectoral level, which requires more targeted efforts to provide incentives for poor families and girls to enroll and stay in school. International evidence shows that reaching the poorest children, children with disabilities, and girls requires more tailored efforts accompanied by dedicated resources (UKAID 2018). The lack of attention to raising awareness about population issues and reproductive health in the curriculum is another missed opportunity for building understanding and changing behaviors from an early age.

At the societal level, traditional and cultural norms have a strong influence on daily life in Egypt and are a contributing factor to sustained gender norms and attitudes around the roles of women and men, women's subordinate social status, and men's influence on decisions related to fertility and desired family size. Male bias also remains the norm in many spheres, although it is less prevalent in education.

On the economic front, low rates of female labor force participation are persistent at approximately 23 percent, which is contrary to the evidence in the literature that points to a positive correlation between girls' education and female employment. The rate is largely the result of structural issues in labor market demand, but supply-side conditions also notably create a mismatch between female education and skills demanded in the labor market. Most women in Egypt are employed in the public sector, but with a reduction in public sector jobs, job opportunities are scant. On the demand side, the low labor force participation rate indicates a lag in shifting social norms, in promoting the skill sets that can attract women and girls to the changing world of work, and in incentivizing employers to recruit females.

TERTIARY EDUCATION

In recent years, there has been a significant rise in tertiary education enrollment in Egypt, largely because of the higher number of secondary school graduates and school- and university-age population growth. From 2015 to 2020, enrollment in tertiary education grew from 2.7 million to 3.2 million. Although this expansion is an achievement, it poses a substantial financial and logistical challenge. Moreover, the gross enrollment rate (GER) for higher education is expected to increase by 25 percent—from 31 percent in 2014 to almost 39 percent in 2025 (figure 4.1).

Given the current trend, and assuming full capacity of existing provision without fundamental changes to delivery models, over 4 million seats for higher education students will be needed by 2025 (figure 4.2).

The substantial increase in female tertiary education enrollment is an important achievement. Female enrollment in public universities accounts for 55 percent of the total enrollment, highlighting impressive advances in female educational attainment over the past few years. There has also been substantial progress in terms of gender equity in higher education. The ratio of females to males with higher education degrees increased from 7 to 10 in 2015 to 12 to 10 in 2017.[2]

Over the past two years, the government of Egypt has launched several initiatives meant to expand access to tertiary education as well as improve the quality and relevance of the sector to better match labor market needs. Initiatives to increase access to tertiary education include increasing enrollment in nonpublic universities and launching nonprofit "for fee" branches of

FIGURE 4.1

Gross enrollment rate for tertiary education, current and projected, 2014–25

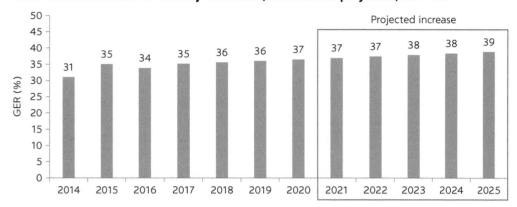

Source: World Bank, School enrollment tertiary (% gross)—Egypt, Arab Rep., https://data.worldbank.org/indicator/SE.TER.ENRR?locations=EG.
Note: GER projections 2018 to 2025. GER by World Bank based on average annual growth rate from 2001 to 2017. GER = gross enrollment ratio.

FIGURE 4.2

Trends in secondary-school-age population, and secondary and tertiary education enrollment, current and projected, 2014–25

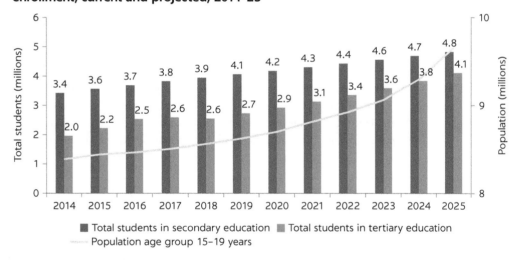

Sources: Population data and estimates from World Bank Health, Nutrition, and Population Statistics: Population estimates and projections, https://databank.worldbank.org/source/population-estimates-and-projections. Data on enrollment from CAPMAS (2019), of which 2019 to 2025 enrollment rates are projections by the World Bank based on average annual growth rate from 2013 to 2018.

public universities. Most recently, the president directed the establishment of 15 public universities (in addition to an initial three: Al-Galala, Al-Alamein, and King Salman) to absorb the rise in demand for tertiary education due to population growth.

Attention to the quality of higher education is also important to ensure that graduates meet labor market needs. Many of the government's initiatives target these issues. For example, over the past two to three years, technological universities have been established, similar to the applied science universities and *polytechnique* institutes in many countries,[3] to integrate more practical experiences into programs of study and to offer an open pathway for students of technical secondary education tracks. This initiative is aimed at relieving the pressure on general academic education and ideally enhancing the quality and relevance of graduates to labor market needs. This effort is in addition to establishing branches of international universities (such as Coventry University).

Current challenges

Many challenges persist for tertiary education in Egypt. First, the expansion of the tertiary education system over a relatively short period of time has not been matched by a rise in per student funding or teaching capacity, because of government financing constraints and trade-offs in government budget allocation (notably between basic education and higher education, but also between education and other sectors). This rise in enrollment beyond the absorptive capacity of higher education institutions has given rise to overcrowding in public universities, especially in public universities; where in outlier cases, students have no place to sit or stand.

The rapid growth in tertiary-level education enrollment over such a short period without matching per student increases in financing has adversely affected quality, as measured by the ratio of students to teaching staff, beyond international good practice. For example, the student-to-staff ratio for engineering programs at one public university was 49 to 1, while the ratio for students to faculty of commerce in another public university stood at 489 to 1. Second, the rapid expansion of the higher education system has contributed to increasing the number of graduates entering a relatively constrained labor market every year, which poses another challenge to the labor market in terms of the demand for higher education graduates.

Two main challenges are critical for fertility: unemployment, particularly among female graduates; and skill mismatches between tertiary education graduates and labor market needs. Unemployment among tertiary-level graduates is higher than for any other education level, and even higher for female than for male graduates: unemployment among young people ages 15–29 was 25 percent in 2017, with the highest concentration among recent tertiary-level graduates (38 percent). Moreover, enrollment is concentrated at the diploma or bachelor level and in the humanities and social sciences, especially for female students. In fact, in the field of social sciences and humanities, the gender ratio in tertiary education reached 99 to 1 female to male in 2005, up from 65 to 1 in 1990 (UNDP 2008). However, there are limited opportunities in these fields. University-educated women have a disproportionately higher unemployment rate than their male counterparts. Among every 100 male university graduates, 89 participate in the labor force and 15 of them are unemployed. Among every 100 female university graduates, 66 participate in the labor force and 31 of them are unemployed (UNDP 2008).

Although the public sector was previously able to absorb a large share of tertiary education graduates, the steady decline in public sector employment—from 33 percent in 2004 to 22 percent in 2018—further contributed to the labor market challenges facing tertiary education graduates, in particular female graduates. In 1994, 80 percent of tertiary graduates were employed by the public sector, compared with less than 30 percent in 2015. This rise is also partly due to the substantial increase in the number and share of tertiary education graduates who are women (Assaad, AlSharawy, and Salemi 2019). The share of women with a university education or higher rose from 6 percent in 1998 to 18 percent in 2018 compared with an increase from 13 to 21 percent for men (Labor Force

Survey, various years).[4] Although the ratio of females to males with higher education degrees increased from 7 to 10 in 2015 to 12 to 10 in 2017, the majority were concentrated in the field of social sciences and humanities. In fact, the gender ratio in the social sciences and humanities at the tertiary level reached 99 to 1 female to male in 2005, up from 65 to 1 in 1990 (World Bank calculations based on CAPMAS 2019), which contributed to fewer job opportunities for women.

Another way to show this considerable shift of tertiary-level graduates from public to private sector employment is to compare recent graduates (those who graduated in the past five years) with all tertiary education graduates, which includes all graduation cohorts, not just recent graduates (figure 4.3). Research on the rate of return (Krafft, Branson, and Flak 2019) to tertiary education shows that females enjoy a tertiary-level rate of return by working in the private sector while males have a tertiary-level incentive for working in the public sector (figure 4.4).

FEMALE LABOR FORCE PARTICIPATION

Female labor force participation is one of the distal determinants of fertility. Fewer men and women are joining Egypt's labor market. Although this is a new phenomenon for men, women's labor force participation has been decreasing, especially among youth, since 2012 (Amer and Atallah 2019). This decline is driven by several factors, including (a) a decrease in public sector employment that has not been offset by the growth of jobs in the private sector; (b) only a slight growth in jobs in private small and medium enterprises, most of which are low-skill jobs; (c) a large informal sector, which is a main employer of women; (d) a disproportionate burden of childcare and household responsibilities; and (e) poor working conditions (Constant et al. 2020; World Bank 2018).

Youth and women have a significantly lower share of employment than men in prime working-age groups (ages 15–64 years). Women's employment fell from

FIGURE 4.3

Economic activity level, tertiary education graduates, total and recent graduates, 2017

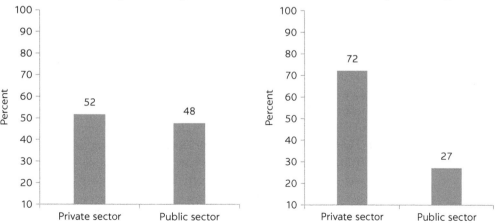

Source: World Bank estimates based on Labor Force Survey 2017, http://www.erfdataportal.com/index.php/catalog/149.
Note: The recent graduates category comprises students who graduated in 2014–17.

FIGURE 4.4

Marginalized rate of return to completion of tertiary education for all tertiary-level graduates (ages 20–54) by gender and public or private sector employment

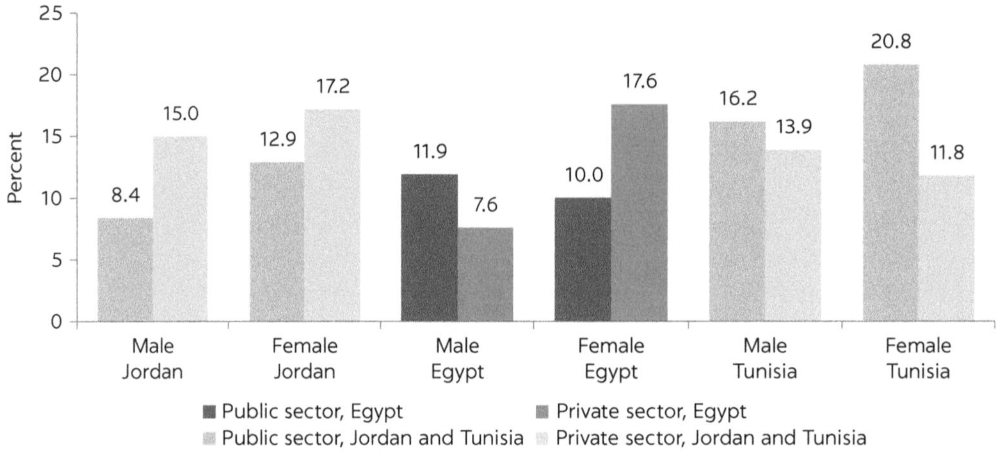

■ Public sector, Egypt ■ Private sector, Egypt
▨ Public sector, Jordan and Tunisia ▨ Private sector, Jordan and Tunisia

Source: Krafft, Branson, and Flak 2019.
Note: Annualized marginal rate of return to completion of tertiary education compared with only secondary education.

22 percent in 2006 to 18 percent in 2012, and then slightly more, to 17 percent in 2018. An estimated 21 percent of those are on part-time contracts (WEF 2019). Similarly, male employment declined from 77 percent in 2012 to 72 percent in 2018 (Krafft and Kettle 2019).

Moreover, a large portion of Egyptian youth are not in education, employment, or training (NEET; Amer and Atallah 2019). Women form the largest share of this group. The proportion of women ages 15–29 years who are NEET increased from 56.4 percent in 2006 to 60.0 percent in 2018, while the share of young men ages 15–29 years who are NEET increased from 7.2 percent to 8.9 percent in the same period. The largest share of NEET is in the 25- to 29-year-old age group, with significantly more NEET young women (82.2 percent) than men (9.8 percent) (Amer and Atallah 2019).

Although unemployment rates remain stable, the proportion who are the "discouraged unemployed"—people who are no longer searching for jobs—is on the rise. Unemployment among men and women, including the discouraged, rose from 9.6 percent in 2012 to 11.1 percent in 2018. Joblessness increased among men from 4.7 percent to 5.8 percent, and among women from 25.8 percent to 27.8 percent, during the same period (Krafft, Assaad, and Keo 2019).

Despite improvements in education levels—with higher enrollment and graduation rates—labor force participation did not increase for either men or women, but in fact decreased, leaving a large portion of the country's human resources untapped. Women with tertiary education, especially, are entering the labor market at increasingly lower rates, while less educated women continue to participate in low-paying job at low rates. Between 1998 and 2018, for example, the rate of women workers who had an intermediate education plummeted from over 40 percent to 20 percent. This decrease in female labor force participation has, unsurprisingly, coincided with the increase in the TFR of the country. As discussed in the previous section, poor labor market prospects for women are likely to have contributed to this outcome, acting as incentives to stay out of the labor market and instead invest in marriage and in raising a family.

Current challenges

Egypt ranks 140th out of 153 countries for women's economic participation (WEF 2019). Women face a host of challenges that hinder their participation in the labor market. While female labor force participation was already very low, it has declined even further, primarily because of the decline in public sector jobs, which represent the main employer for women with higher education. In addition, the low quality of vacancies in the private sector, and the difficulty of reconciling responsibilities at home and work, act as barriers to women's employment (Assaad, Krafft, and Selwaness 2017; Barsoum 2015; Selwaness and Krafft 2018).

A main challenge to female participation in the labor market, and especially in the private sector, is the lack of a working environment that is attractive or hospitable to or supportive of women. Persistent barriers exist, such as the lack of access to childcare, availability of safe and affordable transportation, and concerns about sexual harassment. These may have a direct negative effect on women's desire to participate in the labor market. The skills mismatch (as discussed previously) and the role of influencers who might push girls to study in certain fields may affect their job opportunities. Moreover, gender social norms, perceptions, and attitudes also affect women's ability to join the labor force. Greater flexibility, including family-friendly policies in the private sector, are needed in order to attract more women, such as sufficient maternity leave with reentry guaranteed (within a reasonable and specified time frame), availability of time-saving technologies, remote-work opportunities, and support for childcare. These are essential to encourage women to participate in the labor market (Amer 2015).

The trade-off between work and home is the second challenge. Egypt's strong social and cultural norms imply a certain belief that the most important role for women is that of being mothers, taking care of their families, and fulfilling domestic responsibilities. There is a clear competition or tension between the reproductive and productive roles that women play. About 81 percent of Egyptians believe that a woman doing her work as a housewife is just as satisfying as her paid work, for instance (Girgis and Adel 2021). Evidence also highlights the impact of marriage on women's participation in the labor market. Among working women, 11 percent were previously married, and 25 percent never married. Nearly 66 percent of women outside the workforce are housewives. Further, 87 percent of women who have university degrees but no jobs cite family as being the reason for not working. This reflects a certain conflict between work and family, as even women with a university education tend to sacrifice work for family responsibilities (Baseera, NPC, and UNFPA 2017).

Fluctuations in fertility rates have resulted in inconsistent but growing pressure on the labor market. The rise and fall in fertility rates have led to a disproportionate share of youth in the population over recent decades. A fundamental aspect of Egypt's changing demographics since 1998 has been the broadening of the youth stratum. The number of youth increased in Egypt when mortality rates plunged years before fertility dropped (Assaad and Roudi-Fahimi 2007; Miller and Hirschhorn 1995; Rashad 1989; Robinson and El-Zanaty 2006).

The rise in fertility rates in the late 1970s and 1980s led to the creation of a large cohort of youth ages 10–19 years that placed immense pressure on the labor market by 1998. This pressure further increased in 2006 as the majority of this cohort began entering the labor market. Six years later, the pressure eased with youth having settled into the labor market. However, there would be unanticipated consequences to fertility, as it was around this time that Egypt's TFR began to rise again (see chapter 1). According to Egypt's EDHS series, in 2008, Egypt's TFR was at 3.0 births per woman, and it rose to 3.5 births per woman by 2014.

At the same time, with the implementation of the new population policy and wider use of contraceptives, TFR began to decline, but it stabilized at 3.1 births per woman by 2018 (ERF and CAPMAS 2018). In fact, the Egypt Labor Market Panel Survey (ELMPS) of 2018 stated that 62.6 percent of married women ages 15-49 years take action to prevent pregnancy (Krafft, Assaad, and Keo 2019), up from 58.5 percent in the 2014 EDHS (MOHP, El-Zanaty and Associates, and ICF International 2015).

A demographic echo had begun in 2012, when youth started forming families and having children of their own. The echo was noted that year with the population peak between 0 and 4 years, which grew to be 5–9 years in 2018, putting additional pressure on the education system. Toward the end of this decade, these children will reach working age, placing immense pressure on the labor market (Krafft and Kettle 2019).

Such labor market challenges can be best resolved when demographic changes work in the market's favor. There is a window of opportunity that Egypt must take advantage of. The current eased demographic pressure—with the largest group of youth having aged and the echo cohort still at school—is the chance Egypt needs to resolve the structural challenges of its labor market.

POVERTY AND SOCIAL PROTECTION

Poverty and lack of social protection contribute to increased fertility. About 3.2 percent of Egyptians live below the level of the international poverty line of US$1.90 (2011 PPP US$) per day; only 4.1 percent of Egyptians are considered multidimensionally poor, which reflects Egypt's strong performance relative to other countries on dimensions such as consumption, schooling, and access to basic utilities. On the other hand, the share of the poor when measured using national poverty lines (US$3.80 per day) rose from 25.2 percent in 2010 to 32.5 percent in 2017/18 (World Bank 2020). It is estimated to have declined to 29.7 percent in 2019/20 (CAPMAS 2020), which is still high.

In 2014, among the lowest two wealth quintiles, the fertility rate was 3.6 children per woman, higher than the national average of 3.5; the age at marriage was the lowest among all wealth quintiles (18.9 years and 19.6 years, respectively); and contraceptive use was lower than the national average (55.9 and 55.7 percent, respectively) (MOHP, El-Zanaty and Associates, and ICF International 2015). Different social reasons may explain these trends. Poorest families consider children as a source of income, and having more children guarantees more income to the families (which could also lead to high rates of school dropouts) and a source of safety nets for parents in old age.

The poorest population is concentrated in Upper Egypt, especially in rural areas, where there is limited coverage of health units, which translates into lack of access to family planning services and products, particularly female service providers. The poverty rate in rural Upper Egypt was 51.94 percent, according to the Household Income, Expenditure, and Consumption Survey (HIECS) for 2017/18 (Economic Research Forum and CAPMAS 2021). With the limited income, families are faced with the burden of paying the direct and indirect expenses for FP services, if available; and with the high level of illiteracy, mass communication campaign messages may not be as effective. Such regions are where social protection programs come in (box 4.1).

Tackling fertility-related issues through cash transfer programs

Social protection programs—that is, cash transfer programs—can have an influence on fertility, although the evidence is mixed. Global evidence shows either that cash transfers have no impact on fertility or that they support reductions in fertility or changes in factors that can help reduce fertility over time (UNICEF 2017). Cash transfer programs are widely used to alleviate poverty and help families meet their basic needs. They are typically designed to increase support incrementally with the aim of reducing poverty and economic and social risks and promoting resilience. They may, therefore, influence fertility through several tracks. For example, grant-related income could foster economic independence and increase access to health services, job prospects, and education for girls and women, creating incentives and opportunities for lower pregnancy rates.

Some have argued that cash transfer programs could have a negative impact because they may motivate families to have larger families to access larger cash transfers (Stecklov et al. 2007). The argument suggests that cash transfers may encourage families to keep having children to remain in the program or to get benefits for each child. This is why many countries put a cap on the number of children that can be supported through such a program (Palermo 2016).

Cash transfers could help increase income, thereby reducing fertility in the longer term. Further, they can increase demand and ease access to health care and FP services, which can have both short- and long-term effects on fertility, especially given that in many countries women's lack of access to such services limits their ability to make reproductive choices (Stecklov et al. 2007). This effect is especially relevant for Egypt, where approximately 16 percent of births in 2014 were not wanted (Baseera, NPC, and UNFPA 2017). Moreover, cash transfers may also improve girls' access to education, which in the longer term can result in women having fewer children over their lifetime through delayed marriages and better access to information and services related to FP (UNICEF 2017). This longer-term effect occurs because some cash transfer programs are conditional upon ensuring that children of families enrolled in the program attend school regularly.

Egypt has launched several programs to tackle fertility-related issues that are focused on gender, social protection, or other aspects. The national cash transfer system, the "Takaful and Karama" program (TKP), launched in 2015, was initially designed to support families with up to three children under the Takaful conditional cash transfer subprogram.[a] In 2018, the government revised the cap to make it two children only, to support FP efforts. This subprogram targets households with children under 18 years of age and provides them with income support that is tied to improvement in specific behaviors related to education and health care. It was carefully designed to serve as a "nudge" to influence behavioral changes among Egypt's poorest groups.

Finally, the Ministry of Social Solidarity has adopted an integrated family development strategy including a life-cycle approach to provide childcare services in the first 1,000 days and equal education opportunities. It has also launched behavioral change programs targeting TKP beneficiaries called "Waaei" (meaning awareness) and "Mawaddah" (meaning cordiality), which use rural leaders and social workers to advocate 12 key messages, including combating female circumcision, encouraging FP and girls' education, and discouraging early marriage in addition to educating young people about marriage and the value of family through counseling services.

a. Takaful means solidarity; Karama means dignity.

GENDER AND SOCIAL NORMS

There is a direct correlation between reproductive health, economic development, and gender dynamics. Improved reproductive health is associated with lower total fertility rates, which in turn is one of the main drivers of a population's age structure. Addressing gender barriers can help improve reproductive health outcomes, including fertility, and accelerate Egypt's demographic dividend. Further, women with better reproductive health status tend to invest more resources in their own families' health and education, with better human capital outcomes for their children and for themselves. Evidence shows that, on one hand, the rise in fertility rates can be a challenge for women's empowerment and can have critical implications for human endowment outcomes, economic opportunities, and voice and agency (Baseera, NPC, and UNFPA 2017). On the other hand, several factors can affect women's empowerment and consequently affect fertility rates. In short, enhancing gender equality and women's empowerment can be important for reducing fertility.

Current challenges

Gender and social norms and values affect fertility in different ways. Some religious views related to FP can play a key role in increasing fertility rates, given that the religious discourse among some conservative groups opposes the use of contraceptives. It is also common among some families to prefer boys, which may lead them to keep having children until the woman gives birth to a boy.

Early marriage is also one of the key challenges influencing fertility, because it can have a considerable effect on women's agency, health, and education. Despite laws banning child marriage, the practice is still common in Egypt for several reasons, including social norms, poverty, and low educational attainment. It is estimated that 6 percent of married females are ages 15–17 years and 27 percent are 18–19 years (Baseera, NPC, and UNFPA 2017).

Early marriage usually means childbearing at a young age, leading to higher fertility and more children over a woman's lifetime, relative to women who marry at an older age. Moreover, early marriages usually entail power imbalances, because often young girls are married to considerably older men. Thus they may face difficulties in asserting their preferences, including negotiating safe sexual practices and FP methods, which may also lead to having more children. All these factors have significant consequences for fertility rates and women's health and well-being.

Early marriage is also a factor contributing to women's lack of participation in the labor market. It curtails educational attainment for girls, thereby reducing their chances of entering the labor market or negatively affecting the types of jobs they can engage in (Wodon, Savadogo, and Kes 2017). Early marriage and early motherhood can therefore create a vicious circle that affects women's agency, endowments, and economic and productive role, and results in increased fertility.

Social and cultural norms have a strong influence on gender roles and therefore on fertility choices and preferences in Egypt. One of these is the cultural perception that having a big family strengthens solidarity (*ezwah*) and creates a support system. For some poor families, children are regarded as an economic asset and a source of income, either current or future. This belief is in line with the literature on economic growth and demographics; that is, in labor-intensive, low-income economies, more hands mean more work gets done. Moving out of this cycle requires investment in education and job creation outside of traditional labor-intensive sectors. It also requires behavior change. However, often these same social and cultural norms stand in the way of having open and frank discussions about these issues, including women's empowerment and reproductive health, as these may be considered sensitive topics.

Cultural misinterpretations and rigidity in the narrow definition of gender roles have also compounded with the rise of the militant religious wave over the past decade. This package of militant norms is translated into consanguinity, early marriages, adolescent childbearing, extended family, and resistance to FP. Although these manifestations are more pronounced among the poor, uneducated, and rural residents of Egypt, they have also crept into the lives and lifestyles of wealthier, educated, and urban residents (World Bank 2018).

Gender bias in access to education and employment still exists. Egypt has succeeded in the last decade in closing the gender gap in health and education, but a lot is still needed to grant women equal opportunities across all these areas (WEF 2019), and especially in labor markets.

Egypt continues to suffer from a gender literacy gap as well. The literacy rate among women stands at 65 percent, which translates into a 15 percent gender gap that needs to be bridged (WEF 2019). The gender gap tends to be wider in rural areas and among the lowest wealth quintiles, which poses a serious challenge to those groups, given that the education level of the population is an important factor influencing perceptions, economic participation and productivity, reproductive behavior, and so on. Because illiteracy is higher among women, the impact on women's empowerment and, accordingly, fertility behavior is highly probable. There is evidence that women who are less educated and less empowered are more likely to bear more children and less likely to be using contraceptives (Baseera, NPC, and UNFPA 2017).

In some contexts, preference for sons may be a contributing factor to these outcomes. Gender-based biases continue throughout the life cycle of women and men. Thus, as children grow and reach school age, some families may send their boys to school, whereas female children may stay at home to help with household chores. In addition to contributing to high illiteracy rates among females, such trends contribute to increases in early marriage and childbearing.

These norms and biases also influence female labor force participation, which, as discussed earlier, continues to pose challenges for women. Educated, working women are more likely to make informed choices regarding their reproductive health and the health of their children. They are also more likely to use FP methods. This choice applies to first birth as well to intervals between births, which tend to be longer among working women (Baseera, NPC, and UNFPA 2017).

CONCLUSIONS

Although considerable progress has been made in improving access to health services, both supply- and demand-side constraints remain. Most important among these constraints are (a) shortage of key health personnel, particularly in rural or remote areas; (b) inconsistency of FP programs as a result of policy changes, with service delivery oscillating between vertical, stand-alone, and integrated sexual and reproductive health services; (c) poor planning and management because of a lack of data; and (d) limited funding resulting from how FP is prioritized, as well as weak intersectoral collaboration on drivers of fertility. On the demand side, constraints to reducing fertility include lack of engagement of men as partners in FP, an increase in childbearing among urban educated women caused by shifting norms, and limited labor market opportunities.

In the education sector (including tertiary education), enrollment and retention are key issues. There is a significant drop in enrollment at the secondary level for both girls and boys (from nearly universal to 68 percent for girls and 71 percent for boys). School dropouts are a persistent risk with children from poor families, with boys more likely to drop out. In schools, quality of education is a big concern. It is estimated that 70 percent of children experience learning poverty (that is, they cannot read and understand a short, age-appropriate text by age 10). Some of the failures of the education sector include its inability to keep pace with the demand for higher education and a mismatch between what is taught in schools and the skills needed in the labor market, especially for female tertiary-level students.

The government is addressing these concerns by expanding capacity of educational institutions, opening community schools and more universities, improving quality of higher education, and supporting blended and distance learning at the lower levels, which is also likely to encourage greater participation of girls. Female labor force participation in the country remains low (under 24 percent), and with the shrinking of the public sector—the main employer for women—there has been a drop in already-low female employment. Female employment in the private sector can increase, but the sector needs to create conditions that are conducive to female employment, such as safe transport, flexible hours and working arrangements, access to childcare, and reduced risk of sexual harassment.

Gender and social norms also pose a challenge, especially when higher value is placed on women's domestic roles and their role as mothers. Early marriages and uneven power structures within households continue to affect women's ability to make decisions about their own reproductive health and fertility and the extent to which they can participate in school or employment.

Social protection programs also play an important role in Egypt's population policy. The country has launched several programs aimed at addressing fertility, such as the TKP, which promotes school attendance, improved family nutrition, and use of primary health care. This effort is strongly aligned with the recently launched Waaei program, which aims to support female empowerment through FP, girls' education, and combating of female genital mutilation and early marriage.

Still, to complement the analysis of the sectoral and social drivers of fertility, it is critical to assess the economic impact of fertility changes in terms of what Egypt has missed out on and what potential gains could be made. The next chapter offers some pointers.

NOTES

1. UIS (UNESCO Institute of Statistics), http://uis.unesco.org/.
2. World Bank calculations based on CAPMAS 2019.
3. For example, Germany, France, Austria, and Canada (community colleges).
4. CAPMAS Labor Force Survey. http://www.erfdataportal.com/index.php/catalog/149.

REFERENCES

Abdel-Tawab, Nahla, Nada Wahba, Gihan Hosny, Salma Abou Hussein, Amr Elshalakani, Denizhan Duran, and Shaimaa Ahmed Ibrahim Mohamed. 2020. "Engaging Men and Boys to Reduce Fertility Rates in Egypt." Washington, DC: World Bank Group.

Amer, Mona. 2015. "Patterns of Labor Market Insertion in Egypt, 1998–2012." In *The Egyptian Labor Market in an Era of Revolution*, edited by Ragui Assaad and Caroline Krafft, 70–89. Oxford, UK: Oxford University Press.

Amer, Mona, and Marian Atallah. 2019. "The School to Work Transition and Youth Economic Vulnerability in Egypt." ERF Working Paper 1353, Economic Research Forum, Cairo. https://erf.org.eg/publications/the-school-to-work-transition-and-youth-economic-vulnerability-in-egypt1/.

Assaad, R., A. AlSharawy, and C. Salemi. 2019. "Is the Egyptian Economy Creating Good Jobs? Job Creation and Economic Vulnerability from 1998 to 2018." ERF Working Paper 1354, Economic Research Forum, Cairo.

Assaad, Ragui, Caroline Krafft, and Irene Selwaness. 2017. "The Impact of Marriage on Women's Employment in the Middle East and North Africa." ERF Working Paper 1086, Economic Research Forum, Cairo.

Assaad, Ragui, and Farzaneh Roudi-Fahimi. 2007. "Youth in the Middle East and North Africa: Demographic Opportunity or Challenge?" Policy Brief. Washington, DC: Population Reference Bureau.

Barsoum, Ghada. 2015. "Young People's Job Aspirations in Egypt and the Continued Preference for a Government Job." In *The Egyptian Labor Market in an Era of Revolution*, edited by Ragui Assaad and Caroline Krafft, 108–126. Oxford, UK: Oxford University Press.

Baseera, NPC (National Population Council), and UNFPA (United Nations Population Fund). 2017. "Population Situation Analysis: 2016 Egypt." Cairo: United Nations Population Fund. https://egypt.unfpa.org/en/publications/population-situation-analysis-egypt-2016-report.

CAPMAS (Central Agency for Public Mobilization and Statistics). 2019. "Statistical Yearbook." December. Cairo: CAPMAS. http://www.capmas.gov.eg/.

CAPMAS (Central Agency for Public Mobilization and Statistics). 2020. *Egypt in Figures 2020*. March. https://www.capmas.gov.eg/Pages/StaticPages.aspx?page_id=5035.

Constant, Louay, Ifeanyi Edochie, Peter Glick, Jeffrey Martini, and Chandra Garber. 2020. "Barriers to Employment That Women Face in Egypt." Santa Monica, CA: RAND. https://www.rand.org/content/dam/rand/pubs/research_reports/RR2800/RR2868/RAND_RR2868.pdf.

Economic Research Forum and CAPMAS. 2021. "Household Income, Expenditure, and Consumption Survey (HIECS) for 2017/18." http://www.erfdataportal.com/index.php/catalog/168.

El-Laithy, Heba. 2021. "Inequality of Education Opportunities in Egypt: Impact Evaluation." Egyptian Center for Economic Studies (ECES). http://www.eces.org.eg/PublicationsDetails?Lang=EN&C=12&T=1&ID=1287&Inequality-of-Education-Opportunities-in-Egypt:-Impact-Evaluation.

El Tawil, Noha. 2021. "'Egypt's Population Growth Has to Be Cut to 400K Yearly So We Can Feel Impact of Public Spending': Pres. Sisi." *Egypt Today*. February 16. https://www.egypttoday.com/Article/1/98679/Egypt-s-population-growth-has-to-be-cut-to-400K.

ERF (Economic Research Forum) and CAPMAS. 2018. Egypt Labor Market Panel Survey. http://www.erfdataportal.com/index.php/catalog.

Girgis, Hanan, and Noha Adel. 2021. "Childcare Service and Its Impact on Women Economic Participation." Cairo: Baseera, The National Council for Women, and The World Bank Group. http://en.enow.gov.eg/Report/144.pdf.

Krafft, Caroline, Ragui Assaad, and Caitlyn Keo. 2019. "The Evolution of Labor Supply in Egypt from 1988–2018: A Gendered Analysis." ERF Working Paper 1358, Economic Research Forum, Cairo.

Krafft, Caroline, Zea Branson, and Taylor Flak. 2019. "What's the Value of a Degree? Evidence from Egypt, Jordan and Tunisia." *Compare: A Journal of Comparative and International Education* 51 (1): 61–80. doi:10.1080/03057925.2019.1590801.

Krafft, Caroline, and Emma Kettle. 2019. "The Future of Labor Supply and Demographics in Egypt: Impending Challenges and Untapped Potential." ERF Policy Brief 43, Economic Research Forum, Cairo. https://erf.org.eg/publications/the-future-of-labor-supply-and -demographics-in-egypt-impending-challenges-and-untapped-potential/?tab=undefined.

Miller, Peter, and Norbert Hirschhorn. 1995. "The Effect of a National Control of Diarrheal Diseases Program on Mortality: The Case of Egypt." *Social Science & Medicine* 40 (10): S1–S30.

MOETE (Ministry of Education and Technical Education). 2020. "Statistical Yearbook 2019/2020." MOETE, Cairo. http://emis.gov.eg/Site%20Content/book/019-020/main _book2020.html. In Arabic.

MOETE (Ministry of Education and Technical Education). 2021. "Statistical Yearbook 2020/2021." MOETE, Cairo. http://emis.gov.eg/Site%20Content/book/020-021/main _book2021.html. In Arabic.

MOF (Ministry of Finance). 2021a. "Analytical Separated Statement 2020–2021," table 2-A.8. http://www.mof.gov.eg/MOFGallerySource/Arabic/budget2020-2021/Analytical -Separated-Statement-2020-2021.pdf (table 2-A.8, page 112). In Arabic.

MOF (Ministry of Finance). 2021b. "Financial Statement 2020–2021," table 1. http://www.mof .gov.eg/MOFGallerySource/Arabic/budget2020-2021/Financial-Statement2020-2021.pdf (table 1, page 64). In Arabic.

MOHP (Ministry of Health and Population), El-Zanaty and Associates, and ICF International. 2015. *Egypt Demographic and Health Survey*. Cairo: MOHP and ICF International.

Palermo, Tia. 2016. "Cash Transfers and Fertility: New Evidence from Africa." *UNICEF Connect* (blog). February 24. https://blogs.unicef.org/blog/cash-transfers-and-fertility-new -evidence-from-africa/#:~:text=The%20family%20benefits%20from%20the,%2C%20 in%20fact%2C%20increase%20fertility.

Rashad, Hoda. 1989. "Oral Rehydration Therapy and Its Effect on Child Mortality in Egypt." *Journal of Biosocial Science* 21 (Suppl 10): 105–13.

Robinson, Warren, and Fatma El-Zanaty. 2006. *The Demographic Revolution in Modern Egypt*. Lanham, MD: Lexington Books.

Selwaness, Irene, and Caroline Krafft. 2018. "The Dynamics of Family Formation and Women's Work: What Facilitates and Hinders Female Employment in the Middle East and North Africa?" ERF Working Paper 1192, Economic Research Forum, Cairo.

Stecklov, Guy, Paul Winters, Jessica Todd, and Ferdinando Regalia. 2007. "Unintended Effects of Poverty Programmes on Childbearing in Less Developed Countries: Experimental Evidence from Latin America." *Population Studies* 61 (2): 125–40. https://doi.org /10.1080/00324720701300396.

UKAID. 2018. "Lessons from the Field: Sexual and Reproductive Health and Rights in the GEC." Girl's Education Challenge. London, UK: UKAID. https://girlseducationchallenge.org /what-we-are-learning/.

UNDP (United Nations Development Programme). 2008. *Egypt Human Development Report. Egypt's Social Contract: The Role of Civil Society*. Cairo: UNDP. https://www.eg.undp.org /content/egypt/en/home/library/human_development/publication_3.html.

UNICEF (United Nations Children's Fund). 2017. "Addressing the Myths: Social Protection and Fertility." *Social Policy Summaries*. New York: United Nations Children's Fund. https:// static1.squarespace.com/static/56588879e4b0060cdb607883/t/5bb6761b104c7bc 51c145001/1538684444162/Myth+1_UNICEF_Sept+15_2017.pdf.

WEF (World Economic Forum). 2019. *Global Gender Gap Report 2020*. Geneva: World Economic Forum. http://www3.weforum.org/docs/WEF_GGGR_2020.pdf.

Wodon, Quentin, Aboudrahyme Savadogo, and Aslihan Kes. 2017. "Economic Impacts of Child Marriage: Work. Earnings, and Household Welfare." World Bank and International Center for Research on Women. http://documents1.worldbank.org/curated/en /31276149851278450/pdf/116835-BRI-P151842-PUBLIC-EICM-Brief-WorkEarnings Household-PrintReady.pdf.

World Bank. 2018. *Women Economic Empowerment Study.* Washington, DC: World Bank. http://documents.worldbank.org/curated/en/861491551113547855/Women-Economic-Empowerment-Study.

World Bank. 2019. *Ending Learning Poverty: What Will It Take?* World Bank, Washington, DC.

World Bank. 2020. "Poverty & Equity Brief. Arab Republic of Egypt." World Bank, Washington, DC. https://databank.worldbank.org/data/download/poverty/33EF03BB-9722-4AE2-ABC7-AA2972D68AFE/Global_POVEQ_EGY.pdf.

Additional Reading

Assaad, Ragui, Shaimaa Yassin, and Caroline Krafft. 2018. "Job Creation or Labor Absorption? An Analysis of Private Sector Job Growth by Industry in Egypt." ERF Working Paper 1237, Economic Research Forum, Cairo.

Mullis, I. V. S., Martin, M. O., Foy, P., Kelly, D. L., and Fishbein, B. 2020. "TIMSS 2019 International Results in Mathematics and Science." https://timssandpirls.bc.edu/timss2019/international-results/.

World Bank. 2020. World Development Indicators (database). Washington, DC: World Bank. https://databank.worldbank.org/source/world-development-indicators.

5 The Economic Impact—Forgone Savings and Potential Gains

SAMEH EL-SAHARTY, HEBA NASSAR,
MARIAM M. HAMZA, AND YI ZHANG

Before 2008, the Arab Republic of Egypt had been on a path of declining fertility, increasing the share of its working-age population and potentially maximizing its demographic dividend. However, this advance halted, hurting the country's potential for economic growth and burdening the government through increased public expenditures. This chapter aims to quantify the economic effects of the change in fertility in monetary terms, which goes beyond analyzing the relationships between age structure and economic factors. This approach is vital for evidence-based population policy making, as this type of quantification can inform policy dialogue and help in understanding the economic implications of supporting investment in cost-effective population policies.

The chapter relies on two methods of analysis: a *retrospective analysis* that assesses the costs of Egypt's population growth over 2007/08–2019/20 in terms of forgone savings and opportunity costs for the economy caused by the reversal in fertility decline; and a *prospective analysis* that estimates the potential savings in public expenditure and potential gains in national income under two hypothetical scenarios of different rates of fertility decline ("moderate" and "accelerated") over 2021–30. Population projections are made using data from the UN World Population Prospects database and the DemProj software model. The methodology used for estimating the relationships between age structure, GDP, and savings was described in Cruz and Ahmed (2018).

DEMOGRAPHIC AND MACROECONOMIC TRENDS IN EGYPT

An inverse correlation between GDP per capita and the total dependency ratio (that is, dependency of young and old combined) can be observed for Egypt (figure 5.1). With a sharp decline in the total dependency ratio, driven by the sharp decline in fertility and the child dependency ratio during 1990–2010, GDP per capita continued to grow. The old-age (65 and above) dependency ratio remained stagnant over the entire period at around 7 percent, implying that there are no significant changes in life expectancy to notably increase the small proportion of the older population. One of the commonly used criteria for determining the occurrence of the demographic dividend is whether the value of the total dependency ratio is less than 0.5, that is, one dependent for two workers

FIGURE 5.1

Dependency ratio and GDP per capita, 1960–2019

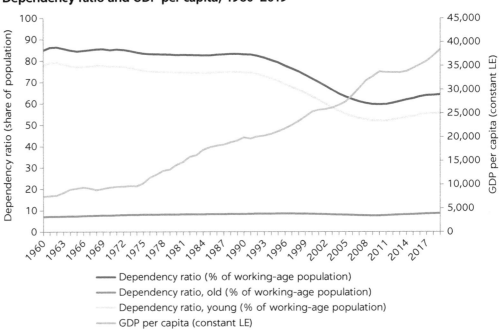

Source: World Development Indicators Database, https://datacatalog.worldbank.org/dataset/world-development -indicators.
Note: GDP = gross domestic product; LE = Egyptian pound.

(Cheung et al. 2004). Between 1990 and 2010, the dependency ratio sharply declined from 83.0 percent to 59.6 percent, the lowest in five decades (figure 5.1).

Another key demographic metric—the working-age share of the population (ages 15–64 years as a share of the total population)—saw an increase in Egypt from 1990 to 2010 but then started to decline. It had hovered around 54 percent over the previous three decades (1960–90). Then, fertility declined significantly, accelerating the growth of the working-age share of the population, which increased by approximately 0.5 percentage points annually. This increase continued through 2010, when the working-age share reached an all-time high of 62.6 percent. Then, driven by higher fertility, population momentum, and a significant increase in the number of children in the population, the share fell, and it was projected to have reached approximately 61 percent in 2020 (figure 5.2).

As demonstrated by the methodology used in Cruz and Ahmed (2018), Egypt followed the global trend and was starting to experience the first phase of its demographic dividend; however, instead of this dividend phase lasting for decades, the working-age share of the population started to decline (figure 5.2), thus slowing economic growth. The trend was initially similar in terms of periods, with the demographic dividend starting around 1966 (shown by the first blue dotted line), when the share of the working-age population started to increase, before peaking in 2010 (second blue dotted line) at 62.6 percent.

Crucially, had fertility continued to decline, Egypt would have maximized its demographic dividend, continuing to reap economic benefits and, in a hypothetical continued fertility decline scenario, even doing better than the global trend, as shown by the orange and green lines in figure 5.2. In this hypothetical "continued decline" scenario, the working-age share of the population would have seen a continued increase past 2011.

FIGURE 5.2

Demographic dividend and the working-age share of the population, globally and for Egypt, actual outcome and continued fertility decline scenario, 1960–2020

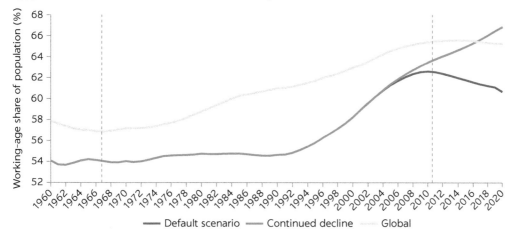

Source: Estimates using World Development Indicators Database, https://datacatalog.worldbank.org/dataset /world-development-indicators.

POPULATION TRENDS: ACTUAL OUTCOME AND CONTINUED DECLINE SCENARIO

If, after 2000, the total fertility rate (TFR) had followed the declining trend of 1970–2000 (appendix B), it would have been 1.96 instead of 3.26 births per woman in 2020 (figure 5.3 and table B.2), and Egypt's population in 2020 would have been about 9 percent less, at 92.6 million, not 101.7 million. The comparison of population sizes between the actual outcome (based on a simulation from 2000 using UN World Population Prospects data and the Spectrum DemProj model) and the modeled continued decline scenario (based on the simulation from 2000 using UN population estimates with the continued fertility decline assumption) is summarized in table B.2. The population distribution across ages and sex is summarized in the population pyramid in figure 5.4.[1]

Had Egypt's TFR continued to decline after 2000, the dependency ratio would have fallen to 0.50 by 2020—a 22.52 percent reduction from 0.64 in the actual outcome (figure 5.5 and table B.2). The dependency ratio is critical for understanding the impacts of changes in population structure—a lower ratio presents opportunities for improving, for example, public spending on health, housing, education, and job opportunities, as it means a greater share of working people to support dependents.

ESTIMATING FORGONE SAVINGS IN PUBLIC EXPENDITURE AND WELFARE OPPORTUNITY COSTS, 2007/08–2019/20: A RETROSPECTIVE ANALYSIS

This section estimates savings forgone because of the effects of the reversal in fertility decline, in public expenditures on health, housing, and education, as well as the welfare opportunity costs. The methodology is described in appendix C. A similar exercise on the creation of job opportunities is summarized in box 5.1.

FIGURE 5.3

Total fertility rate, actual outcome and continued decline scenario, 2000–20

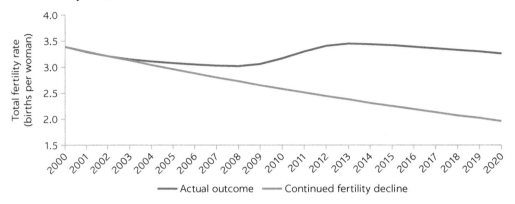

Source: Original calculations based on UN World Population Prospects (https://population.un.org/wpp/) database and Spectrum DemProj model.

FIGURE 5.4

Population distribution by age and sex, actual outcome and continued decline scenario, 2020

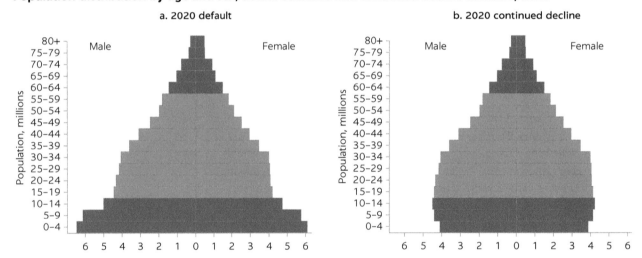

Source: Original calculations based on UN World Population Prospects database (https://population.un.org/wpp/) and Spectrum DemProj model.

FIGURE 5.5

Dependency ratio, actual outcome and continued decline scenario, 2000–20

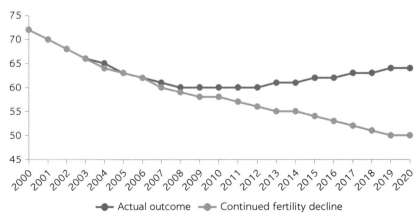

Source: Original calculations based on UN World Population Prospects database (https://population.un.org/wpp/) and Spectrum DemProj model.

Box 5.1

A retrospective analysis for employment

Creating jobs is a key challenge facing the Egyptian economy, given the increase in population and the weak link between GDP growth and unemployment caused by decades of industrial policies that have discouraged investment in employment-generating activities. Industrial policies have, on the contrary, led to growth in sectors that are not labor intensive.

The reason underlying the results of the retrospective analysis in appendix E is the investment in infrastructure since 2015, particularly in 2017, with a relatively small increase in new jobs. Public investment is necessary for creating job opportunities in both the public and private sectors. The increase in employment was fluctuating and, in several years, very small (2010/11 and after 2017).

The change in employment (default or continued decline scenario) shows small, fluctuating increases in new job opportunities, on the assumption that the employment rate is the same in both scenarios and ranges between 0.39 and 0.43. Also, the public cost of creating job opportunities shows a trend toward growth with the same or decreasing employment level.

The savings in the new job opportunities needed as a result of the retrospective population projection was seen only in the three years 2017–20. Thus the total real possible savings in total public investment needed to create new jobs is also small, at LE 0.116 million in 2019/20, or LE 0.399 million in total over the three years 2017–20.

Health

We used data from the Ministry of Finance for calculating public health expenditure for 2007/08–2019/20 (appendix C, table C.1). Cumulative real actual public expenditure on health (2007/08–2019/20) was LE 586,200 million versus LE 558,837 million according to the real retrospective projections under the continued fertility decline scenario. The real forgone savings in public expenditure on health (2007/08–2019/20), if the fertility decline had not reversed, comes to LE 27,363 million, averaging 4.69 percent of real actual public expenditure on health—quite a significant amount. For 2019/20, real retrospective projections amounted to LE 42,434.57 million.

We also examined the increase in population welfare with actual public expenditure on health distributed among a smaller population, based on the continued decline scenario. The result is higher per capita expenditure on health, rising from 0.64 percent in 2007/08 to 9.81 percent in 2019/20. So, per capita real public expenditure on health would have been LE 503 in 2019/20.

Housing

A similar analysis was conducted for public expenditure on housing (table C.2). Cumulative real actual public expenditure on housing (2007/08–2019/20) was LE 423,841 million versus LE 405,047 million according to the retrospective projections under the continued fertility decline scenario. The real forgone savings in public expenditure on housing (2008/08–2019/20), if fertility decline had not reversed, comes to LE 18,794 million, averaging 4.43 percent of the actual public expenditure on housing. Per capita real public expenditure on housing reached LE 397.42 in 2019/20 versus LE 436.39 based on the continued fertility decline scenario.

To estimate the increase in population welfare, public expenditure on housing was distributed among a smaller population, per the continued decline scenario. The result is higher per capita public expenditure on housing, rising from 0.64 percent in 2007/08 to 9.81 percent in 2019/20, and yielding per capita real public expenditure of LE 436 in 2019/20.

Education

For education, we used the same methodology for the calculation of public expenditure for pre-university and university but confined the analysis to the population cohort of ages 5–24 years—the school-age population from primary to tertiary levels (table C.3). In 2019/20, per capita real actual expenditure on education was, at LE 2,175.35, lower than the LE 2,461.50 based on the retrospective projections.

Given the decrease in size of the population (as in the continued decline scenario of the population projections), real retrospective projections of public expenditure on education came to LE 74,418.82 million in 2019/20, with the equivalent per capita figure of LE 2,461.50.

The cumulative real actual public expenditure on education (2007/08–2019/20) was LE 1,319,538 million compared with LE 1,272,352 million based on the retrospective projections. The real forgone savings in public expenditure on education (2007/08–2019/20), if the fertility decline had not reversed, comes to LE 47,185 million. Forgone savings in public expenditure on education as a share of the total real actual figure was quite high, at 11.62 percent in 2019/20, and 3.58 percent on average between 2007/08 and 2019/20.

In terms of population welfare, if expenditure on education was distributed among a smaller population (per the continued decline scenario), the result again is rising per capita real actual expenditure, from 0.12 percent in 2008/09 to 13.15 percent in 2019/20.

Forgone savings on health, housing, and education combined due to the reversal in fertility decline

The estimated amount of LE 93,343 million in real public expenditure on health, housing, and education together could have been saved had the population growth rate followed the declining trend in the retrospective population projection for 2007/08–2019/20 (table C.4). These forgone savings in such expenditure were estimated at 8.93 percent of real expenditure for health and housing and 11.62 percent of real expenditure for education in 2019/20. Had fertility continued to decline, the government would have saved LE 17.6 billion in real terms on all three sectors in 2019/20. The education sector would have witnessed the highest savings, with approximately LE 9.8 billion, followed by health and housing (figure 5.6 and table C.4).

Figure 5.7 shows the additional potential benefit—namely, the impact of the decline in population size on the welfare of individuals as seen by the percentage increase in per capita real expenditure in the three sectors—given the assumption that total public expenditure was not reduced over the period. It was estimated at 9.81 percent for health and housing and 13.15 percent for education.

FIGURE 5.6

Forgone savings in real actual public expenditure on health, housing, and education, 2007/08–2019/20

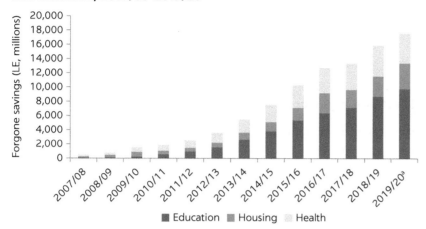

Source: Original calculations based on actual expenditures, https://www.mof.gov.eg/ (in Arabic).
a. Original estimates based on the planned budget, https://www.mof.gov.eg/ (in Arabic).

FIGURE 5.7

Retrospective projections of percentage increase in per capita real expenditure on health, housing, and education, 2007/08–2019/20

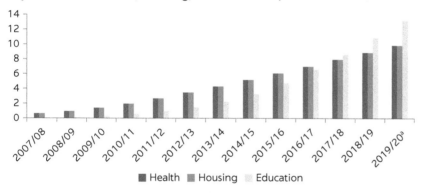

Source: Original calculations based on actual expenditures from the Ministry of Finance, https://www.mof.gov.eg/ (in Arabic).
a. Original estimates based on the planned budget, https://www.mof.gov.eg/ (in Arabic).

Estimating opportunity costs for the economy as a whole

This section's analysis estimates the effect of a relationship between the share of the working-age population and dependency ratios on per capita GDP growth and savings, and to quantify this effect for the hypothetical continued decline scenario. It follows the methodology of Cruz and Ahmed (2018) as outlined in appendix D. More specifically, the aim of the analysis is to:

• Assess whether heterogeneous effects exist for Egypt, given its unique context, when examining the impact of the share of the working-age population and dependency ratios on per capita growth and gross domestic savings.

- Estimate the impact of the share of the working-age population and dependency ratios on per capita growth and gross domestic savings for Egypt.
- Quantify the opportunity cost of the reversal in Egypt's fertility decline on GDP and gross domestic savings through estimating GDP under a hypothetical scenario of continued fertility decline.

The following section describes the effects noted in the analysis.

Effect of a high dependency ratio on GDP

Egypt experiences additional economic pressure resulting from a high dependency ratio. In appendix D, table D.1 shows the regression results based on the empirical model shown in equation (1) in that appendix, revealing a significant negative relationship globally between the dependency ratio and GDP per capita. When looking at heterogeneous effects using the binary variable for Egypt, a significant negative coefficient is also yielded, implying that a high dependency ratio further exacerbates the negative relationship.

Effect of a hypothetical continued decline on GDP

On the basis of the above results and using the population projections estimated under the hypothetical scenario of a continued fertility decline (table B.2), we estimated the opportunity cost of the fertility-decline reversal. A continued decline in fertility would have made GDP per capita grow approximately 4.4 percentage points faster, resulting in 2019 GDP some LE 150 billion higher.

Using the regression results (appendix D), it is estimated that a 1 percentage point increase in the dependency ratio decreases GDP per capita growth by 0.37 percentage point. Using the hypothetical continued decline scenario results (table B.2), the dependency ratio would have been 51 percent instead of 63 percent in 2018, which would have lifted GDP per capita annual growth to approximately 7.9 percent from 3.5 percent. Using this higher hypothetical growth rate and multiplying it by 2018's GDP yields the hypothetical 2019 GDP per capita,[2] which is approximately LE 40,000 instead of LE 38,000 (in constant prices), a difference of about 5 percent.[3] This difference multiplied by the hypothetical population in 2019 yields an aggregate GDP of LE 4.1 trillion instead of LE 3.9 trillion (at constant prices).[4] Figure 5.8 summarizes the results.

FIGURE 5.8

Effect of a continued fertility decline on 2019 GDP

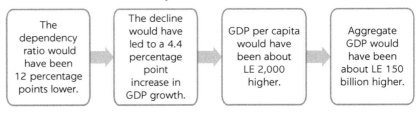

Source: Original figure for this publication following the methodology of Cruz and Ahmed 2018.
Note: GDP = gross domestic product; LE = Egyptian pound.

FIGURE 5.9

Forgone savings in 2019 due to the reversal in fertility decline

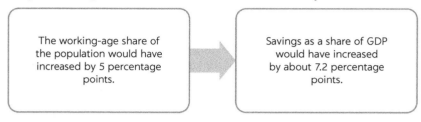

> The working-age share of the population would have increased by 5 percentage points.

> Savings as a share of GDP would have increased by about 7.2 percentage points.

Source: Original figure for this publication following the methodology of Cruz and Ahmed 2018.

Effect of population age structure on gross domestic savings

Corroborating the theory that an increase in the working-age share of the population lifts savings, a 1 percentage point increase in the working-age population share in Egypt increases gross domestic savings as a share of GDP by approximately 1.44 percentage points (table D.2, column S3).

Effect of a hypothetical continued fertility decline on gross domestic savings

Using the results discussed above and as presented in table D.2, along with the population projections estimated under the hypothetical scenario of a continued fertility decline, we estimated the opportunity cost of this reversal (along lines similar to the above).

Using the difference between the actual and hypothetical working-age share of population under a continued decline of fertility (table B.2), the working-age share of the population would have been 66 percent instead of 61 percent in 2018, resulting in gross domestic savings as a share of GDP of approximately 21.05 percent in 2019 instead of 13.85 percent (figure 5.9). This potential increase in savings would have had a significant effect on investment and economic growth.

PROJECTING EGYPT'S POPULATION THROUGH 2030: A PROSPECTIVE ANALYSIS

For the prospective analysis, further population projection modeling was conducted, focusing on 2021–30 (appendix F). It estimates the potential savings and socioeconomic gains under two hypothetical scenarios of fertility decline: a moderate decline to a TFR of 2.5, and an accelerated decline to a TFR of 2.1—replacement level—in 2030. The modeled populations were produced based on the assumptions of reduced fertility rates from different levels of future policy interventions and were compared with the "medium-fertility variant" projection from the UN Population Division—hereinafter called the "default" scenario—in which by 2030, Egypt's TFR will have fallen to 2.9 births per woman. The TFRs for 2030 in the moderate and accelerated decline scenarios represent 14 percent and 28 percent reductions, respectively, from the default scenario. For both hypothetical scenarios, TFRs for 2021 to 2029 were estimated through the interpolation feature in the Spectrum DemProj software (appendix B) using the historical TFR of 2020 and targeted TFRs for 2030.

On the basis of these modeled populations, Egypt's projected population in 2030 will be 119.1 million in the moderate decline scenario and 117.3 million in the accelerated decline scenario—a 1.4 percent and 2.9 percent reduction from the UN's default forecast of 120.8 million (table F.1). Figure 5.10 summarizes the model's TFR assumptions for 2020–30 for the three scenarios. Other population parameters for the two hypothetical scenarios were the same as they were for the default scenario.

Dependency ratios were calculated for each scenario. The only factors driving the differences in dependency ratios among the three scenarios were the assumptions about TFRs for the period between 2021 and 2030. The UN projects Egypt's dependency ratio in 2030 to be 0.6. If Egypt's TFRs decline according to either the moderate or accelerated decline scenario over the next 10 years or so, the dependency ratio is forecast to decline to 0.57 or 0.55, representing a 3.8 percent or 7.8 percent reduction from the default scenario (figure 5.11).

For estimating the potential savings in public expenditure on health, housing, and education through 2030, we used the same approach as for calculating the retrospective savings. The projections ran from 2019/20 through 2029/30 and depended on the rate of growth in real actual per capita expenditure over 2008/09–2018/19, which fluctuated across the years. For this reason, we used the average expenditure growth for each sector, which was 2.25 percent for health, 8.39 percent for housing, and 4.91 percent for education (table G.1). These rates were used to estimate growth in each sector for the next decade.

Building on the retrospective analysis of jobs needed, results of a similar exercise on creating job opportunities are summarized in box 5.2.

Health

Using the projected population 2020–30 (table F.1), we calculated projected real public expenditure in these scenarios. Table G.2 shows an average growth rate for real public expenditure of 3.96 percent under the default scenario and 3.65 percent

FIGURE 5.10

TFR assumptions for the default, moderate, and accelerated decline scenarios, 2020–30

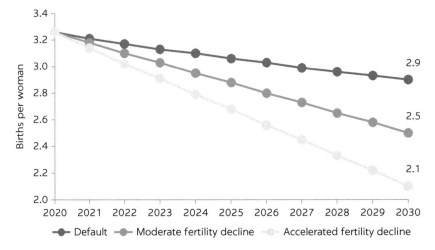

Source: Original calculations based on UN World Population Prospects database (https://population.un.org/wpp/) and Spectrum DemProj model.
Note: TFR = total fertility rate.

FIGURE 5.11

Dependency ratios for the default, moderate, and accelerated decline scenarios, 2020–30

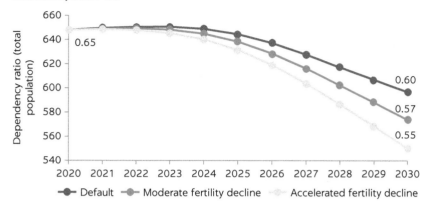

Source: Original calculations based on UN World Population Prospects database (https://population.un.org/wpp/) and Spectrum DemProj model.

Box 5.2

A prospective analysis for employment

Employment policies have never focused on mitigating labor market failures and distortions to promote the emergence of fast-growing, high-productivity jobs. Policy makers therefore need to look beyond supply-side labor-market policies to accelerate employment growth. Similar to the retrospective analysis in appendix E, the prospective analysis for 2019/20–2029/30 (details not shown) reveals that heavy public investment will be needed to create jobs.

Investment under various fertility decline scenarios was not estimated because of the lack of variation in the population size of entrants into the labor market under different scenarios through 2030. Changes in fertility will affect the number of those under 10 by 2030, while investment for job creation is needed for those above 15.

The public cost of generating one new job opportunity grows very fast, at 21.16 percent, taking the public cost to generate one new job in 2030 to LE 25,713—a total of LE 21,194 billion given the population size. Although over 10 years fertility declines would not alter this large figure because the changes are in the younger population who do not work, this figure shows the rough size of public expenditure needed to create job opportunities.

---

under the accelerated scenario that resulted from the decline in population growth. This population-growth decline presents potential savings, as shown in figure 5.12 (details in table G.2). Cumulative potential savings increase with the decrease in the population growth rate, from LE 4,250.03 million in 2020–30 in the moderate scenario to LE 8,791.44 million in the accelerated scenario. All these projections assume that all other conditions are constant.

Housing

Table G.3 shows an average growth rate for real public expenditure on housing of 10.2 percent in the default scenario and 9.87 percent in the accelerated scenario due to fertility decline.

FIGURE 5.12

Potential total savings in real public expenditure on health relative to the default scenario, 2019–20 through 2029–30, LE millions, 2017 prices

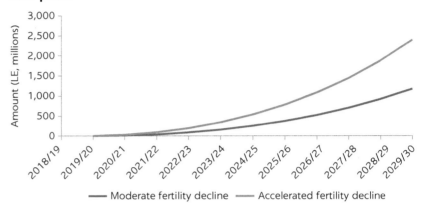

Sources: For 2018/19, actual expenditures, and 2019/20, planned budget, https://www .mof.gov.eg/ (in Arabic); for other years, original estimates based on https://www.mof .gov.eg.

FIGURE 5.13

Potential savings in real public expenditure on housing relative to the default scenario, 2019–20 through 2029–30, LE millions, 2017 prices

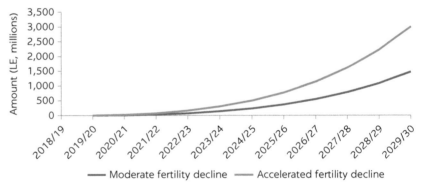

Sources: For 2018/19, actual expenditures, and 2019/20, planned budget, https://www .mof.gov.eg/ (in Arabic); for other years, original estimates based on https://www.mof .gov.eg.

The increase in public expenditure on housing due to the higher population growth rate and higher fertility rates is reflected in the potential savings in public expenditure, which increases over time (figure 5.13 and table G.3). The savings is projected to rise with the decrease in population growth rate from LE 4,758.40 million in 2020–30 in the moderate scenario to LE 9,826.17 million in the accelerated scenario, in constant 2017 prices—assuming that all other variables are constant.

Education

Using the population projections for 2020–30, we calculated the number of pre-university and university students in the age group 4–25 years, rather than

FIGURE 5.14

Potential savings in real public expenditure on education relative to the default scenario, 2019–20 through 2029–30, LE millions, 2017 prices

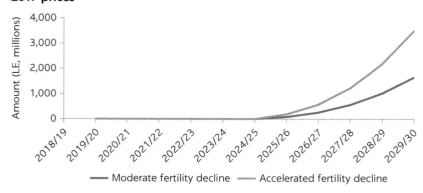

Sources: For 2018/19, actual expenditures, and 2019/20, planned budget, https://www .mof.gov.eg/ (in Arabic); for other years, original estimates based on https://www.mof .gov.eg.

the whole population. We then calculated real public expenditure on education in the scenarios (figure 5.14 and table G.4). This shows an average growth of 6.82 percent in the default and 6.62 percent in the accelerated scenario due to the decline in the population growth rate, reflecting the decline in fertility. The lower rate for the accelerated scenario compared with the moderate scenario is because the younger age group is affected first by the fertility decline.

The increase in cumulative public expenditure in the education sector due to the higher population growth rate and higher fertility rates is reflected in the projected potential savings in public expenditure (table G.4), which increases with the decrease in population growth rate from LE 1,444.16 million in 2020–30 under the moderate scenario to LE 7,686.42 million under the accelerated scenario in constant 2017 prices—on the assumption that all other variables are constant.

Summary of cumulative potential savings on health, housing, and education

As this analysis indicates, the highest potential for savings in public spending from a fertility decline will be in housing, followed by health and then education (figure 5.15). Savings in education spending will be the least, simply because of the population momentum that will lead to an increase in the number of young children even with the fertility decline. According to calculations based on UN World Population Prospects data and the Spectrum DemProj model, the number of children in the age group 5–9 years is estimated to be 12,223,000 in 2020 and will continue to increase until 2025, reaching 12,698,866 under all scenarios. It will only start declining in 2026. So even with efforts to reduce fertility, the government will continue to face upward pressure on public financing for education. The cumulative potential savings in the three sectors over the next decade will amount to LE 12.6 billion under the moderate scenario or LE 26.3 billion under the accelerated scenario (figure 5.15).

FIGURE 5.15

Cumulative potential savings by sector and scenario, 2020–30, LE millions, 2017 prices

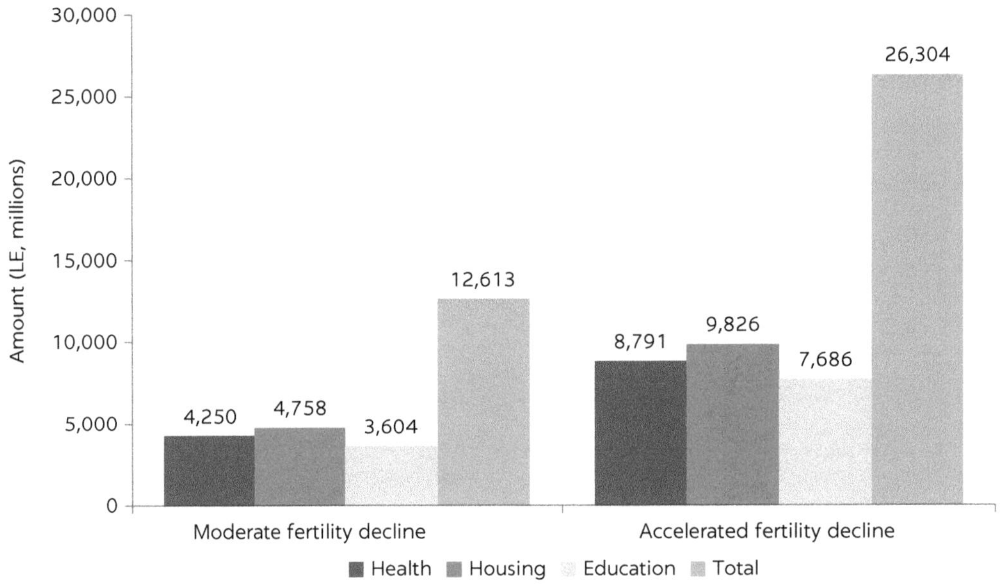

Sources: For 2018/19, actual expenditures, and 2019/20, planned budget, https://www.mof.gov.eg/ (in Arabic); for other years, original estimates based on https://www.mof.gov.eg.

Potential gains in national income under two TFR scenarios through 2030

After estimating the impact of the share of the working-age population and dependency ratios on per capita growth (appendix D), we now use this relationship to estimate the difference in income growth by 2030 under the two hypothetical scenarios with TFR decline—the moderate scenario with a TFR of 2.5 and the accelerated scenario with a TFR of 2.1—assuming constant growth in GDP per capita of 3.5 percent (that of 2019). The steps followed are in figure 5.16, and the results are in tables H.1 and H.2.

Using the same regression results shown in table D.1, a 1 percentage point increase in the dependency ratio is expected to decrease GDP per capita growth by 0.37 percentage points. This is attributable to changes in fertility and the age structure, and is multiplied by the difference in the dependency ratio between the default scenario and the hypothetical fertility decline scenario to attain the higher GDP per capita growth figure. The constant growth rate of GDP per capita is used to calculate annual GDP per capita under the default scenario, while the higher growth rate is used to calculate the hypothetical annual GDP per capita values. Finally, the GDP per capita values are multiplied by the population values under the default and hypothetical scenarios to attain aggregate GDP.

Figure 5.17 shows the different variables of interest under each scenario for the constant growth rate of 3.5 percent. (Detailed results are in tables H.1 and H.2.) GDP per capita consistently grows annually, growing at a higher rate under the hypothetical fertility decline scenarios. However, the difference in aggregate GDP under the hypothetical fertility decline is negative for at least the first three years. This can be explained by the lower population size in the hypothetical

FIGURE 5.16

Estimating the potential gain in income under a hypothetical accelerated fertility decline scenario and constant 3.5 percent per capita GDP growth

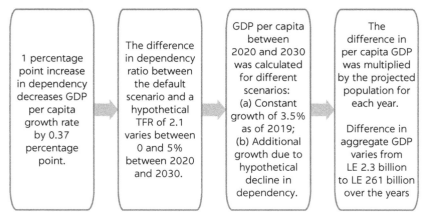

| 1 percentage point increase in dependency decreases GDP per capita growth rate by 0.37 percentage point. | The difference in dependency ratio between the default scenario and a hypothetical TFR of 2.1 varies between 0 and 5% between 2020 and 2030. | GDP per capita between 2020 and 2030 was calculated for different scenarios: (a) Constant growth of 3.5% as of 2019; (b) Additional growth due to hypothetical decline in dependency. | The difference in per capita GDP was multiplied by the projected population for each year. Difference in aggregate GDP varies from LE 2.3 billion to LE 261 billion over the years |

Source: Original estimates following the methodology of Cruz and Ahmed 2018.
Note: GDP = gross domestic product; LE = Egyptian pound; TFR = total fertility rate.

FIGURE 5.17

Differences in GDP under two TFR scenarios at constant 3.5 percent per capita GDP growth

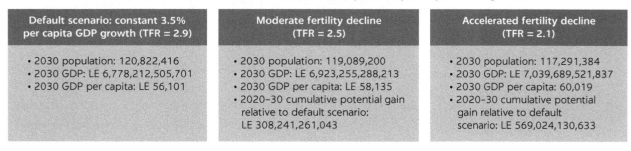

Default scenario: constant 3.5% per capita GDP growth (TFR = 2.9)	Moderate fertility decline (TFR = 2.5)	Accelerated fertility decline (TFR = 2.1)
• 2030 population: 120,822,416 • 2030 GDP: LE 6,778,212,505,701 • 2030 GDP per capita: LE 56,101	• 2030 population: 119,089,200 • 2030 GDP: LE 6,923,255,288,213 • 2030 GDP per capita: LE 58,135 • 2020–30 cumulative potential gain relative to default scenario: LE 308,241,261,043	• 2030 population: 117,291,384 • 2030 GDP: LE 7,039,689,521,837 • 2030 GDP per capita: 60,019 • 2020–30 cumulative potential gain relative to default scenario: LE 569,024,130,633

Sources: Original calculations based on World Development Indicators Database (https://datacatalog.worldbank.org/dataset/world-development-indicators) and UN World Population Prospects database (https://population.un.org/wpp/); Spectrum DemProj model.
Note: GDP = gross domestic product; LE = Egyptian pound; TFR = total fertility rate.

scenarios, which when multiplied by GDP per capita yields a lower GDP. This negative effect is then reversed when the difference in the dependency ratios between the scenarios increases. After 2025, GDP under the two hypothetical scenarios climbs higher than under the default.

For robustness, to ensure that results are not driven by the high per capita GDP growth rate, the analysis was replicated assuming a 2.5 percent growth rate in GDP per capita (tables H.3 and H.4, and figure 5.18). The potential gain was still significant, showing that the results are not driven by the choice of growth rate.[5]

These projections assume that all else is equal, in that nothing changes in the economy except for fertility, showing the radical impact of a fertility decline. Yet a drawback of these projections is precisely this assumption, because it does not control for other factors in the economy that will have additional effects on GDP per capita and aggregate GDP. Still, under this assumption and accounting for only the dependency ratio, the potential gain and differences between GDP per

FIGURE 5.18

Differences in GDP under two TFR scenarios at constant 2.5 percent per capita GDP growth

Default scenario: constant 2.5% per capita GDP growth (TFR = 2.9)	Moderate fertility decline (TFR = 2.5)	Accelerated fertility decline (TFR = 2.1)
• 2030 population: 120,822,416 • 2030 GDP: 6,091,634,701,346 • 2030 GDP per capita: LE 50,418	• 2030 population: 119,089,200 • 2030 GDP: LE 6,224,140,773,312 • 2030 GDP per capita: LE 52,265 • 2020–30 cumulative potential gain relative to default scenario: LE 284,956,453,319	• 2030 population: 117,291,384 • 2030 GDP: LE 6,330,769,170,734 • 2030 GDP per capita: LE 53,975 • 2020–30 cumulative potential gain relative to default scenario: LE 526,085,858,490

Sources: Original calculations based on World Development Indicators Database (https://datacatalog.worldbank.org/dataset/world-development-indicators) and UN World Population Prospects data (https://population.un.org/wpp/); Spectrum DemProj model.
Note: GDP = gross domestic product; LE = Egyptian pound; TFR = total fertility rate.

capita are stark, emphasizing the criticalness and magnitude of the opportunities at hand.

Potential savings at the household level

A fertility decline will see savings not only in public finance but also among households. For example, a family with fewer children will save on spending on health, education, and clothing for each additional child (box 5.3).

Long-term impact of population changes

Egypt's population will inevitably continue to grow for the foreseeable future. This growth is linked to population momentum—that is, the increase in population size driven by the youth bulge when they reach reproductive age and begin childbearing. According to UN population projections, Egypt's population will grow to 120.8 million in 2030 and to 159.9 million in 2050. However, if fertility decline were to match the above accelerated fertility decline scenario, Egypt's population would grow to 117.3 million in 2030 and 141.0 million in 2050 (figure 5.19). The population increase to 141.0 million is due to population momentum, while the rest of the increase to 159.9 million is due to a fertility rate exceeding replacement level.

More important than population size is the population age structure. An accelerated fertility decline would yield a huge youth bulge, resulting in a favorable ratio of working-age population and paving the way to achieving the demographic dividend (figure 5.20).

The dramatic difference in population size and age structure between the 2030 and 2050 scenarios has massive implications for economic growth. Using the same methodology as used to estimate the potential gain in GDP till 2030, the analysis estimated the potential gain in GDP till 2050.

Were Egypt to continue at its current momentum, as opposed to shifting toward accelerated fertility decline, the economy would risk forgoing approximately LE 103.5 trillion in GDP gains between 2020 and 2050 (figure 5.21). This is equivalent to 25 times Egypt's GDP for 2020. The potential gain in GDP is small in the early years, but it grows exponentially to reach LE 13,739 billion in

Box 5.3

Potential savings for households due to fertility decline

Using the results of the unpublished Household Income, Expenditure, and Consumption Survey (HIECS) for 2020 conducted by the Central Agency for Public Mobilization and Statistics (CAPMAS n.d.), we estimated private per capita expenditure on health and education as an example for the potential economic impact at household level.

Household expenditure on health per child averaged LE 2,376, ranging from LE 3,106 in urban Lower Egypt to LE 1,584 in frontier governorates (figure B5.3.1). Similarly, household expenditure on education per enrolled child averaged LE 2,944 in 2020, with a wide range between LE 6,525 in metropolitan areas to LE 1,085 in rural Upper Egypt (figure B5.3.2).

FIGURE B5.3.1

Household expenditure on health per child, 2020, LE

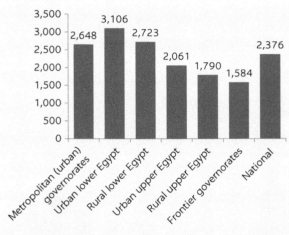

FIGURE B5.3.2

Household expenditure on education per enrolled person, 2020, LE

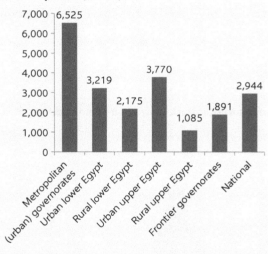

Source: CAPMAS Household Income, Expenditure, and Consumption Survey (HIECS) for 2020, n.d.
Note: LE = Egyptian pound.

The total expenditures on health and education were LE 5,320 per child, which constitutes about 10 percent of average total household expenditures (estimated at LE 52,646 in 2020). Considering other expenses that a child would entail, a family of two children would, therefore, potentially save this amount when compared with another family with three children.

Source: CAPMAS Household Income, Expenditure, and Consumption Survey (HIECS) for 2020, n.d.

2050—the difference between the default scenario of LE 17,851 billion and the accelerated fertility decline scenario of LE 31,590 billion.

The potential gain in income per capita is even more telling, as the larger income value is distributed among a smaller population, thus increasing the potential welfare gain per person. GDP per capita under the accelerated fertility decline scenario is roughly double GDP per capita under the default scenario in 2050—LE 111,600 versus LE 222,000 (figure 5.22).

FIGURE 5.19

Egypt population forecasts to 2050, millions

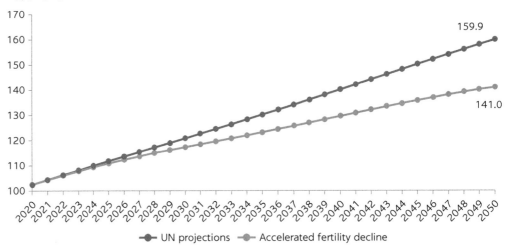

Source: Original calculations based on UN World Population Prospects data and Spectrum DemProj model.

FIGURE 5.20

Changes in population structure under different scenarios

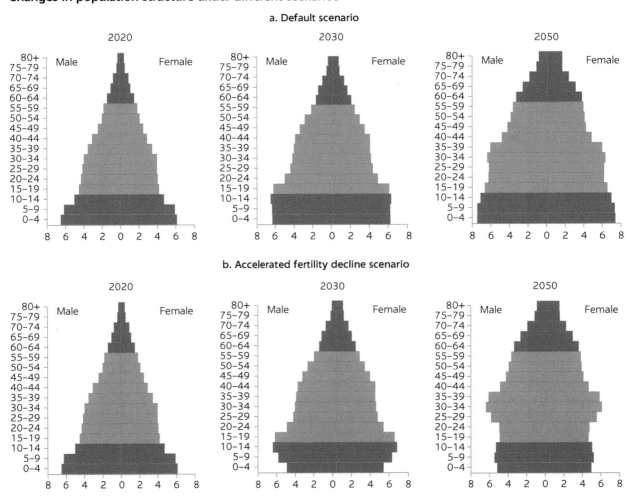

Source: Original calculations based on UN World Population Prospects database (https://population.un.org/wpp/) and Spectrum DemProj model.

FIGURE 5.21
Egypt's potentially forgone GDP through 2050, LE, billions

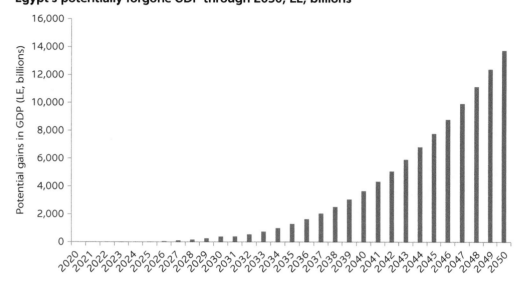

Source: Original calculations.
Note: GDP = gross domestic product; LE = Egyptian pound.

FIGURE 5.22
GDP per capita under the default and accelerated fertility decline scenarios through 2050, LE, 1,000

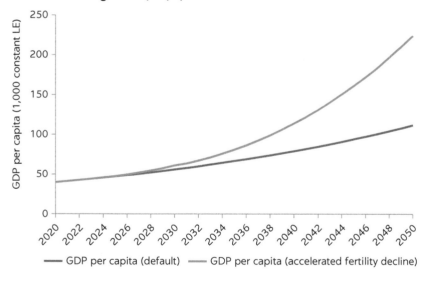

Source: Original calculations.
Note: GDP = gross domestic product; LE = Egyptian pound.

CONCLUSION

The economic impact associated with the demographic dividend is highly significant in magnitude and duration globally, but Egypt has missed large economic gains by narrowing its demographic dividend opportunity. The country was on a path of declining fertility and an increasing share of its working-age population, maximizing its demographic dividend. But it came off that path and hurt its economy—by an estimated LE 150 billion in 2019 GDP—because of a high dependency ratio. Additionally, very large savings in public expenditure were forgone in health, education, and housing, amounting to a cumulative loss of LE 93,456.8 million in real terms.

The path forward *can* be different, though, and estimating potential gains from policies is vital for estimating their cost-effectiveness. This chapter has shown that Egypt could see very large savings in public expenditure by 2030, reaching LE 26.3 billion in housing, education, and health under an accelerated fertility decline scenario. Additionally, the economy could see potential gains in income—for example, increasing its 2030 GDP per capita by up to LE 3,918—depending on the particular fertility scenario projection.

Similarly, under different specifications, assumptions, and fertility decline scenarios, Egypt's potential cumulative gain in GDP between 2020 and 2030 could be between LE 284.9 billion and LE 569.0 billion. Potential gains increase exponentially, highlighting the vitality and time-sensitivity of adopting effective policies. The economy could potentially forgo approximately LE 103.5 trillion in GDP between 2020 and 2050 by *not* adopting policies to pursue the accelerated fertility decline scenario.

The government therefore needs to tailor policies to ensure that the fertility decline of 1990–2010 is repeated and sustained, so as to benefit from increased GDP per capita, potentially improved human capital, and a reduction in poverty.[6]

The actual outcome will, of course, largely depend on the policies that the government adopts both to slow population growth and benefit from the youth bulge—including socioeconomic interventions that affect people's decisions on the number of children—and to create productive jobs, drawing on global best practices as necessary. In short, solving Egypt's demographic challenge will require a government whose various ministries can come together with a strong population program and plan of action, a human capital development program, and concerted development efforts. These themes are taken up in the following chapters.

NOTES

1. The UN population data were used for the retrospective and prospective population projections as it provides detailed yearly projections by age group until 2050, which are needed to populate the DemProj model. CAPMAS data are relatively limited and could not therefore be used.
2. 2018 GDP and dependency ratios are used to be able to compare with the latest data available, from 2019.
3. Based on the WDI database, which deflates prices based on Egypt's National Accounts base year of 2016/17.
4. This is not the cumulative effect, but only the effect in 2019, assuming that a shock occurred.
5. This calculation was also carried out for a growth rate of 2.0 percent, and results yielded similar estimates in potential gain, albeit lower (not shown in this report).
6. A poverty analysis could not be conducted for Egypt because of the limited data available on poverty; however, given the findings on GDP per capita and additional channels through which demographic changes affect poverty, it is likely that poverty would also decline with a decrease in dependency ratios.

REFERENCES

Cheung, S. L. K., P. Yip, I. Chi, A. Golini, and J. M. Robine. 2004. "Change in Demographic Window in Low Fertility Countries." Paper presented at the International Seminar on Demographic Window and Healthy Aging: Socioeconomic Challenges and Opportunities, organized by the IUSSP Committee on Longevity and Health and the Asian MetaCentre in collaboration with Peking University and the Center for Healthy Aging and Family Studies, Beijing, China, May 10–11.

Cruz, Marcio, and S. Amer Ahmed. 2018. "On the Impact of Demographic Change on Economic Growth and Poverty." *World Development* 105: 95–106. https://ideas.repec.org/a/eee /wdevel/v105y2018icp95-106.html.

Annex: Additional Reading

CAPMAS (Central Agency for Public Mobilization and Statistics). 2020. "Statistical Yearbook." December 2020. Cairo: CAPMAS. http://www.capmas.gov.eg.

IDSC (Information and Decision Support Center). Undated. Data and Statistics Database. Council of Ministers, Government of Egypt. https://www.idsc.gov.eg/IDSC/DMS/List .aspx, accessed December 20, 2020.

Lee, Ronald, and Andrew Mason. 2006. "What Is the Demographic Dividend?" *Finance and Development* 43 (3). https://www.imf.org/external/pubs/ft/fandd/2006/09/basics.htm.

Mason, Andrew, and Tomoko Kinugasa. 2008. "East Asian Economic Development: Two Demographic Dividends." *Journal of Asian Economics* 19 (5–6): 389–99. https://doi .org/10.1016/j.asieco.2008.09.006.

6 Global Evidence and Best-Practice Review of Programs That Spur Fertility Decline

SAMEH EL-SAHARTY AND ABDO S. YAZBECK

Central to policy recommendations in any field are full knowledge and appreciation of the documented and published evidence on what has worked. Failure to take such best-practice knowledge into account robs a country of accumulated global knowledge and increases the likelihood of it repeating its own mistakes and those of other countries. The previous chapters presented a detailed account of population issues in the Arab Republic of Egypt; this chapter aims to summarize global practice and evidence to inform the policy recommendations in chapter 7.

Of course, no two countries or their problems are identical, and even the same country has different geographic locations or preconditions for success or failure at different points in time. What has been shown to work in that and other countries, therefore, while critical for consideration, should always be approached with humility and balanced with a view of country and time heterogeneity.

This chapter focuses on what methods have been proven empirically to work around the world in accelerating the decline in fertility. That does not mean that other policies or actions are unimportant, just that they have not been evaluated—and some are simply hard to evaluate. It is still critical, however, to prioritize policies in areas with documented evidence of success, starting with by far the most important.

FAMILY PLANNING PROGRAMS

Family planning programs are responsible for much of the fertility decline

Family planning (FP) programs aimed at increasing the contraceptive prevalence rate (CPR) are associated with a decline in fertility rates. Global evidence suggests a strong inverse correlation between the CPR and total fertility rate (TFR). Data from 286 Demographic and Health Surveys (DHSs) in 86 countries between 1985 and 2019 suggest that a 1 percentage point increase in the CPR is associated with a decline of 0.071 point in the TFR (figure 6.1).[1] This approach is most effective when the increase is in modern contraceptive methods. For example, the Republic of Korea started a vertical FP program as part of its population strategy that was embedded in its five-year economic development plans in the

FIGURE 6.1

Relationship between CPR and TFR between 1985 and 2019

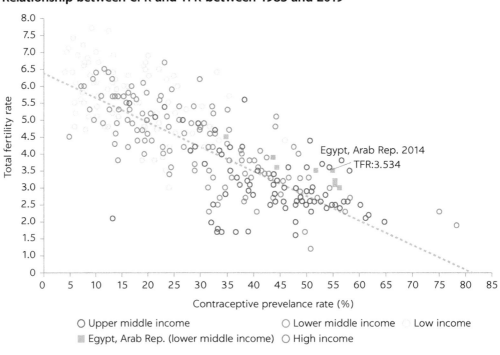

Source: Original calculations based on Demographic and Health Survey (DHS) data from 86 countries.
Note: CPR = contraceptive prevalence rate; TFR = total fertility rate.

1960s and 1970s. This program was responsible for one-third of the total reduction in fertility during its implementation period (Whang 1981). An analysis of data from all countries—aggregated and grouped according to their maximum rate of fertility decline over a 20-year period—showed that the group of countries with rapid fertility decline (exceeding 1.5 births per decade) achieved rapid economic development that picked up pace as the fertility decline accelerated. These countries adopted voluntary FP measures around the time that their birth rates began to fall, although not all maintained these measures until reaching replacement-level fertility (O'Sullivan 2017).

Unmet need is strongly correlated with the CPR

Globally, 214 million women of reproductive age in developing regions who want to avoid pregnancy are not using a modern contraceptive method and are considered to have an unmet need (Guttmacher Institute 2018). Unmet need is strongly inversely associated with the CPR (figure 6.2).

Unmet need does not decrease linearly when FP programs improve and desired fertility decreases. Initial improvements in FP programs can actually increase demand for contraception, which often causes demand to exceed supply, increasing unmet need until supply shifts in response (Bongaarts 1991). This curvilinear relationship between unmet need and CPR makes it necessary to use unmet-need and CPR measures together to capture the intersection of FP policies and practices. In the longer term, unmet need declines, and this progressive satisfaction of need remains the main driving force behind a rising CPR and falling fertility (Becker, Pickett, and Levine 2006).

FIGURE 6.2

Relationship between unmet need and the CPR between 1985 and 2019

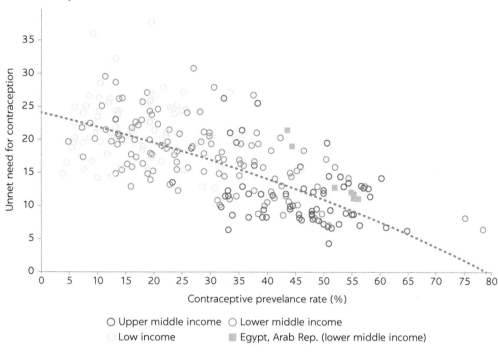

Source: Original calculations based on Demographic and Health Survey (DHS) data from 86 countries.
Note: CPR = contraceptive prevalence rate.

However, measuring unmet need contains numerous assumptions and imprecisions (Cleland, Harbison, and Shah 2014). Some researchers have suggested a related indicator, the satisfaction of demand for FP services, which consists of the percentage of total demand for FP at any time being satisfied by current contraceptive use.[2]

FP is one of the most cost-effective development interventions

Multiple studies have highlighted the cost-effectiveness of FP in terms of health outcomes and healthcare costs (for example, FP2020 n.d.). The Copenhagen Consensus Center compared the cost-effectiveness of development interventions, including FP, and concluded that every $1 invested in meeting the unmet need for contraceptives yields, in the long term, an average of $120 in accrued annual benefits: $30–50 in benefits from avoiding unintended pregnancies and averting infant and maternal mortality, and $60–100 in long-term benefits from putting countries on a path toward a demographic dividend and economic growth (FP2020 n.d.). Several evidence-based FP high-impact practices (HIPs) are either *proven* or *promising* as means to increase contraceptive use (box 6.1).

Postpartum FP services, particularly facility-based, have the highest impact among all FP service delivery approaches

Postpartum FP (PPFP) services can be provided in four different settings: facility-based with antenatal care or delivery; facility-based with immediate postpartum care; community-based counseling and services; and integration of services with child immunization programs. PPFP is a proven practice backed by enough

Box 6.1

High-impact practices (HIPs) in family planning

Enabling environment HIPs
- *Galvanize commitment* to support FP programs.
- Develop, implement, and monitor supportive government *policies*.
- Increase allocation and efficient use of *domestic, public financing* for voluntary FP at national and subnational levels.
- Develop an effective *supply-chain management system* for FP so that women and men can choose, obtain, and use the contraceptive methods they want throughout their reproductive life.
- Develop and support capacity to *lead and manage* FP programs.
- *Keep girls in school* to improve health and development.

Service delivery HIPs
Proven
- Integrate trained, equipped, and supported *community health workers (CHWs)* into the health system.
- Proactively offer voluntary contraceptive counseling and services at the same time and location where women receive facility-based *postabortion care*.
- Support distribution of a wide range of FP methods and promotion of healthy contraceptive behaviors through *social marketing*.

- Support *mobile outreach* service delivery to provide a wide range of contraceptives, including long-acting reversible contraceptives and permanent methods.
- *Immediate postpartum FP:* Offer contraceptive counseling and services as part of care provided during childbirth at health facilities.

Promising
- Train and support *drug shop and pharmacy staff* to provide a wider variety of FP methods and information.
- *Integrate FP and immunization services:* Offer FP information and services proactively to women in the extended postpartum period.
- *Social franchising:* Organize private providers into branded, quality-assured networks to increase access to provider-dependent contraceptive methods and related services.

Social and behavior change HIPs
Proven
- Use *mass media* channels to support healthy reproductive behaviors.

Promising
- *Community group engagement:* Engage and mobilize communities in group dialogue.
- Use *digital technologies* to support healthy sexual and reproductive behaviors.

Source: HIPs 2019.

evidence to recommend widespread implementation as part of a comprehensive FP strategy, provided that there is monitoring of coverage, quality, and cost, as well as implementation research, to strengthen the impact.

Facility-based childbirth services offer an ideal platform to reach women and their partners with FP information, counseling, and services before discharge from the health facility, if women's right to make a full and informed choice is respected. When Mexico added FP education to its national clinical guidelines for prenatal care, the likelihood of postpartum use of contraception significantly increased (Barber 2007). Evidence from several studies has shown that if women are provided with comprehensive counseling and are proactively offered contraception from a range of choices as part of childbirth care, 20–50 percent of them will leave the facility with a method (HIPs 2017a). A review of impact shows that facility-based immediate PPFP has the highest odds ratio of 2.03 out of 14 interventions, followed by community-based PPFP (1.96), then facility-based antenatal care (1.67). PPFP integrated with child immunization services is a promising strategy (HIPs 2017a) with an odds ratio of 1.15 (Weinberger et al. 2019).

Expanding the method mix is associated with increased use of contraceptives

Expanding the method mix helps ensure that methods are available for women with different needs. The need for contraception may vary throughout the reproductive life cycle, and individuals may have different preferences. For example, one study has shown that only 14 percent of women wish to cease childbearing and thus limit future pregnancies, while 25 percent of women want to space their pregnancies, reflecting a need for shorter-term or reversible methods (Van Lith, Yahner, and Bakamjian 2013). Another study has found that 62 percent of women with unmet need have never used contraception (Jain et al. 2013), and that a wider range of options may be appealing enough to some women to try contraception. Evidence has shown that the addition of one new method to the available method mix can increase contraceptive prevalence by as much as 8 percentage points (Ross and Stover 2013).

Integrating community health workers into the health system is a proven high-impact FP practice

When appropriately designed and implemented, community health worker (CHW) programs can increase use of contraception, particularly where unmet need is high, access is low, and geographic or social barriers to use of services exist.[3] CHWs are particularly important for reducing inequities in access to services by bringing information, services, and supplies to women and men in the communities where they live and work, rather than requiring them to visit health facilities, which may be distant or otherwise inaccessible (Shekar et al. 2016). The level of education and training, scope of work, and employment status of CHWs vary across countries and programs.

CHW programs are a proven practice that has sufficient evidence to recommend widespread implementation as part of a comprehensive FP strategy, provided that—as with PPFP services—there is monitoring of coverage, quality, and cost, as well as implementation research to strengthen impact (HIPs 2015). CHW programs increase contraceptive use in places where use of clinic-based services is not universal. A review of community-based programs in Sub-Saharan Africa found that six of seven experimental studies demonstrated a significant increase in contraceptive use or reduction in fertility rates (Phillips, Greene, and Jackson 1999).

The magnitude of effect varies by context and design of the CHW program. In Madagascar, individuals who had direct communication with CHWs were 10 times more likely to use modern contraceptives than individuals who did not (Stoebenau and Valente 2003). In Afghanistan, a CHW program increased contraceptive use by 24–27 percentage points in areas where initial contraceptive prevalence was very low, at 9–24 percent (Huber, Saeedi, and Samadi 2010).

Further, CHW programs may reduce unmet need in countries with large rural populations. Countries such as Bangladesh and Indonesia have strong CHW programs, in which CHWs deliver a significant share of modern methods to their communities. In Bangladesh, 34.9 percent of modern contraceptive users indicate CHWs as their most recent source of contraceptive supply, and in Indonesia 19.4 percent do so. In both these countries, there is also comparatively low unmet need for FP in rural areas (14 and 11 percent, respectively) (Prata et al. 2005).

In Ghana, in communities where CHWs operated alongside community volunteers, the total fertility rate was reduced by one birth per woman after eight years, compared with communities with the typical health care system (Phillips, Bawah, and Binka 2006).

The Matlab region of Bangladesh has seen perhaps the most concentrated, long-term FP program in the world. Between 1976 and 1985, Bangladesh recorded an estimated 25 percent reduction in fertility rates among women who were visited every two weeks by a trained CHW. When the program was scaled up, contraceptive use increased hugely; there was also greater demand for spacing methods for women with higher educational attainment and increased earnings, and women had on average 1.5 fewer births over a 20-year period than counterparts in the control area. The program also achieved a statistically significant reduction in maternal mortality ratios among the intervention group during the same period (Gribble and Voss 2009; Koenig et al. 1987).

Programs that link CHWs with clinic-based service delivery can be cost-effective. Cost and cost-effectiveness of CHW programs vary largely by program setting, worker compensation, maturity of the program, strategies used for training and supervision, and the number of clients served (FRONTIERS, FHI, and Advance Africa 2002). A review of FP programs in 10 developing countries found that programs that combined CHWs with clinic-based service delivery were more cost-effective than either clinic-based programs or CHW programs alone (Prata et al. 2005). A review of impact found that provision of pills and condoms in a community by CHWs had an odds ratio of 1.56 for the uptake of contraception, which increased to 1.70 when the provision of injectables was added to the other methods (Weinberger et al. 2019).

Supporting mobile outreach services to provide a wide range of contraceptives boosts contraceptive use

Mobile outreach services can increase contraceptive use, particularly in areas of low contraceptive prevalence, high unmet need for FP, and limited access to contraceptives, and where geographic, economic, or social barriers limit service uptake. When mobile outreach services are well designed, they help programs broaden the mix of contraceptive methods available to clients, including increasing access to long-acting reversible contraceptives and permanent methods; yet these two types are typically unavailable in most rural or hard-to-reach areas because of a lack of skilled providers, commodities, and equipment.

Delivery of mobile outreach services can address these access barriers by bringing information, services, contraceptives, and other supplies to where women and men live and work, generally free or at a subsidized rate. Mobile outreach programs may also leave a lasting legacy that strengthens existing health systems when the model includes developing and supporting local health workers' knowledge and skills to provide a wider range of methods (HIPs 2014). A review of evidence suggested that outreach and community-based distribution are effective and acceptable ways of increasing access to contraceptives, particularly injectables and long-acting and permanent methods (Mulligan et al. 2010).

In Tunisia, a study concluded that mobile units contributed one-third of the total output of the national FP program and a greater share of the national program's activities in rural areas (Coeytaux et al. 1989). In 2011 in Nepal, 13 percent of all users of modern methods obtained their contraception method from government mobile clinics (MOHP, New ERA, and ICF International 2012). In Uganda, mobile services within existing clinic-based services led to increased use of modern contraception, from 7 percent in 2007 to 23 percent in 2010, including increased use of long-acting reversible contraceptives and permanent methods, from 1 percent to 10 percent (Casey et al. 2013). In Egypt, a study of the cost-effectiveness of mobile clinics concluded that, though they cost more per facility than static clinics, they also generated more contraceptive use, particularly intrauterine devices, which required fewer FP visits (Al-Attar, Bishai, and El-Gibaly 2017).

Cost-reduction mechanisms have also seen some success, particularly with vulnerable groups like adolescents

Demand-side interventions that decrease the cost of FP services have been both theorized, and found in operational research, to increase the use of FP services. Different forms of cost-reduction interventions depend on how systems are set up (for example, if there are official user fees) and which costs are most important to clients (real costs such as transport costs and lost wages due to clients missing work, versus official medical costs faced by clients). Cost-reduction mechanisms include incorporating FP services in existing health insurance programs and providing FP vouchers.

Health insurance can increase the use of FP services by reducing costs of services for users. For example, an analysis of FP programs in universal health coverage plans in Latin America found that the contraceptive prevalence rate was 16.5 percentage points higher among insured women than uninsured women (Fagan et al. 2017). In the United States, 54 percent of insured women were using prescription contraception, compared with only 45 percent of those who did not have health insurance (Culwell and Feinglass 2007). In the United Kingdom, a wide range of contraceptive methods is provided free under the National Health Service.

FP vouchers have been associated with an increase in contraceptive use. In Pakistan, vouchers were associated with a net increase of 26 percent in contraceptive use (Ali et al. 2019). A Nicaraguan program that distributed vouchers to adolescents for free FP services led to a significant increase in the use of reproductive health services, greater knowledge of contraceptive methods, and some increase in use of FP methods (Meuwissen, Gorter, and Knottnerus 2006). An impact review found that the distribution of vouchers for free or subsidized FP services was associated with an increase in contraceptive use, with an odds ratio of 1.33. Vouchers for pills and condoms distributed in a community with easy access to CHWs increased the contraceptive uptake by an odds ratio of 1.56, which increased to 1.70 when the provision of injectables was added to the other methods (Weinberger et al. 2019).

Mass media FP interventions contribute to increased contraceptive use

Several country studies have pointed toward the positive influence of mass media messaging on FP uptake. During the 1990s, for instance, Tanzania aired a radio soap opera about FP and HIV/AIDS, with storylines developed after formative research with religious and youth groups. The result was increased self-efficacy around FP, positive attitudes about and approval of FP, and increased use of contraception among married women (Rogers et al. 1999).

An observational study in Kyrgyzstan and Tajikistan concluded that viewing FP messages on television improved the probability of using modern contraception by 8–11 percent, but listening to FP messages on radio did not have a significant effect (Habibov and Zainiddinov 2017). A similar study in the Philippines concluded that a national mass media campaign was associated with a 6.4 percent increase in modern contraceptive use (Kincaid and Do 2006).

A synthesis of several studies reported differences in contraceptive use between those exposed, or not, to mass media, ranging from 5 to 27 percentage points. Those exposed to mass media were more likely to use contraception; and studies on odds ratios found that those exposed to mass media were 25 percent to 2 times more likely to use modern contraception than those not exposed (HIPs 2017b).

All these findings are consistent with a systematic review that concluded that exposure to mass media programs can increase modern contraceptive use in a variety of settings (Naugle and Hornik 2014), and with an impact review that concluded that social and behavior change programs through mass media campaigns had an odds ratio of 1.29, which increased to 1.51 when coupled with interpersonal communication channels (Weinberger et al. 2019).

The largest fertility changes due to FP programs occur in settings with both demand- and supply-side interventions

A consistent finding in the literature has been that multipronged programs that tackle both demand- and supply-side drivers of use of FP services have a higher success rate than those moving along one dimension at a time (box 6.2).

Box 6.2

Different pathways, different results

Bangladesh and Pakistan had similar fertility rates in the 1960s and early 1970s. In the early 1980s, Bangladesh launched a national family planning program with door-to-door provision of contraceptives by health workers. This was accompanied by a widespread communications campaign, including one hour each day on Radio Bangladesh dedicated to family planning and to population health topics. By 2012, Bangladeshi women were bearing on average 1.8 fewer children than their Pakistani counterparts.

Kenya and Uganda had the same fertility rate in the late 1970s. Kenya then launched a national program of community-based distribution of low-cost contraceptives, combined with a communications campaign on limiting family size and on using family planning. Kenyan families are nowadays smaller by about two children than Ugandan families. This program was, however, scaled back in the mid-1990s, which explains in part the stall in declining fertility rates in Kenya since then.

The Islamic Republic of Iran and Jordan had similar fertility rates in the 1980s. The former then introduced a national program to provide free contraception through village health workers, coupled with a media campaign on the importance of small family size, and by 2010 its fertility rate was 1.8 births per woman lower than Jordan's.

Source: Bongaarts et al. 2012.

GIRLS' EDUCATION

Policy changes for encouraging school enrollment for girls appear to have strong effects on reducing fertility

Promoting girls' education through the secondary level is effective in supporting fertility reduction by delaying the age of marriage and enabling young women to make informed decisions about FP, including increased use of contraceptive methods.

For example, in Brazil, improvements in schooling of girls accounted for about 70 percent of the fertility decline observed in the country during the 1960s and 1970s (Lam and Duryea 1999). In Turkey, a study on the extension of compulsory schooling from five to eight years in 1997 found that, at age 17, the proportion of married women fell from 15.2 to 10.0 percent and that the share of adolescent girls who had given birth by age 17 declined from 6.2 to 3.5 percent as a result of this new policy. Those findings imply that the impact of increased schooling on marriage and early fertility persists beyond the completion of compulsory schooling for an "important duration" (Kirdar, Tayfur, and Koç 2009). In Kenya, increased mandatory primary schooling from seven to eight years led to an increase in overall education attainment, a delay in marriages and births past adolescence, an increase in modern contraceptive use, and early evidence of decreased fertility (Chicoine 2012).

In Bangladesh, a stipend policy was introduced to increase girls' schooling. A study to assess this policy showed that girls with higher levels of schooling were estimated to have 12 percent lower fertility than the baseline (Hahn et al. 2018). In Nigeria, increasing female education by one year through eliminating primary school fees—alongside investments to increase teacher and classroom volume—reduced early fertility by 0.26 births (Osili and Long 2007) and increased use of contraceptive methods. However, an evaluation of Bolsa Família—a welfare program in Brazil that provides low-income households with income conditional on school attendance, as well as on childhood immunization, prenatal visits for pregnant women, and other conditions—found strong education attendance effects but no corresponding decline in adolescent fertility (Olson, Gardner Clark, and Reynolds 2019).

AGE AT MARRIAGE

Legal and policy changes intended to delay age at first marriage had limited effect on subsequent fertility reduction

A comparative analysis of approaches to increase the age at marriage found weak evidence to support the impact of legal and policy changes on the age at marriage (Malhotra et al. 2011). This outcome may be due to study design, including long, required follow-up periods, and implementation challenges for legal measures.

One evaluation of legal reform of the age at marriage—in Indonesia in 1975—found that the law did not significantly decrease child marriage (Cammack, Young, and Heaton 1996). In India, an assessment of a similar law indicated that enforcement and accountability mechanisms were ineffective, and that awareness among all government levels and within communities remained low for several years after the law's passage (Das Gupta et al. 2008).

Box 6.3

Evidence from Egypt on successful FP programming

Family planning (FP) was introduced as part of the National Population Policy for Egypt in 1973 and was later integrated with reproductive and maternal health care to align with the International Conference on Population and Development of 1994, held in Cairo. Between 1980 and 2008, the total fertility rate in Egypt declined from 5.6 to 3.0 births per woman, which coincided with an expansion of contraceptive choices and an increase in the contraceptive prevalence rate (CPR) from 23 percent to 60 percent (USAID 2011).

- The national "Gold Star" program, implemented from 1995 to 2000, was successful in improving the quality and usage of family planning services.
- In addition to the direct effect on fertility, family planning is credited with contributing to 3.8 million fewer infant deaths and over 7 million fewer child deaths, and for saving 18,000 maternal lives, between 1980 and 2008.
- According to a World Health Organization policy brief (WHO 2009), the incentive payment program, implemented under the 1997 health sector reform program, had a positive effect on the performance of FP providers, including the provision of more information about contraceptive methods available. Moreover, women who visited FP clinics and who received incentive payments were more likely to report having participated in the choice of the contraceptive method than those in nonintervention sites. The authors of the policy brief concluded that "providers respond to payment incentives, and, on the whole, they respond in the way policy makers would like."
- Exposure to the mass media campaign "Your Health, Your Wealth," disseminated via television and radio, increased the likelihood of spousal discussions about contraception by 14.4 percentage points and had a large, statistically significant effect on modern contraceptive use of 27.4 percentage points (Hutchinson and Meekers 2012).
- Mass media also played a key part in creating support for the FP program, in which the religious leadership issued specific edicts on the role and limits of family planning, thus creating space for use of family planning by couples interested in managing the timing and number of births (Cortez et al. 2014).

Some successful initiatives, however, have combined individual- and community-based programs. For example, an assessment of the "Safe Age of Marriage" program in Yemen that focused on delaying marriage among children and adolescents through community engagement concluded that the program successfully decreased young marriage in the targeted community (Freij 2010). In addition, Egypt was once one of the best performers in increasing contraceptive use and reducing fertility (box 6.3).

CONCLUSION

Showcasing global—and domestic—experiences on best practices in family planning programming, this chapter suggests lessons that may be applicable to Egypt. While no "one size" works to reduce fertility rates—over time, by geography, countries differ in their needs and responses—there are clearly different pathways to achieving population goals. This review has outlined some of the main policy areas documented as effective within their individual time and place, that may provide some useful insights for refocusing the Egypt National Population

Strategy 2015–2030. In this light, the next chapter focuses on policy and strategic priorities that may support the country in accelerating its progress on population goals.

NOTES

1. The TFR also tends to decrease with an increase in a country's income.
2. Satisfaction of demand for FP = CPR / (CPR + unmet need).
3. CHWs are referred to by a wide range of titles, such as a village health worker, community-based distributor, community health aide, community health promoter, health extension worker, and lay health adviser.

REFERENCES

Al-Attar, Ghada S. T., David Bishai, and Omaima El-Gibaly. 2017. "Cost-Effectiveness Analysis of Family Planning Services Offered by Mobile Clinics versus Static Clinics in Assiut, Egypt." *African Journal of Reproductive Health* 21 (1): 30–38.

Ali, Moazzam, Syed Khurram Azmat, Hasan Bin Hamza, Md. Mizanur Rahman, and Waqas Hameed. 2019. "Are Family Planning Vouchers Effective in Increasing Use, Improving Equity and Reaching the Underserved? An Evaluation of a Voucher Program in Pakistan." *BMC Health Services Research* 19 (1): 200.

Becker, Loren, Jessica Pickett, and Ruth Levine. 2006. "Measuring Commitment to Health: Global Health Indicators Working Group Report." Washington, DC: Center for Global Development. https://www.cgdev.org/sites/default/files/10016_file_FINAL_9_5_06.pdf.

Bongaarts, John. 1991. "The KAP-Gap and the Unmet Need for Contraception." *Population and Development Review* 17 (2): 293–313.

Bongaarts, John, John Cleland, John W. Townsend, Jane T. Bertrand, and Monica Das Gupta. 2012. *Family Planning Programs for the 21st Century: Rationale and Design.* New York: Population Council.

Cammack, Mark, Lawrence A. Young, and Tim Heaton. 1996. "Legislating Social Change in an Islamic Society—Indonesia's Marriage Law." *American Journal of Comparative Law* 45–73.

Casey, Sarah, Shannon McNab, Clare Tanton, Jimmy Odong, Adrienne Testa, and Louise Lee-Jones. 2013. "Availability of Long-Acting and Permanent Family-Planning Methods Leads to Increase in Use in Conflict-Affected Northern Uganda: Evidence from Cross-Sectional Baseline and Endline Cluster Surveys." *Global Public Health* 8 (3): 284–97.

Chicoine, L. 2012. "Education and Fertility: Evidence from a Policy Change in Kenya." IZA Discussion Paper 6778, Institute of Labor Economics, Bonn, Germany.

Cleland, John, Sarah Harbison, and Iqbal H. Shah. 2014. "Unmet Need for Contraception: Issues and Challenges." *Studies in Family Planning* 45 (2): 105–22. https://doi.org/10.1111/j.1728-4465.2014.00380.x.

Coeytaux, Francine, Dayl Donaldson, Touhami Aloui, Taoufik Kilani, and Habib Fourati. 1989. "An Evaluation of the Cost-Effectiveness of Mobile Family Planning Services in Tunisia." *Studies in Family Planning* 20 (3): 158–69. doi:10.2307/1966570.

Cortez, Rafael, Seemeen Saadat, Sadia A. Chowdhury, and Intissar Sarker. 2014. "Maternal and Child Survival: Lessons from 5 Countries." HNP Discussion Paper, World Bank, Washington, DC.

Culwell, Kelly, and Joe Feinglass. 2007. "The Association of Health Insurance with Use of Prescription Contraceptives." *Perspectives on Sexual and Reproductive Health* 39 (4): 226–30. doi:10.1363/3922607.

Das Gupta, Sushmita, Sampuna Mukherjee, Sreela Singh, Rohini Pande, and Sharmishtha Basu. 2008. "Knot Ready: Lessons from India on Delaying Child Marriage for Girls." International Center for Research on Women, Washington, DC. https://www.icrw.org/wp-content/uploads/2016/10/Knot-Ready-Lessons-from-India-on-Delaying-Marriage-for-Girls.pdf.

Fagan, Thomas, Arin Dutta, James Rosen, Agathe Olivetti, and Kate Klein. 2017. "Family Planning in the Context of Latin America's Universal Health Coverage Agenda." *Global Health, Science and Practice* 5 (3): 382–98.

FP2020. n.d. "Family Planning's Return on Investment." Fact Sheet. Washington, DC: Family Planning 2020. https://www.familyplanning2020.org/sites/default/files/Data-Hub/ROI /FP2020_ROI_OnePager_FINAL.pdf.

Freij, Leah S. 2010. *"Safe Age of Marriage" in Yemen: Fostering Change in Social Norms.* Washington, DC: Pathfinder International.

FRONTIERS (Frontiers in Reproductive Health Program), FHI (Family Health International), and Advance Africa. 2002. *Best Practices in CBD Programs in Sub-Saharan Africa: Lessons Learned from Research and Evaluation.* Washington, DC: FRONTIERS.

Gribble, James, and Maj-Lis Voss. 2009. "Family Planning and Economic Well-Being: New Evidence from Bangladesh." Policy Brief, Population Reference Bureau, Washington, DC. https://www.prb.org/pdf09/fp-econ-bangladesh.pdf.

Guttmacher Institute. 2018. "Adding It Up: Investing in Contraception and Maternal and Newborn Health, 2017." Guttmacher Institute, New York. https://www.guttmacher.org /fact-sheet/adding-it-up-contraception-mnh-2017.

Habibov, Nazim, and Hakim Zainiddinov. 2017. "Effect of TV and Radio Family Planning Messages on the Probability of Modern Contraception Utilization in Post-Soviet Central Asia." *International Journal of Health Planning and Management* 32 (1): e17–e38. doi:10.1002 /hpm.2318.

Hahn, Youjin, Asadul Islam, Kanti Nuzhat, Russell Smyth, and Hee-Seung Yang. 2018. "Education, Marriage, and Fertility: Long-Term Evidence from a Female Stipend Program in Bangladesh." *Economic Development and Cultural Change* 66 (2): 381–415. doi:10.1086/694930.

HIPs (High Impact Practices in Family Planning). 2014. "Mobile Outreach Services: Expanding Access to a Full Range of Modern Contraceptives." Washington, DC: USAID. http://www .fphighimpactpractices.org/briefs/mobile-outreach-services.

HIPs (High Impact Practices in Family Planning). 2015. "Community Health Workers: Bringing Family Planning Services to Where People Live and Work." Washington, DC: USAID. http:// www.fphighimpactpractices.org/briefs/community-health-workers.

HIPs (High Impact Practices in Family Planning). 2017a. "Immediate Postpartum Family Planning: A Key Component of Childbirth Care." Washington, DC: USAID. https://www .fphighimpactpractices.org/briefs/immediate-postpartum-family-planning/.

HIPs (High Impact Practices in Family Planning). 2017b. "Mass Media: Reaching Audiences Far and Wide with Messages to Support Healthy Reproductive Behaviors." Washington, DC: USAID. https://www.fphighimpactpractices.org/briefs/mass-media.

HIPs (High Impact Practices in Family Planning). 2019. "Family Planning High Impact Practices List." Washington, DC: The High Impact Practices Partnership. https://www .fphighimpactpractices.org/wp-content/uploads/2020/11/HIP_List_Eng.pdf.

Huber, Douglas, Nika Saeedi, and Abdul Khalil Samadi. 2010. "Achieving Success with Family Planning in Rural Afghanistan." *Bulletin of the World Health Organization* 88 (3): 227–31. http://dx.doi.org/10.2471 percent2FBLT.08.059410.

Hutchinson, P. L., and D. Meekers. 2012. "Estimating Causal Effects from Family Planning Health Communication Campaigns Using Panel Data: The 'Your Health, Your Wealth' Campaign in Egypt." *PLoS One* 7 (9): e46138. doi:10.1371/journal.pone.0046138.

Jain, Anrudh, Francis Obare, Soumya Ramarao, and Ian Askew. 2013. "Reducing Unmet Need by Supporting Women with Met Need." *International Perspectives on Sexual and Reproductive Health* 39 (3): 133–41. doi:10.1363/3913313.

Kincaid, D. Lawrence, and Mai Phuong Do. 2006. "Multivariate Causal Attribution and Cost-Effectiveness of a National Mass Media Campaign in the Philippines." *Journal of Health Communication* 11 (Suppl 2) 69–90. doi:10.1080/10810730600974522.

Kirdar, Murat G., Meltem Dayıoğlu Tayfur, and İsmet Koç. 2009. "The Impact of Schooling on the Timing of Marriage and Fertility: Evidence from a Change in Compulsory Schooling Law." Research Paper. Economic Research Forum, Cairo. https://www.economicdynamics .org/meetpapers/2009/paper_809.pdf.

Lam, David, and Suzanne Duryea. 1999. "Effects of Schooling on Fertility, Labor Supply, and Investments in Children, with Evidence from Brazil." *Journal of Human Resources* 34 (1): 160. https://doi.org/10.2307/146306.

Malhotra, Anju, Ann Warner, Allison McGonagle, and Susan Lee-Rife. 2011. "Solutions to End Child Marriage: What the Evidence Shows." International Center for Research on Women, Washington, DC. https://www.icrw.org/wp-content/uploads/2016/10/Solutions-to-End -Child-Marriage.pdf.

Meuwissen, L. E., A. C. Gorter, and A. J. A. Knottnerus. 2006. "Impact of Accessible Sexual and Reproductive Health Care on Poor and Underserved Adolescents in Managua, Nicaragua: A Quasi-Experimental Intervention Study." *Journal of Adolescent Health: Official Publication of the Society for Adolescent Medicine* 38 (1). doi:10.1016/j.jadohealth.2005.01.009.

MOHP (Ministry of Health and Population), New ERA, and ICF International. 2012. Nepal Demographic and Health Survey 2011. Kathmandu, Nepal: MOHP. Copublished by ICF International. http://dhsprogram.com/pubs/pdf/FR257/FR257[13April2012].pdf.

Mulligan J., P. Nahmias, K. Chapman, A. Patterson, M. Burns, M. Harvey, et al. 2010. "Improving Reproductive, Maternal and Newborn Health: Reducing Unintended Pregnancies. Evidence Overview. A Working Paper (version 1.0)." Department for International Development (DFID), London. http://r4d.dfid.gov.uk/Output/185828/Default.aspx.

Naugle, Danielle A., and Robert C. Hornik. 2014. "Systematic Review of the Effectiveness of Mass Media Interventions for Child Survival in Low- and Middle-Income Countries." *Journal of Health Communication* 19 (Suppl 1): 190–215. https://www.ncbi.nlm.nih.gov /pmc/articles/PMC4205927/.

Olson, Zachary, Rachel Gardner Clark, and Sarah Anne Reynolds. 2019. "Can a Conditional Cash Transfer Reduce Teen Fertility? The Case of Brazil's Bolsa Família." *Journal of Health Economics* 63 (January): 128–44. https://doi.org/10.1016/j.jhealeco.2018.10.006.

Osili, Una O., and Bridget. T. Long. 2007. "Does Female Schooling Reduce Fertility? Evidence from Nigeria." NBER Working Paper 13070, National Bureau of Economic Research, Cambridge, MA.

O'Sullivan, Jane N. 2017. "The Contribution of Reduced Population Growth Rate to Demographic Dividend." Paper presented at the 27th International Population Conference, Cape Town, October 30–November 3. https://uaps2015.princeton.edu/papers/150981.

Phillips, James F., Ayaga A. Bawah, and Fred N. Binka. 2006. "Accelerating Reproductive and Child Health Programme Impact with Community-based Services: The Navrongo Experiment in Ghana." *Bulletin of the World Health Organization* 84 (12): 949–55. http:// www.who.int/bulletin/volumes/84/12/06-030064.pdf.

Phillips, James F., Wendy L. Greene, and Elizabeth F. Jackson. 1999. *Lessons from Community- Based Distribution of Family Planning in Africa*. New York: Population Council. http://www .popcouncil.org/pdfs/wp/121.pdf.

Prata, Ndola, Farnaz Vahidnia, Malcolm Potts, and Ingrid Dries-Daffner. 2005. "Revisiting Community-Based Distribution Programs: Are They Still Needed?" *Contraception* 72 (6): 402–07.

Rogers, Everett M., Peter W. Vaughan, Ramadhan M. A. Swalehe, Nagesh Rao, Peer Svenkerud, and Suruchi Sood. 1999. "Effects of an Entertainment-Education Radio Soap Opera on Family Planning Behavior in Tanzania." *Studies in Family Planning* 30 (3): 193–211.

Ross, John, and John Stover. 2013. "Use of Modern Contraception Increases When More Methods Become Available: Analysis of Evidence from 1982–2009." *Global Health Science and Practice* 1 (2): 203–12.

Shekar, Meera, Abdo Yazbeck, Rifat Hasan, and Anne Bakilana. 2016. "Population and Development in the Sahel: Policy Choices to Catalyze a Demographic Dividend." Health, Nutrition, and Population (HNP) Discussion Paper, World Bank, Washington, DC.

Stoebenau, Kirsten, and Thomas W. Valente. 2003. "Using Network Analysis to Understand Community-Based Programs: A Case Study from Highland Madagascar." *International Family Planning Perspectives* 29 (4): 167–73. http://www.guttmacher.org/pubs/journals /2916703.html.

USAID (US Agency for International Development). 2011. *Egypt Health and Population Legacy Review*, Vol. 1. USAID: Washington, DC.

Van Lith, Lynn M., Melanie Yahner, and Lynn Bakamjian. 2013. "Women's Growing Desire to Limit Births in Sub-Saharan Africa: Meeting the Challenge." *Global Health, Science and Practice* (1): 97–107. doi:10.9745/ GHSP-D-12-00036.

Weinberger, Michelle, Jessica Williamson, John Stover, and Emily Sonneveldt. 2019. "Using Evidence to Drive Impact: Developing the FP Goals Impact Matrix." Avenir Health. *Studies in Family Planning* 50 (4): 289–316.

Whang, In-Joung. 1981. "Korean National Family Planning Program: A Case History," No. 6. East-West Resource Systems Institute, Honolulu. http://hdl.handle.net/10125/48061.

WHO (World Health Organization). 2009. "Impact of Provider Incentive Payments on Reproductive Health Services in Egypt." *Policy Brief.* World Health Organization, Geneva. https://www.who.int/reproductivehealth/publications/health_systems/rhr_09_04/en/.

Annex: Additional Reading

Barber, Sara L. 2007. "Family Planning Advice and Postpartum Contraceptive Use among Low-Income Women in Mexico." *International Family Planning Perspectives* 33 (1): 6–12.

Constant, Louay, Ifeanyi Edochie, Peter Glick, Jeffrey Martini, and Chandra Garber. 2020. "Barriers to Employment That Women Face in Egypt." Santa Monica, CA: RAND Corporation. https://www.rand.org/content/dam/rand/pubs/research_reports/RR2800/RR2868/RAND_RR2868.pdf.

Koenig, Michael A., James F. Phillips, Ruth S. Simmons, and Mehtab A. Khan. 1987. "Trends in Family Size Preferences and Contraceptive Use in Matlab, Bangladesh." *Studies in Family Planning* 18 (3): 117–27.

Valente, Thomas W., Young Mi Kim, Cheryl Lettenmaier, William Glass, and Yankuba Dibba. 1994. "Radio Promotion of Family Planning in The Gambia." *International Family Planning Perspectives* 20 (3): 96–100.

World Bank. 2018. "Women Economic Empowerment Study." Washington, DC: World Bank. https://openknowledge.worldbank.org/handle/10986/31351.

7 Policy and Strategic Priorities in Making the Choice

SAMEH EL-SAHARTY, AMR ELSHALAKANI, NAHLA ZEITOUN,
BRIDGET CRUMPTON, AMIRA KAZEM, CORNELIA JESSE, AND
SOURAYA EL-ASSIOUTY

Achieving the first phase of the demographic dividend within a decade through fertility decline is possible for the Arab Republic of Egypt—*if* it coordinates policies and strategies across multiple sectors in a sustained manner, and does so as a deliberate choice, not through acceptance of destiny.

Countries where the total fertility rate (TFR) has fallen (to somewhere between four children per woman and the replacement level) have made real efforts to complete the fertility transition through health and family planning (FP) programs (Gertler and Molyneaux 1994; World Bank 2010; Goodkind et al. 2018). This decline is often accompanied by a rise in the proportion of the working-age population, which contributes to economic growth and human capital accumulation (World Bank and IMF 2016).

On the basis of our analysis of the demographic dynamics, the sectoral drivers, the economic impact, and the evidence presented in the earlier chapters, we propose the following six policy and strategic priorities that—if implemented in a concerted manner—should yield the greatest reduction in fertility and in turn achieve the first phase of the demographic dividend:

1. Increasing the contraceptive prevalence rate (CPR)
2. Reducing school dropouts
3. Increasing female labor force participation
4. Delaying age of marriage
5. Leveraging social protection programs
6. Improving governance of the population program

In addition, it is also imperative to adopt broad-based socioeconomic development policies to achieve the second phase of the demographic dividend.

Figure 7.1 illustrates the theory of change, showing the transmission channels of the proposed priorities and the achievement of the demographic dividend. The central priority is increasing contraceptive use, which can be achieved through strengthening family planning programs. Social programs can be leveraged to reduce school dropouts and provide job opportunities to women.

Reducing school dropouts, for girls, would increase the potential of female labor force participation, delay marriage, and contribute to increased contraceptive use and delayed or spaced childbearing. Improving governance of the

FIGURE 7.1

Theory of change for achieving the demographic dividend in Egypt

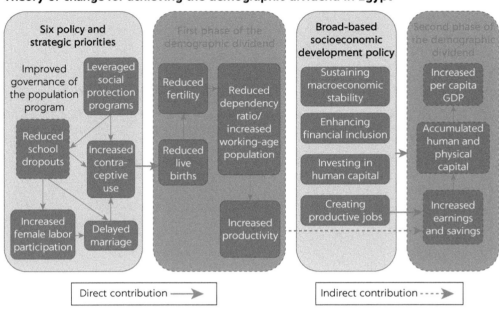

Source: Original illustration for this publication.
Note: GDP = gross domestic product.

population program will be critical to ensure the coordination of these priorities across sectors.

Increased contraceptive use will reduce the crude birth rate, contributing to reduced fertility, an increased share of the working-age population, and increased productivity. These achievements would fulfill the first phase of the demographic dividend.

This first phase is transitory, however, and cannot be sustained except through broad socioeconomic policies that entail creating productive jobs, investing in human capital, enhancing financial inclusion, and sustaining macroeconomic stability. These are the policies needed to achieve the second phase in terms of increased earnings and savings, accumulation of human and physical capital, and increased per capita GDP.

INCREASING THE CPR

In chapter 6, strong evidence was presented on the inverse correlation between the CPR and TFR. In figure 6.1, Egypt is above the trendline, meaning that it has a higher TFR than the average CPR achieved in other countries, reflecting the underperformance of its FP program. According to the latest Egypt Demographic and Health Survey (EDHS) of 2014, Egypt's CPR was only 58.5 percent (MOHP, El-Zanaty and Associates, and ICF International 2015). However, according to the Egypt Labor Market Panel Survey 1998–2018, the CPR was estimated to have reached 62.6 percent in 2018 (Krafft, Assaad, and Keo 2019). This positive trend should continue.

The centerpiece for reducing fertility and curbing population growth is the expansion of FP coverage to reach a CPR of 75 percent within the next decade, or a reduction of 0.88 point in the TFR, taking it to roughly 2.3—near replacement level. This would require two primary challenges to be addressed: meeting unmet need for contraception and reducing contraceptive discontinuation.

Meeting unmet need. Egypt's unmet need for contraception has been consistently higher than the average for other countries at the same CPR (see figure 6.2). Using the 2014 EDHS, if unmet need for currently married women is 12.6 and the CPR is 58.5, the share of satisfied demand for FP is 82.3 percent, leaving unsatisfied demand for FP at 17.7 percent. The unmet need and the high rate of unsatisfied demand mean that these high levels may not be related just to the FP program but also to social factors outside the program. The supply side of FP programs should therefore focus on identifying women at risk of unintended pregnancy who are interested in and willing to use contraception, and who represent a target population in need of contraceptive services (Moreau et al. 2019). Further, owing to the heterogeneity of the causes of unmet needs—with a sizable proportion attributed to husband or male guardian interference—programs that address husbands and young boys should be considered.

Reducing contraceptive discontinuation. Some women discontinue contraceptive use even though they want to avoid pregnancy (Ali, Cleland, and Shah 2012). Reasons include side effects, myths, contraceptive failure, or the service environment, including service quality and availability of a sufficient choice of methods (Castle and Askew 2015). As shown in the 2014 EDHS, 30 percent of contraceptive users discontinued within 12 months of initiating a method. Among these discontinuers, 35 percent of women discontinuing modern methods were still in need of contraception to prevent unintended pregnancy. Efforts to increase demand should therefore address the reasons that women are discontinuing while still in need. According to the 2014 EDHS, the most common reasons for contraceptive discontinuation were related to fear of side effects and health concerns. One option is to provide a wide choice of contraceptives that can meet the needs of some discontinuers, giving them the option of switching, including the introduction and promotion of self-administered long-term methods (box 7.1). One estimate suggests that

---

Box 7.1

Some self-administered long-term methods

Studies have shown that self-administered subcutaneous, long-acting hormonal injections can be provided by grassroots health cadres and by users themselves, thus reducing reliance on health care systems (Burke et al. 2014). Studies also suggest that women find these self-administered hormonal injections to be a feasible and acceptable choice of contraception, which is being introduced, scaled up, or piloted in more than 15 countries (FP2020 n.d.).

Other new product categories include vaginal rings that women can insert themselves, which can be offered through supply outlets ranging from drug stores to tertiary-level facilities (Merkatz et al. 2014). The levonorgestrel (LNG) intrauterine system and emerging technologies such as a biodegradable implant and longer-lasting injectables hold the promise of an even wider choice of methods.

broadening method availability can reduce contraceptive discontinuation by 8 percent (Jain et al. 2013).

Increasing the CPR and overcoming these two primary challenges would require the government to undertake the following seven strategies.

Expanding the capacity of the MOHP to provide FP services

A key constraint to expanding use of contraception is the lack of female service providers, a shortage that can be remedied by expanding the base of providers to include female nurses and by shifting some service tasks, such as providing injectables or subdermal implants. In many countries, allowing community health workers to provide such injectables and implants has expanded access to, and increased voluntary use of, both methods (HIPs 2015).

These moves should be preceded by training and counseling in client-oriented service provision for a range of methods in both clinical and community settings (Sathar et al. 2005). Comprehensive counseling for clients lets them learn more about contraceptive choices, management of side effects, and options of switching (Jain 2016).

Another constraint is the lack of services and providers in remote and rural areas, which can be overcome though mobile clinics and teams. The MOHP expanded FP services through mobile clinics but only reached 80 percent of the target. More concerted efforts and increased resources are needed to reach the underserved population, complemented with mobile teams from district hospitals to primary health care units (PHCUs) or village facilities deployed once or twice a week to provide FP services.[1]

Further, FP should be integrated into other health services so that all encounters with public providers may be capitalized on to educate women (and their husbands) about FP. This includes the use of social workers and counselors through "in-reach" within the outpatient clinics and services of the MOHP general and district hospitals to provide counseling and referral of women to FP services.

Integrating FP into postpartum care

Increasingly, women are giving birth in health facilities, creating more opportunities for women to initiate an FP method before they leave the facility. In fact, the first 12 months after giving birth are one of the most vulnerable times in a woman's life. It is when her need for FP is greatest, as her health and that of her children depend on it, but it is also when that need is least likely to be met. On the basis of 60 Demographic and Health Surveys (DHSs), it was estimated that more than 90 percent of postpartum women wanted to delay or avoid another pregnancy, yet some two-thirds were not using contraception (Ali, Cleland, and Shah 2012).

Integrating FP services with the existing postpartum care provided during childbirth and up to 12 months after delivery is the time when women are in increased contact with the health system, from antenatal checkups to early childhood immunizations—and each encounter is an opportunity for providers to ensure that women's contraceptive needs are being met. Further, improved quality of intrauterine devices (IUDs) and implants and their safer insertion make the process of getting an immediate postpartum IUD simpler and easier.

General and district hospitals of the MOHP can provide an expanded base for postpartum FP services through their ob/gyn departments, and make FP methods available on ob/gyn wards for women who choose to use FP immediately after giving birth. Further, and because more than 63 percent of all births in Egypt are provided in the private sector (Pugliese-Garcia et al. 2020), measures must be taken to ensure that postpartum FP services and consultation have been offered to mothers in private facilities. These services could be expanded by including the associated costs in the benefit package under the newly introduced universal health insurance system.

Expanding FP services in the public sector

Initiatives to establish FP clinics and services at university hospitals and other public sector organizations have been partly undertaken, but FP clinics and services need to be established at *all* hospitals and clinics of the Health Insurance Organization (HIO), the emerging General Authority for Healthcare (GAH), Curative Care Organization, Teaching Hospital Organization, and other public sector provider organizations. The roles of HIO and the GAH are critical not only because of their wide network of hospitals but also because of their clinics in big public sector companies that can serve a large segment of working women.

Engaging non-public-sector providers

Increasing the variety of providers allows users to choose convenient service delivery points. Engaging nongovernmental organizations (NGOs) was one of the factors that contributed to increasing access and coverage of FP services in Egypt in the late 1980s and early 1990s. Similarly, engaging the private sector, particularly pharmacies, can also increase access to oral contraceptive pills, including those for emergency contraception, and injectables, especially for underserved populations (HIPs 2013). The MOHP should outline the FP service standards, quality guidelines, and the needed supply mix of methods with NGOs. Further, NGOs must be mandated to report on progress on their services to the public. Finally, training for private sector pharmacists to provide better information on FP methods is needed to increase service availability to the public.

Improving the supply chain and quality of methods

From the 1980s, the United States Agency for International Development (USAID) was Egypt's major supplier of free or reduced-cost contraceptive commodities, in particular IUDs (Riggs-Perla et al. 2011). From the 2000s, however, USAID scaled down support for FP in Egypt, phasing out commodity distribution by end-2007 (Alterman 2012), as part of a broader waning of US government support for the FP program. The US government continued to fund contraceptive distribution, but its support for mass media and incentives for FP service providers fell off (Radovich et al. 2018). Between the 2008 and 2014 EDHSs, use of IUDs declined, while the proportion of women using the contraceptive pill or injectables increased. Although all are effective modern methods, there is evidence that women using the pill and other short-acting modern methods have shorter birth intervals, by choice or by contraceptive failure (table 7.1), than those using IUDs (Baschieri and Hinde 2007).

TABLE 7.1 **Contraceptive failure rates by method (as used in the Spectrum model)**

METHOD	FAILURE RATE (%)
Female sterilization	0.50
Male sterilization	0.15
Oral pill	6.90
IUD	1.60
Injections	2.90
Implants	0.05
Male condom	9.80
Lactational amenorrhea	24.00
Traditional methods	78.00

Source: Stover and Winfrey 2017.
Note: The failure rate is defined as the proportion of women using a method who will become pregnant in a year because of failure of the method.

The shift in method mix between the two most recent EDHSs may point to fundamental changes in FP access—particularly for IUD insertion—following USAID's phaseout of subsidized contraceptive commodity distribution and provider training. Today, ensuring supply-chain robustness and contraceptive-supply availability at points of care close to clients is essential. Robust supply chains that eliminate stockouts and engage multiple manufacturers to ensure high-quality, low-cost contraceptive products are critical for uptake and continuation (HIPs 2012).

Expanding the method mix in the public and private sector

Expanding the mix can ensure that methods are available for women with different needs. A key intervention is removing the MOHP monopoly on the distribution of some FP methods and allowing the methods' official statutory pricing for subsequent use through community pharmacies.

New contraceptive technologies have been developed to satisfy the diverse preferences of women and their partners and to overcome the challenges of providing some methods in low-resource settings. Introducing new contraceptives to the FP program, with a focus on long-term methods, is key to avoiding the high failure rates of short-term methods (see table 7.1). One immediate action is allowing the private sector to import and distribute subdermal implants (as the most effective contraceptives) and allowing private doctors to insert them—a practice currently confined to the MOHP.

Generating demand

Even with a well-informed provider base, an expanded method mix can reach its full potential only with continued demand from users. For example, just half of women who have current unmet need for contraception intend to use contraception in the future, suggesting that lack of demand substantially contributes to unmet need (Moreau et al. 2019).

Experience with FP programs suggests that demand generation through media campaigns and mobile services can increase contraceptive use and intention to use modern contraceptives by improving community and individual knowledge and attitudes, and by promoting partner communication. Satisfied contraceptive users who speak to others about their experience are also highly effective in generating demand and changing social norms related to FP (Belaid et al. 2016).

Such shifts in norms, ideas, and knowledge play a fundamental role in changing reproductive behavior and fertility levels. Historical patterns suggest that the beginning of a fertility transition often takes place simultaneously among similar cultural groups. In Egypt, when change occurred in one village, similar shifts were taking place in neighboring villages, whether fertility increased or decreased (Weeks 2004). Overall, strategies should also aim to enhance women's agency in a comprehensive manner. Changing attitudes and addressing stereotypes and social norms are key approaches, achievable by mobilizing communities on the ground through local structures and grassroots organizations.

Demand generation should not be a "one size fits all" approach, but instead should be tailored for different regions and subgroups depending on the underlying factors that reduce demand, which may be related to early marriage, culture, husband/mother-in-law, religion, social values, or restrictive gender norms. It is also important to have a gender-sensitive approach that distinguishes between men's and women's FP needs.

REDUCING SCHOOL DROPOUTS

Increasing girls' enrollment and their completion of upper-secondary education is an internationally proven strategy for addressing fertility challenges, requiring both sectoral interventions and a combination of social and cross-sectoral responses to halt Egypt's atypical rise in fertility rates among higher-educated, wealthier, urban women. The following four areas stand out.

Increasing girls' enrollment

Egypt has experienced one of the fastest global expansions of education. Enrollment is near universal at primary level, and the net enrollment rate was 97.6 percent at lower-secondary level and 76.6 percent at upper-secondary level—75.9 percent girls and 77.3 percent boys (MOETE 2020). Accelerating expansion of girls' enrollment at secondary level requires increased investment to expand the supply of schooling at secondary level. Further, additional measures will be needed to ensure that schools are accessible and safe, and to address parental concerns and risks to girls' safety on the way to and from school, and at school. Promotion of community schools is another option as an alternative to public schools, because these can be more tailored to the needs of girls and students in underserved areas, draw female teachers from the community, and build family confidence in the education safety of girls.

Reducing girls' dropouts

Once girls are enrolled in school, the priority is to keep them enrolled. Dropouts in Egypt are far higher at upper- than lower-secondary level, and are 4.7 percentage points higher for girls than boys—17.3 percent compared with 12.6 percent—at 15 percent overall (El-Laithy 2021). A critical international strategy to reduce dropouts and increase retention is to improve the quality of education and relevance to employability (Krafft, Branson, and Flak 2019). Egypt is moving in this direction as part of MOETE's "Education 2.0 reform," which prioritizes quality, and which is aimed at improving learning and equipping students with critical thinking skills and the ability to make informed life choices, including those relating to early marriage and fertility.

International evidence also demonstrates the value added of strategies to keep girls in school, especially at upper-secondary level (where risk of dropping out is highest). Among these strategies are girls' clubs to promote girls' empowerment, life skills, awareness of sexual reproductive health and gender issues in a safe, peer, or mentoring environment; boys' clubs to raise awareness of similar issues; menstrual management in schools and access to sanitary and hygiene products; and school-based monitoring systems to track girls' attendance in real time and act as an early warning system of who is at risk of dropping out, to flag patterns and barriers to attendance, and to develop local feedback loops and individualized responses to female students and their families, involving school and community leaders and parents (UKAID 2018).

Prioritizing education on sexual and reproductive health

International evidence shows that programs in education on sexual and reproductive health (SRH) play a vital and multifaceted role in providing accurate information on SRH, dispelling myths and misinformation, reinforcing values and positive attitudes, and strengthening decision-making and communication skills. But too often, these programs focus on the physical aspects of SRH over broader social and emotional issues. Too often, they target girls and women only, rather than involving boys and men.

The Egyptian government is introducing population issues and reproductive health into the school curriculum. These topics will need to build on pedagogical research on developing age-appropriate material to inform the development of the curriculum, backed up by teacher training. They can include norms around gender and sexuality, equality, and empowerment, which have been shown to positively affect health-related behaviors, such as the use of contraception, alongside health and nonhealth outcomes, such as critical-thinking skills.

Other key approaches include addressing gender bias and stereotyping in both the school and teacher-training curricula. To address the reality that many young people are not enrolled in formal education, an important policy recommendation is to extend the outreach of SRH and population education to out-of-school or other groups of young people. Partnering with young people and building on youth organizations to serve as trainers can be effective at promoting peer learning and youth leadership, when adopted with a range of mechanisms such as setting up youth clubs and using mass communication (like radio and television) or social media (such as blogs) to raise awareness (UNFPA 2012).

Creating an enabling environment to incentivize girls' retention in education

Further, the COVID-19 pandemic may have wider implications for continuity of learning for girls than boys as a result of MOETE's strategy of promoting distance learning and transitioning to blended learning. Initial analysis of the impacts of the pandemic suggests that many families are adopting negative coping mechanisms to manage its fallout, including spending less on education and health or requiring their children to work. Children from low-income households have less access to remote learning devices, and parents may be less likely to have time or skills to support their children's learning. An emerging issue is that girls may have less access to digital learning than boys because of social fears that they will access inappropriate material.

Policy recommendations include expanding social protection programs; reducing the digital divide so that all children can continue learning; designing remote learning programs that are accessible to all children and adapted for households that do not have access to broadcast or digital media; supporting and training teachers and parents to manage remote virtual classrooms and help children learn at home, at all levels of education; and targeting girls' access and bias against online learning for girls, including more real-time analysis and surveys to assess implications for girls' learning and to inform more customized learning content and training materials (El-Laithy 2021).

INCREASING FEMALE LABOR FORCE PARTICIPATION

Increasing the female labor force participation rate (LFPR) in Egypt, particularly among urban, educated women, is critical for addressing the fertility challenge. Women's participation has not increased, despite improvements in their education attainment and the relatively large share of women holding a university degree. The reasons are not only structural but also normative, with values and practices associated with gendered roles and relations acting as barriers to the female LFPR. It is crucial to reduce these barriers and expand job opportunities for women through reforms that facilitate childcare and mandate equal pay. Increased female labor force participation thus calls for a comprehensive approach in the following main areas.

Improving women's employability

Female enrollment in higher education has increased in recent years, but it needs to shift toward disciplines that offer higher rates of employment for females, as opposed to the current majority in humanities. Higher education institutions need to create career guidance mechanisms that specifically target female secondary students to inform their decisions about which field of study to pursue, encouraging them to enroll more in science, technology, engineering, and mathematics (STEM) disciplines or other more labor-market-relevant programs. Their employability could be further enhanced through targeted support by university career services, to ease their transition into jobs. This would ideally be coupled with behavioral training targeting teachers at all grade levels to address gender-biased stereotyping and establish a more gender-sensitive mind-set early on. MOETE is committed to a more gender-sensitive approach in its Education 2.0 reform.

Providing support services that facilitate female employment

Although data indicate that the returns to female higher education are significant (and higher than that of males), women are often challenged by lack of affordable childcare (nurseries or kindergarten, for example). As household chores—particularly care for family members (child and elderly care)—virtually always fall on women's shoulders, better policies to support the care economy would no doubt boost the female LFPR. A growing body of research has investigated this impact and confirms that childcare is indeed an instrumental factor in lifting the female LFPR, for two reasons: first, the childcare industry is an employer of women, and expanding it would create more opportunities for women; and second, the expansion would allow mothers to return to the labor market in other sectors. In addition, female graduates may require targeted career counseling (in addition to shifting to higher rates of employment disciplines) to help them find job opportunities and become employed.

Creating an enabling and conducive environment for female employment

One key policy direction here would be targeted awareness and/or an incentives package primarily focused on employers to reduce biased decision-making that negatively affects female employment (including promotions). A more conducive and safe environment for women in the workplace starts with addressing employers' stereotyping of female employees that either drives candidates away or offers them a lower-value package of salary and benefits. A combined package of awareness on the value added of female workers, as well as incentives to recruit females, is needed.

In an effort to incentivize and institutionalize gender equity in the private sector in Egypt, the National Council for Women, with support from the World Bank, revived the Egyptian Equity Seal certification, a model that was successfully implemented in Latin America. The model promotes gender equity in the private sector by building a series of good practices in recruitment, career development, family–work balance, and sexual harassment.

Combating violence against women and girls

Women and girls face gender-based violence in both the public and private spheres, and addressing it is crucial to increasing the female LFPR. This could be achieved by enforcing the legislation on violence against women and girls and sexual harassment in public spaces, including on transportation and in the workspace, as this will encourage women's uptake of job opportunities. Another key measure is sharing information with the public on the law against violence against women and girls and sexual harassment. Grievance-redress mechanisms in organizations, when implemented properly, including respectfully treating victims and maintaining their privacy, are also important, not only to ensure justice but also to send a strong signal to communities that such behaviors are unacceptable.

Addressing the social norms and values system

Sociocultural norms and stereotypes that shape gender roles and identify women with restrictive characteristics and capabilities in the labor market reinforce existing inequalities. Changing them is therefore critical for a higher female LFPR. Such norms justify discrimination in the labor market—despite improvements in female education and skills—and, inevitably, shape women's engagement and preferences. Such rigid gender roles influence the types of work women and men do, the amount of work they do, and how well they are compensated. This is especially troublesome given that women bear the burden of unpaid care and household labor. Unless investments are made to translate gender equality policy into actions, these deeply entrenched informal social norms will undermine the best policies and plans for advancing gender justice. These actions can be achieved through designing and implementing initiatives using a behavioral lens approach to change and social norms, and to the expectations that shape gender roles and behaviors.

Addressing impediments in the private sector

While women are well represented—36 percent—in the government and public sector combined in Egypt, only 18 percent of the country's female workforce is employed in the private sector. The representation of women across economic sectors also varies considerably. Further, women on average get paid 34 percent less per hour than their male counterparts, and they are underrepresented on boards of companies and in managerial positions (9.7 percent and 7.1 percent, respectively).

Against this backdrop, and in view of a shrinking public sector and a private sector that is increasingly playing a central role in employment creation and economic growth, it is imperative that the private sector become more hospitable to women to encourage their employment, be reconcilable with women's domestic responsibilities, and improve their working conditions. This demands concerted efforts to address biases and to enhance inclusiveness and gender equality in the workplace, achievable through gender-sensitive policies and measures that need to be institutionalized within the company. Examples include creating safe working spaces for women; ensuring access to childcare; promoting flexible working arrangements; addressing biases in recruitment and making proactive efforts to recruit qualified women; and creating a culture of open communication where concerns and challenges can be discussed and corrective measures taken.

Further, the Closing the Gender Gap Accelerator—launched by the Ministry of International Cooperation with the National Council for Women (NCW) and the World Economic Forum (WEF), and in partnership with the private sector—is a step in the right direction. It aims to help the government and businesses close economic gender gaps; design innovative plans that will encourage growth and shape the workforce landscape; advance gender parity, diversity, and inclusion; and improve the ability of families and individuals to increase their income through economic mobility (UN Women 2020).

Boosting women's participation in promising new sectors

In examining opportunities for expanding women's employment in the private sector, the "Women Economic Empowerment Study" identifies the top 12 industries in Egypt that hire women intensively or have the potential to grow and could employ more women, including social care, education, human health, garments, computers and electronics, pharmaceuticals, financial services, travel agencies, business services, real estate, information and communications technology, and retail trade (World Bank 2018). These sectors are also export oriented and would create good jobs that are attractive to increasingly educated women.

DELAYING AGE OF MARRIAGE

In traditional societies, the competition between the reproductive and productive roles of women is usually in favor of the former. Early marriage and early motherhood limit the chances and options available to women, and a vicious circle results in increasing fertility levels among women who too often take low-paid jobs and lack career prospects. Experience from other countries suggests the types of interventions that can delay or prevent early marriage.

Empowering girls

These interventions are aimed at empowering girls through information sharing, life-skills teaching, vocational and livelihoods skills training, mentored learning spaces to facilitate the acquisition of core academic skills, and support networks to enhance opportunities for continued schooling.

Engaging parents and communities

Efforts in this direction are essential so that an enabling environment is created and the stigma associated with delaying marriage is reduced. Interventions would aim to change social norms and reduce the pressure to marry early. Engaging with parents and communities will mitigate any potential unintended negative consequences of girls' participation in empowering activities and programs. It is also vital to tap into existing government platforms, whether through the social units under the Ministry of Social Solidarity or the governorate offices of the National Council for Women.

Improving formal schooling and education opportunities for girls

Such improved opportunities could be achieved by preparing, training, and supporting girls for enrollment or re-enrollment in school, in addition to reforming education so that academic skills are aligned with labor market needs, creating an enabling environment for girls to stay in school.

Enforcing laws and policies

In Egypt, although early marriage is prohibited by law, the practice is still prevalent in rural areas, especially in Upper Egypt. An Early Marriage Strategy 2015–2020 was designed to reduce the share of early marriages by 50 percent, focusing on geographic areas with high prevalence (Samari 2017). This strategy needs to be revised and updated, given the persistent correlation between child marriage and fertility. It is imperative to enforce existing child protection laws more rigorously and close any legal loopholes that allow families to marry off girls who are below the legal age of marriage. And unless these laws are accompanied by mechanisms to enforce them, and are complemented with multisectoral interventions that include raising awareness among leaders at all levels, the practice will be difficult to root out.

LEVERAGING SOCIAL PROTECTION PROGRAMS

The existing Takaful and Karama program (TKP) presents a strong opportunity for expanding its reach. With its tight focus on supporting women's access to health (especially FP services) and on promoting girls' education, the TKP can be leveraged to optimize the impact on fertility reduction by creating platforms for "cash plus" interventions. That is, the TKP programs affect other aspects of people's lives, including those that influence fertility.

The TKP database hosts over 8 million households (31 million individuals), encompassing all those who have applied to the program. Of those who applied, 3.4 million households (12 million individuals) were found eligible and enrolled in the program. Seventy-five percent of the cardholders are women, and 67 percent of the cash is dedicated to Upper Egypt. In 2018, the government decided to have the TKP support up to two children only, which became effective in January 2019, echoing a clear message that the government is promoting smaller families to curb fertility and enhance social transformation. This is further emphasized through a program called "Two Is Enough" (box 7.2).

Policy interventions targeted at lower-quintile households to incentivize demand for schooling and attendance have proved effective in Egypt. They should be reinforced and diversified through the TKP, an effective mechanism for rewarding school attendance and health clinic visits. Other incentivizing

---

Box 7.2

"Two Is Enough"—Egypt's campaign to address high fertility

The "Two Is Enough" program was launched in 2018 by the MOHP and the Ministry of Social Solidarity, in coordination with the United Nations Population Fund (UNFPA). It is meant to curb fertility rates by targeting Takaful beneficiaries, encouraging them to have only two children, raising their awareness of FP, and providing them with subsidized access to birth control. The initiative relies on awareness-raising sessions in addition to printed material, which is distributed among target groups to address social and health beliefs of FP.

The program includes a strong communication component, where messages are disseminated through TV, radio, and social media campaigns to reach out to 1 million Takaful households in the poorest 10 governorates experiencing the highest poverty and fertility rates. The program's outreach depends largely on community involvement. Over 2 million home visits were conducted by community workers, resulting in over 400,000 women visiting FP clinics, where they receive counseling and FP supplies free of charge. The role of community health workers has proved central to this agenda, along with the provision of quality services and access to subsidized birth control. NGOs also played a key role in establishing clinics on their premises and training staff to support beneficiaries. Over 40,000 women visited such clinics, 25,000 of whom have started using FP methods because of the intervention.

Source: UNFPA 2019.

options could include on-the-job training and adult literacy programs (El-Laithy 2021). Another TKP program, "Forsa" (meaning opportunity), has a strong focus on women to help generate female employment and sustainable livelihoods.

Further, there is a strong opportunity to leverage the existing TKP infrastructure to address broader issues pertaining to women and girls. For instance, the program has a grievance-redress mechanism, which is advertised to communities to allow for submission of complaints through multiple channels (hotline, website, and local units). In addition, social accountability tools and mechanisms, such as Social Accountability Committees at the village level, allow for regular feedback from citizens.

IMPROVING GOVERNANCE OF THE POPULATION PROGRAM

In the past few decades, Egypt curbed population growth only during 1986–93, when the government shouldered the burden, reflecting four concurrent factors (Dawood and Abdel Latif 2019):

- Strong political will;
- A comprehensive population policy with quantitative objectives;
- A strong, independent, and stable institutional framework—the National Population Council (NPC)—responsible for population; and
- The provision of financial resources from the government and donors.

One key factor was the authority and powers of the NPC, which mobilized different government sectors and ministries as part of a coordinated national plan. Improving the governance of the national population program would require all these elements, as most priorities require actions beyond the remit of any one ministry. Thus, for 2021 and beyond, the following four fundamental interventions are proposed.

Establishing a strong institutional framework

The first intervention is to establish a "strong, independent, stable institutional framework" for the national population program, comprising the following (Dawood and Abdel Latif 2019):

- An existing national body headed by a ministerial-level official—the "Champion"—should report to the president or at least to the prime minister and should comprise a core team of key ministers such as those for finance, planning, health, education, and social solidarity.
- This body will be the sole government entity responsible for preparing the coordinated national plan and for coordinating across ministries and organizations. It will also monitor performance indicators, on the basis of which the performance of all the government organizations will be evaluated. The body's decisions must be binding on all concerned organizations executing the plans.
- The body should have a technical team or secretariat responsible for preparing background technical studies, coordinating preparation of implementation plans, and conducting monitoring and evaluation.
- The body should have a lean organizational structure, and staffing can be seconded from other ministries or public organizations to minimize the creation of bureaucratic layers.

- The body can enlist independent experts in health, population, economics, social protection, and human development, as well as have cooperation agreements with think tanks, universities, and research centers for conducting background technical studies.
- Local coordinating committees that report to the national body will be established in each governorate and made up of representatives from ministries and public entities. They will be responsible for overseeing implementation, for coordinating provision of population services and follow-up, and for troubleshooting local issues.
- The implementation plans should be adequately funded through a budget for the national program and an allocation for each governorate, depending on its demographic profile (see table 7.2).

Providing legal and regulatory support

Many of the proposed policy and strategic priorities require a critical examination of existing laws and regulations. For example, new regulations are needed to allow qualified health workers, such as nurses, to provide FP services; to contract out FP services to the private sector; to allow the private sector to import and/or distribute some FP methods monopolized by the MOHP; and to fast-track the registration of new FP methods.

Developing differentiated subnational implementation plans

The Egypt National Population Strategy (ENPS) 2015–2030 was useful in setting the long-term vision for the population program, and the Egypt First Five-Year Population Implementation Plan (EPIP) 2015–2020 provided an implementation framework. But the population program failed to achieve its planned targets, largely because it did not consider Egypt's geographic variations.

TABLE 7.2 **Demographic profile of the high-burden governorates**

NAME	LIVE BIRTHS		MARRIAGE CONTRACT		SCHOOL DROPOUT		UNEMPLOYMENT		ILLITERACY
	LIKELIHOOD	CONC.	LIKELIHOOD	CONC.	LIKELIHOOD	CONC.	LIKELIHOOD	CONC.	LIKELIHOOD
Sharqia	U	U	G	G	G	G	F	F/M	G
Menia	U	R/U	G	G	G	G	F/M	F/M	G
Assiut	U	R/U	G	G	G	G	F	F	G
Aswan	U	U	G	G	G	G	F/M	F/M	G
Alexandria	R	R	G	G	G	G	M	F/M	G
Giza	R	R	G	G	G	G	F	F	G
Qena	R	R	G	G	G	G	F	F	G
Sohag	R/U	R	G	G	G	G	F	F/M	G
Dakahlia	U	U	G	G	G	G	F	F	G
Gharbia	U	U	G	G	G	G	M	M	G
Beheira	U	U	G	G	G	G	F	F	G
Beni Suef	U	U	G	G	G	G	F/M	F/M	G

Source: Original illustration and calculations based on CAPMAS (2020) for live births, marriage contracts, and unemployment; and on CAPMAS (2017) for school dropouts and illiteracy.
Note: See table 3.5. Conc. = concentration; G = governorate level; U = urban; R = rural; F = female; M = male. Red cells denote high rate (>95% CI above national average) and/or distribution exceeding population distribution by >1%. Green cells denote low rates.

Governorates and regions have different demographic profiles (as discussed in chapter 3) and should be categorized and prioritized by these profiles. Implementation plans that address the local conditions should be created, and outputs should be monitored at the subregional level.

For example, table 7.2 presents the high-priority governorates where the likelihood and concentration of live births are high but the associated social determinants vary widely from school dropouts to unemployment. Supply- and demand-side interventions need to be crafted concurrently by the governorates based on local circumstances (including addressing, respectively, high unmet need and discontinuation rates, and early marriage/conception and school dropouts). A bottom-up approach in preparing these implementation plans will have more ownership and ensure accountability.

Developing a national dashboard for the population program

Issues of data generation and use impede planning and decision-making on FP in Egypt, as most plans and studies use the latest EDHS and the Service Provision Assessment data, which are more than seven years old. An EDHS and other service surveys are therefore imperative to update the status of the key demographic indicators and to assess progress. Yet if data from an EDHS are only produced every seven years or so, this long periodicity will not help policy makers and program managers take timely corrective measures.

It is therefore critical to establish a population dashboard with a set of annual key performance indicators (KPIs) that can be collected in a timely manner and reported on a monthly or quarterly basis. Only KPIs that have a baseline measurement can be included, as experience shows it is impossible to improve what is not measured. Data from CAPMAS should constitute the backbone of the dashboard, as these are routinely collected and do not require additional data collection tools.

The annual KPIs established at the national level should be translated into a subset of KPIs at the governorate level, and they should vary depending on the demographic profile of each governorate. Subnational implementation plans should be closely linked to their corresponding KPIs. Finally, the dashboard should be automated to provide near real-time data and to flag any deviations from the planned targets, enabling corrective measures.

ENSURING A BROAD-BASED SOCIOECONOMIC DEVELOPMENT POLICY

The six policy and strategic priorities discussed above can help the government in addressing population growth and achieving the first phase of the demographic dividend through fertility decline, increased share of the working-age population, and increased worker productivity. Increasing the share of the working-age population constitutes a necessary but not sufficient condition for achieving the second phase. Having a large share of the working-age population that is healthy, educated, skilled, and potentially productive is an achievement; but if the economy is not creating *productive* jobs to employ this cohort, so as to boost income and savings that would lead to human and physical capital accumulation and economic growth, the second phase will not materialize.

According to Merotto, Langbein, and Weber (2020), youthful countries face steeper challenges in creating jobs and undertaking structural change. Egypt has a large, youthful population. On top of that, its population growth rate is elevated compared with that of peers (2 percent compared with 1.2 percent on average in middle-income countries in 2004–18). Countries like Vietnam and Sri Lanka maintained average growth well below 1 percent annually during the same period. This points to the urgency of addressing population growth (through family planning) for better per capita growth outcomes in Egypt (Alnashar, El-Ashmawy, and Youssef 2020).

These six priorities therefore need to be backed up by policy imperatives that ensure sustained inclusive growth characterized by strong leadership and governance, macroeconomic stability (so that markets work), a market orientation to guide structural change, an outward orientation to achieve scale and impose discipline, and a future orientation to boost savings and meet investment needs (CGD 2008). For Egypt, this translates into the following four policy imperatives.

Creating productive jobs

Egypt is an early-dividend country, but the first phase of the demographic dividend can be achieved only to the extent that the economy can create productive jobs to absorb the growing working-age population. This step is crucial because income levels tend to rise with higher productivity levels. Merotto and Eberhard-Ruiz (2020) show that labor productivity growth explained 79 percent of the growth in per capita incomes in 95 countries, on average, during 1991–2001.

During 2003/04–2018, Egypt's overall GDP growth averaged 4.5 percent, compared with 5.6 percent for the average of middle-income countries and close to that of many peers. However, when assessed in per capita or per worker terms, growth was quite sluggish: Egypt's GDP per capita growth over this period averaged 2.4 percent, or 2.0 percentage points less than the average in middle-income countries (Alnashar, El-Ashmawy, and Youssef 2020). This underperformance reflects modest labor productivity growth as well as declining employment rates, which can be explained mainly by feeble labor productivity growth, which averaged 1.9 percent, lower than the average for middle-income countries of 4.6 percent in the same period (Alnashar, El-Ashmawy, and Youssef 2020).

Despite having a growing young population, Egypt has been unable to raise its employment rate because the pace of job creation has fallen below the growth in the size of the working-age population. This has in turn weighed on GDP per capita growth, as Egypt has not been able to absorb its growing young population into employment (figure 7.2). The sectoral patterns of growth that have led to such outcomes include the concentration of employment in low-value-added sectors such as private agriculture, which includes subsistence (unpaid) work, and in public social services. Egypt has not been able to tap the potential of the country's large young population because the productive and job-creation capacity of the economy has remained constrained (Alnashar, El-Ashmawy, and Youssef 2020).

FIGURE 7.2

Decomposition of annual average growth in GDP per capita, Egypt and comparators, 2004–18

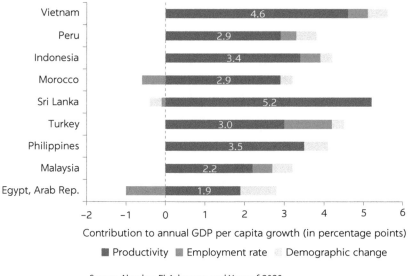

Source: Alnashar, El-Ashmawy, and Youssef 2020.
Note: GDP = gross domestic product.

An economic transformation is therefore needed to increase productivity within sectors as well as increase the reallocation of labor (among other resources) toward more productive sectors, so as to generate high-earning jobs at scale (McMillan et al. 2017). Further, getting the enabling environment right is equally critical to create attractive opportunities for domestic and foreign investment to enhance within-sector productivity growth and to support the movement of workers into higher-value activities and sectors. This step is in addition to resolving some of the impediments to private sector activity through reducing barriers to competition and easing regulations to access loans from commercial banks (Alnashar, El-Ashmawy, and Youssef 2020). Finally, there is a need to accelerate job creation, by ensuring that both the supply side (particularly human capital formation) and the demand side (job-intensive economic growth) of job creation are well aligned to absorb the labor force across different income levels (Troiano 2015; World Bank 2013). These policies would also include the removal of barriers to female labor force participation, given persistent gender gaps in Egypt's labor market.

The bigger challenge on the demand side is informality. Its high share, even among educated workers and especially women, suggests that formal job opportunities are limited. Firms might prefer being informal because the costs of becoming formal may exceed the benefits (for instance, complying with regulations or facing competition from informal firms). For workers, on the other hand, the opposite could be true since formal employment brings greater social protection and job security. Addressing demand-side problems in the labor market would thus require a range of policies addressing the business environment, tax policy, labor regulations, and access to finance (that affect the cost of establishing formal enterprises) to encourage job creation and formal hiring by private firms (World Bank 2019).

Investing in and leveraging human capital

Investing in building, preparing, and protecting human capital will be important to fast-track the economic transformation process, particularly through investing in early child development, investing in technical and vocational education and training, enhancing labor market mobility, promoting healthy lifestyles, and adopting quality standards in production and service delivery. Investment in human development is needed to tackle nonincome deprivations and inequalities of opportunity so that these same groups can gain the capacity to benefit from and contribute to economic growth and prosperity (Paxson and Schady 2007). In the short and medium terms, a program for upskilling and reskilling the workforce will be key to address the skills mismatch in supply and demand for workers, which exists across all levels of educational attainment (figure 7.3).

In the coming decades, global trade flows are projected to continue shifting toward countries earlier in their demographic transition, possibly yielding substantial benefits for these countries. In pursuing their domestic agendas, countries can also arbitrage, and in the process leverage demographic change at the global level through cross-border capital flows and global trade (World Bank and IMF 2016).

For Egypt, investments in developing the skills of its growing working-age population from the first phase of the demographic dividend in more productive industries and in selected value-added services and products may lead to a comparative advantage in trade, and to greater returns to labor and capital.

Enhancing financial inclusion and entrepreneurship

Financial inclusion, particularly for women, is a key enabler for poverty reduction and inclusive growth, and is critical to women's economic empowerment and ability to secure the livelihood of their families.

FIGURE 7.3

Mismatch in supply and demand for workers by educational attainment, 2016

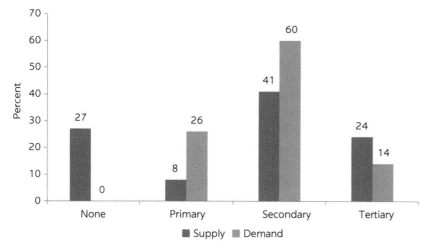

Source: World Bank 2019.

Financial inclusion and entrepreneurship are proven to be game changers for women, but this is subject to a conducive legal, regulatory, and business-enabling environment.

In Egypt, despite the reported progress due to government interventions to improve the regulatory environment for financial inclusion and for women's work, many women, especially poor and rural residents, remain outside the formal financial system. Although there are several factors explaining the financial gap between men and women, the main reason is a lack of awareness of service providers regarding the business reasons for targeting women; another is the weaker financial capability of women. Intersecting with the gap in financial inclusion is the low level of entrepreneurship in Egypt. The inability to access finance limits the size and growth potential of firms and is a major barrier for the establishment of enterprises. The weakness and generic nature of available business development services are also hurdles that small enterprises face, especially women-owned ones (most of which are in the microenterprise sector), the percentage of which is small relative to those in other countries in the region, and globally.

Women's full financial inclusion requires intertwined efforts at three levels:

- At the micro level, focusing on enhancing women's financial literacy and changing their attitudes toward banking;
- At the meso level—where financial institutions and entities produce gender-specific products—encouraging women to use these products and services; and
- At the macro level—where the legislative framework ensures nondiscrimination in access to credit—changing prevailing social norms to support this shift.

Sustaining macroeconomic stability and ensuring policy predictability

Early-dividend countries like Egypt need to lay the foundation for the second phase of the demographic dividend, notably through consolidating the country's public finances and enhancing government fiscal and debt management and transparency.

In recent years, Egypt has made strides in stabilizing the macroeconomy, but persistent structural challenges need to be resolved to safeguard a substantial recovery through the following: resuming fiscal consolidation after the COVID-19 pandemic crisis to pave the way for the private sector to invest and expand; maintaining a market-determined and competitive exchange rate; and achieving low and stable inflation to provide more price visibility and the overall predictability needed by investors (Alnashar, El-Ashmawy, and Youssef 2020).

Other longer-term reforms will be needed to improve the business environment, including cutting red tape, especially that related to taxes and customs (Youssef et al. 2019); incentivizing domestic savings; and facilitating access to land through streamlining procedures to own, register, and transfer land.

These measures will help to reduce fiscal risks and create the fiscal space to strengthen social protection, reduce inequity, and invest in human capital—all necessary for economic transformation. The effects of successful policies in these areas can be mutually reinforcing, helping to create a virtuous circle of sustained growth and enabling Egypt's full claim on its long-delayed demographic dividend.

THE WAY FORWARD

Given the scope and complexity of the proposed policy and strategic priorities, the following time frame aims to ensure optimal sequencing of implementation, harmonization and complementarity across priorities, and expectation-setting about the implementation timeline and expected results from each intervention (table 7.3).

The president's "Decent Life Initiative," launched in January 2019, and the "National Project for the Development of the Egyptian Family," launched in February 2022, can be used as the platform to implement many of the proposed policies and strategies. The initiative aims "to provide a decent life for the most vulnerable groups nationwide and further contributes to enhancing the quality

TABLE 7.3 Proposed time frame for the policy and strategic priorities

	IMMEDIATE (WITHIN 1 YEAR)	SHORT–MEDIUM (1–3 YEARS)	LONG-TERM (2–5 YEARS)
Increasing the contraceptive prevalence rate (CPR)	• Meeting unmet need • Integrating FP services in postpartum care • Improving the supply chain and quality of methods • Expanding the capacity of the Ministry of Health and Population (MOHP) to provide family planning (FP) services • Generating demand for FP use	• Expanding FP services in the public sector • Reducing contraceptive discontinuation • Engaging nonpublic-sector providers • Expanding the method mix in the public and private sector	
Reducing school dropouts	• Reducing girls' dropouts • Prioritizing education on sexual and reproductive health (SRH)	• Increasing girls' enrollment, particularly at secondary level	• Creating an enabling environment to incentivize girls' retention in education
Increasing female labor force participation	• Providing support services that facilitate female employment	• Combating violence against women and girls • Creating an enabling and conducive environment for female employment • Addressing impediments in the private sector	• Addressing the social norms and values system • Boosting women's participation in promising new sectors
Delaying age of marriage	• Enforcing laws and policies • Engaging parents and communities	• Improving formal schooling and education opportunities for girls	
Leveraging social protection programs	• Boosting the "Two Is Enough" program	• Expanding coverage of the Takaful and Karama program (TKP)	• Leveraging the TKP to address broader issues (such as gender violence)
Improving governance of the population program	• Establishing a strong institutional framework • Developing differentiated subnational implementation plans	• Developing a national dashboard for the population program • Providing legal and regulatory support	

continued

TABLE 7.3, *continued*

	IMMEDIATE (WITHIN 1 YEAR)	SHORT-MEDIUM (1–3 YEARS)	LONG-TERM (2–5 YEARS)
Ensuring a broad-based socioeconomic development policy			
Creating productive jobs	• Identifying sectors for potential value-added growth • Easing regulations to access loans from commercial banks • Removing barriers to female labor force participation	• Reallocating labor toward more productive sectors • Reducing barriers to competition • Reducing the cost of establishing formal enterprises	• Increasing productivity within sectors • Encouraging job creation and formal hiring by private firms
Investing in and leveraging human capital	• Reskilling and upskilling the labor force to address the skills mismatch • Investing in technical and vocational education and training • Promoting healthy lifestyles	• Investing in early child development • Adopting quality standards in production and service delivery	• Enhancing labor market mobility
Enhancing financial inclusion and entrepreneurship	• Enhancing women's financial literacy and changing their attitudes toward banking	• Easing regulations to access loans from commercial banks • Encouraging financial institutions to produce gender-specific products and encouraging women to use them	• Ensuring nondiscrimination in access to credit
Sustaining macroeconomic stability and ensuring policy predictability	• Resuming fiscal consolidation plans • Maintaining a market-determined and competitive exchange rate • Achieving low and stable inflation	• Improving the investment climate for domestic and foreign investment in higher-value sectors • Enhancing government fiscal and debt management and transparency	• Incentivizing domestic savings • Facilitating access to land

Source: Original illustration for this publication.

of daily public services provided to citizens, including medical services, with a focus on rural areas. The initiative also aims to develop Egypt's poorest villages, according to the poverty map, provides job opportunities and supports orphan girls to get married" (Decent Life Initiative, presidency.eg). The project aims to improve the quality of life of citizens by controlling population growth and improving population characteristics through several axes including economic empowerment, reproductive health services, cultural awareness and education, digital transformation and evaluation, and legislative interventions (mped.gov.eg).

NOTE

1. Recently, the Visiting Doctors program, supported under the Transforming Egypt's Healthcare System Project of the MOHP, deployed FP-trained female doctors to the areas of most FP need, particularly in Upper Egypt.

REFERENCES

Ali, Mohammad M., John G. Cleland, and Iqbal H. Shah. 2012. *Causes and Consequences of Contraceptive Discontinuation: Evidence from 60 Demographic and Health Surveys.* Geneva, Switzerland: World Health Organization.

Alnashar, Sara, Fatma El-Ashmawy, and Jala Youssef. 2020. "Egypt Economic Monitor: From Crisis to Economic Transformation—Unlocking Egypt's Productivity and Job-Creation Potential." World Bank, Washington, DC. http://documents.worldbank.org/curated /en/256581604587810889/Egypt-Economic-Monitor-From-Crisis-to-Economic -Transformation-Unlocking-Egypt-s-Productivity-and-Job-Creation-Potential.

Alterman, Jon B. 2012. "Egypt and U.S. Health Assistance." CSIS Global Health Policy Center, Center for Strategic and International Studies, Washington, DC. https://csis-website-prod .s3.amazonaws.com/s3fs-public/legacy_files/files/publication/120625_Egypt_US_Health _Assistance.pdf.

Baschieri, Angela, and Andrew Hinde. 2007. "The Proximate Determinants of Fertility and Birth Intervals in Egypt: An Application of Calendar Data." *Demographic Research* 16 (3): 59–96. doi:10.4054/DemRes.2007.16.3.

Belaid, Loubna, Alexandre Dumont, Nils Chaillet, Amel Zertal, Vincent De Brouwere, and Valéry Ridde. 2016. "Implementation and Effects of Demand Generation Interventions in Low- and Middle-Income Family Planning Programs: A Systematic Review." *Cahiers Realisme* 6 (April). http://www.equitesante.org/wp-content/uploads/2016/04/Numero-6 -Apr20161.pdf.

Burke, Holly M., Monique P. Mueller, Catherine Packer, Brian Perry, Leonard Bufumbo, Daouda Mbengue, Bocar Mamadou Daff, and Anthony Mbonye. 2014. "Provider Acceptability of Sayana® Press: Results from Community Health Workers and Clinic-Based Providers in Uganda and Senegal." *Contraception* 89 (5): 368–73. doi:10.1016/j.contraception.2014.01.009.

CAPMAS (Central Agency for Public Mobilization and Statistics). 2017. *Egypt Census 2017.* December. Cairo: CAPMAS. http://www.enow.gov.eg/Report/EgyptCensus2017.pdf.

CAPMAS (Central Agency for Public Mobilization and Statistics). 2020. *Egypt in Figures 2020.* March. Cairo: CAPMAS. https://www.capmas.gov.eg/Pages/StaticPages.aspx ?page_id=5035.

Castle, Sarah, and Ian Askew. 2015. "Contraceptive Discontinuation: Reasons, Challenges and Solutions." FP2020, Washington, DC; Population Council, New York.

CGD (Commission on Growth and Development). 2008. *The Growth Report. Strategies for Sustained Growth and Inclusive Development.* Washington, DC: World Bank.

Dawood, Ahmed, and Abla Abdel Latif 2019. "Population Policy in Egypt: An Analysis of the Constituents for Success and the Optimal Institutional Form, a Comparative Study." Working Paper 203, Egyptian Center for Economic Studies, Cairo. http://www.eces.org.eg /cms/NewsUploads/Pdf/2019_12_8-15_45_41Working%20Paper%20203.pdf. In Arabic.

El-Laithy, Heba. 2021. "Inequality of Education Opportunities in Egypt: Impact Evaluation." Working Paper 216, Egyptian Center for Economic Studies, Cairo, http://www.eces.org.eg /PublicationsDetails?Lang=EN&C=12&T=1&ID=1287&Inequality-of-Education -Opportunities-in-Egypt:-Impact-Evaluation.

FP2020. n.d. "Delivering High-Quality and Rights-Based Services: FP2020 The Way Ahead 2016–2017." Family Planning 2020, Washington, DC. http://2016-2017progress.family planning2020.org/en/fp2020-in-countries/delivering-high-quality-and-rights -based-services.

Gertler, Paul J., and John W. Molyneaux. 1994. "How Economic Development and Family Planning Programs Combined to Reduce Indonesian Fertility." *Demography* 31 (1): 33. doi:10.2307/2061907.

Goodkind, Daniel, Lisa Lollock, Yoonjoung Choi, Thomas McDevitt, and Loraine West. 2018. "The Demographic Impact and Development Benefits of Meeting Demand for Family Planning with Modern Contraceptive Methods." *Global Health Action* 11 (1): 1423861. doi:10 .1080/16549716.2018.1423861.

HIPs (High-Impact Practices in Family Planning). 2012. "Supply Chain Management: Investing in Contraceptive Security and Strengthening Health Systems." Toolkit. USAID, Washington, DC.

HIPs (High-Impact Practices in Family Planning). 2013. "Drug Shops and Pharmacies: Sources for Family Planning Commodities and Information." USAID, Washington, DC. https:// www.fphighimpactpractices.org/briefs/drug-shops-and-pharmacies/.

HIPs (High-Impact Practices in Family Planning). 2015. "Community Health Workers: Bringing Family Planning Services to Where People Live and Work." USAID, Washington, DC. https://www.fphighimpactpractices.org/briefs/community-health-workers/.

Jain, Anrudh. 2016. "Examining Progress and Equity in Information Received by Women Using a Modern Method in 25 Developing Countries," *International Perspectives on Sexual and Reproductive Health* 42 (3): 131–40.

Jain, Anrudh, Francis Obare, Soumya Ramarao, and Ian Askew. 2013. "Reducing Unmet Need by Supporting Women with Met Need." *International Perspectives on Sexual and Reproductive Health* 39 (3): 133–41. doi:10.1363/3913313.

Krafft, Caroline, Ragui Assaad, and Caitlyn Keo. 2019. "The Evolution of Labor Supply in Egypt from 1988–2018: A Gendered Analysis." ERF Working Paper 1358, Economic Research Forum, Cairo.

Krafft, Caroline, Zea Branson, and Taylor Flak. 2019. "What's the Value of a Degree? Evidence from Egypt, Jordan and Tunisia." *Compare: A Journal of Comparative and International Education* 51 (1): 61–80. https://doi.org/10.1080/03057925.2019.1590801.

McMillan, Margaret, John Page, David Booth, and Dirk Willem te Velde. 2017. "Supporting Economic Transformation: An Approach Paper." Overseas Development Institute, London. https://odi.org/en/publications/supporting-economic-transformation-an-approach -paper/.

Merkatz, Ruth B., Marlena Plagianos, Elena Hoskin, Michael Cooney, Paul C. Hewett, and Barbara S. Mensch. 2014. "Acceptability of the Nestorone®/Ethinyl Estradiol Contraceptive Vaginal Ring: Development of a Model; Implications for Introduction." *Contraception* 90 (5): 514–21. doi:10.1016/j.contraception.2014.05.015.

Merotto, Dino, and Andreas Eberhard-Ruiz. 2020. "#1 Better, Not More Jobs Are Associated with Increased Per Capita Income." Jobs and Development Partnerships. https://www .jobsanddevelopment.org/better-notmore-iobs-are-associated-with-increased-per -capita-income/.

Merotto, Dino, Jörg Langbein, and Michael Weber. 2020. "#11 Youthful Countries Face Steeper Challenges Creating Better Jobs With Structural Change" Jobs and Development Partnership. https://www.jobsanddevelopment.org/youthful-countries-face-steeper -challenges-creating-better-jobs-with-structural-change/.

MOETE (Ministry of Education and Technical Education). 2020. "Statistical Yearbook 2019/2020." MOETE, Cairo. http://emis.gov.eg/Site%20Content/book/019-020/main _book2020.html. In Arabic.

MOHP (Ministry of Health and Population), El-Zanaty and Associates, and ICF International. 2015. *Egypt Demographic and Health Survey 2014*. Cairo: MOHP. https://dhsprogram.com /publications/publication-fr302-dhs-final-reports.cfm.

Moreau, Caroline, Mridula Shankar, Stephane Helleringer, and Stanley Becker. 2019. "Measuring Unmet Need for Contraception as a Point Prevalence." *BMJ Global Health* 4: e001581.

Paxson, Christina, and Norbert Schady. 2007. "Cognitive Development among Young Children in Ecuador: The Roles of Wealth, Health, and Parenting." *Journal of Human Resources* 42 (1): 49–84.

Pugliese-Garcia, Miguel, Emma Radovich, Oona M. R. Campbell, Nevine Hassanein, Karima Khalil, and Lenka Benova. 2020. "Childbirth Care in Egypt: A Repeat Cross-sectional Analysis Using Demographic and Health Surveys between 1995 and 2014 Examining Use of Care, Provider Mix and Immediate Postpartum Care Content." *BMC Pregnancy Childbirth* 20, article 46. doi:10.1186/s12884-020-2730-8.

Radovich, Emma, Atef el-Shitany, Hania Sholkamy, and Lenka Benova. 2018. "Rising Up: Fertility Trends in Egypt before and after the Revolution." *PLoS ONE* 13 (1): e0190148. doi:10.1371/journal.pone.0190148.

Riggs-Perla, Joy, Carol Carpenter-Yaman, Leslie B. Curtin, Andrew Kantner, Pinar Senlet, Mona El Shafei, and Mellen Duffy Tanamly. 2011. *Egypt Health and Population Legacy Review,* Vol. 1. Washington, DC: USAID.

Samari, Goleen. 2017. "Women's Agency and Fertility: Recent Evidence from Egypt." *Population Research and Policy Review* 36 (4): 561–82. doi:10.1007/s11113-017-9427-3.

Sathar, Zeba, Anrudh Jain, Soumya Ramarao, Minhaj ul Haque, and Jacqueline Kim. 2005. "Introducing Client-Centered Reproductive Health Services in a Pakistani Setting." *Studies in Family Planning* 36 (3): 221–34.

Stover, John, and William Winfrey. 2017. "The Effects of Family Planning and Other Factors on Fertility, Abortion, Miscarriage, and Stillbirths in the Spectrum Model." *BMC Public Health* 17 (Suppl 4): 775. doi:10.1186/s12889-017-4740-7.

Troiano, Sara. 2015. "Population Dynamics and the Implications for Economic Growth, Poverty and Inequality—What Is Relevant for Southern Africa." World Bank, Washington, DC.

UKAID. 2018. "Lessons from the Field: Sexual and Reproductive Health and Rights in the GEC." Girl's Education Challenge. London, UK: UKAID. https://girlseducationchallenge.org /what-we-are-learning/.

UNFPA (United Nations Population Fund). 2012. "United Nations International Youth Day 2012. Education on Sexual and Reproductive Health: Building Partnerships with and for Youth." Fact sheet. https://www.un.org/esa/socdev/unyin/documents/UNFPA SexualReproductiveHealth.pdf.

UNFPA (United Nations Population Fund). 2019. "Review of the Executive Plan 2015–2020: In the Context of the National Population and Development Strategy 2015–2030." UNFPA, Cairo. https://egypt.unfpa.org/sites/default/files/pub-pdf/exectives_english_aug20.pdf.

UN Women. 2020. "Report on the Policy Measures Adopted by the Egyptian Government to Ensure a Gender-Sensitive National Response to the COVID-19 Crisis." UN Women, Cairo. Egypt.unwomen.org.

Youssef, H., S. Alnashar, J. Youssef, A. Elshawarby, and C. Zaki. 2019. *Egypt Economic Monitor: From Floating to Thriving—Taking Egypt's Exports to New Levels.* Washington, DC: World Bank Group.

Weeks, John. 2004. "The Role of Spatial Analysis in Demographic Research." In *Spatially Integrated Social Science,* edited by Michael. F. Goodchild and Donald G. Janelle. New York: Oxford University Press.

World Bank. 2010. "Experiences with Fertility Reduction in Five High-Fertility Countries." World Bank, Washington, DC. https://openknowledge.worldbank.org/handle/10986 /27498.

World Bank. 2013. *World Development Report: Jobs.* Washington, DC: World Bank.

World Bank. 2018. "Women Economic Empowerment Study." World Bank, Washington, DC. https://openknowledge.worldbank.org/handle/10986/31351.

World Bank. 2019. "Understanding Poverty and Inequality in Egypt." World Bank, Washington, DC. https://openknowledge.worldbank.org/handle/10986/32812.

World Bank and IMF (International Monetary Fund). 2016. *Global Monitoring Report 2015/2016: Development Goals in an Era of Demographic Change.* Washington, DC: World Bank. doi:10.1596/978-1-4648-0669-8.

Annex: Additional Reading

Becker, Loren, Jessica Pickett, and Ruth Levine. 2006. "Measuring Commitment to Health: Global Health Indicators Working Group Report." Center for Global Development, Washington, DC. https://www.cgdev.org/sites/default/files/10016_file_FINAL_9_5_06.pdf.

Bongaarts, John. 1991. "The KAP-Gap and the Unmet Need for Contraception." *Population and Development Review* 17 (2): 293–313.

Cleland, John, Sarah Harbison, and Iqbal H. Shah. 2014. "Unmet Need for Contraception: Issues and Challenges." *Studies in Family Planning* 45 (2): 105–22. doi:10.1111/j.1728-4465 .2014.00380.x.

Guttmacher Institute. 2018. "Adding It Up: Investing in Contraception and Maternal and Newborn Health, 2017." Fact sheet. Guttmacher Institute, New York. https://www .guttmacher.org/fact-sheet/adding-it-up-contraception-mnh-2017.

May, John F. 2012. *World Population Policies: Their Origin, Evolution, and Impact.* Dordrecht Netherlands; New York: Springer.

Ross, John, and John Stover. 2013. "Use of Modern Contraception Increases When More Methods Become Available: Analysis of Evidence from 1982–2009." *Global Health Science and Practice* 1 (2): 203–12.

WHO (World Health Organization). 2017. "Family Planning Evidence Brief: Expanding Contraceptive Choice." WHO, Geneva. https://apps.who.int/iris/handle/10665/255865.

Progress to Date on EPIP 2015–2020

This appendix details the progress in implementing activities and achieving the targets for each of the five axes under the first goal of the Egypt First Five-Year Population Implementation Plan 2015–2020 (EPIP 2015–2020). This goal aims to reduce population growth rates, with a focus on fertility. Progress in activities is based mainly on the results of an unpublished evaluation by the National Population Council (NPC), conducted by independent consultants for NPC, and on a published paper (in Arabic) of a study conducted by the Egyptian Center for Economic Studies (Dawood and Abdel Latif 2019). Progress against the targets was measured using quantitative data in national statistics and data in the above two studies. The assessment period was generally 2015–18.

A.1 FAMILY PLANNING AND REPRODUCTIVE HEALTH

The first axis, Family Planning and Reproductive Health, is the most critical one for reducing fertility in the Arab Republic of Egypt. Although ENPS 2015–2030 and EPIP 2015–2020 stress multisectoral cooperation in engaging national stakeholders to achieve the objectives under this axis, the Ministry of Health and Population (MOHP) has the largest share of responsibilities and activities, with a few being conducted jointly with the NPC.

Specifically, in terms of multisectoral cooperation, this axis aims to promote cooperation with the Ministry of Communications and Information Technology, the Ministry of Planning and Economic Development, and the Ministry of Finance, especially in the field of developing databases and information systems, developing and equipping the main warehouses and linking them electronically, and allocating land for building primary health care units (PHCUs). EPIP 2015–2020 also considers cooperation with the Ministry of Higher Education and with schools of medicine for training and capacity building. The General Information Authority, the Ministry of Religious Endowment, and the Ministry of Information have also been involved in organizing media meetings, led by the NPC. The axis also defines partnership between the Ministry of Planning and Economic Development, civil society organizations, the private sector, and the Social Fund for Development to ensure the integrity of the services and to provide the means and outlets for service provision at the national level.

The budget for this axis in EPIP 2015–2020 is estimated at LE 561,695,130 annually for all activities (2.2 percent of the total budget for all activities) and LE 446,123,220 annually for priority activities (6.2 percent of the total budget for priority activities), under the first scenario of continuing the current fertility rate (see table 2.1 in the main report).

The axis has six general objectives (table A.1). General objective 1 has nine specific objectives and general objective 5 has three specific objectives. Because the principal aim of our review was to identify progress toward reducing population growth, it focused on three general objectives (1, 2, and 4) and six specific objectives (1.1 through 1.6).

TABLE A.1 **General and specific objectives of the Family Planning and Reproductive Health axis**

	GENERAL OBJECTIVES		SPECIFIC OBJECTIVES
1.	Raise the rate of use of family planning methods from 58.5 percent to 64.0 percent within five years	1.1	Ensure availability of family planning services in primary health care units at a rate of 100 percent for five years
		1.2	Ensure availability of family planning services in 100 percent of deprived and remote places at the end of five years
		1.3	Ensure availability of family planning services through the Health Insurance Organization, the Curative Care Organization, hospitals affiliated with other sectors, and public and central hospitals, at a rate of 100 percent in the first year
		1.4	Provide adequate quantities of equipment in 100 percent of clinics in all sectors, according to the standards
		1.5	Raise the skills and capabilities of service providers 100 percent according to standards annually in all service delivery outlets
		1.6	Reduce the gap between knowledge and practice to reduce unmet need within five years
		1.7	Add some reproductive health services to family planning services
		1.8	Activate the family medicine system that provides the basic package of services, including reproductive health services
		1.9	Accredit family planning, maternal, and childcare clinics to provide services, especially in deprived areas
2.	Amend legislation, laws, and regulations in line with constitutional rights and Egypt's ratified international obligations		
3.	Commit to apply the referral system between levels of care to the required standards in 100 percent of the primary care units		
4.	Provide safe maternity services and breastfeeding awareness for priority areas, especially rural and disadvantaged areas		
5.	Offer support services for HIV/AIDS patients at all levels of health care	5.1	Build research and technical capacity for HIV/AIDS
		5.2	Provide health services to HIV/AIDS patients
			Build research and technical capacity for HIV/AIDS
		5.3	Provide health services to HIV/AIDS patients
6.	Provide high-quality basic care services		

Source: EPIP 2015–2020 (in Arabic).

General objective 1: Raise the rate of use of family planning methods from 58.5 percent to 64.0 percent within five years

This general objective has three activities that focus on developing databases, raising the capabilities of statisticians, and participating in developing a central system to obtain information on family planning. Funding for these activities was either insufficient or unavailable.

Data on population and family planning (FP) are collected from the public sector using only a paper-based system at the PHCU level. Electronic registration is then done at the governorate and central levels, and this had been initiated as of the end of 2018. The sector has trained statisticians at the central and governorate levels to administer the FP program, extract reports, and analyze them. By end-2018, 38 training courses had been conducted for 580 participants.

This general objective has three indicators:

- *The rate of contraceptive use.* There have been no data on this, however, since the Egypt Demographic and Health Survey 2014 (2014 EDHS).
- *The rate at which reports are issued from the FP database, that is, monthly, quarterly, and annually, but only for the public sector and not for civil society or the private sector.*
- *The percentage of health service providers (in MOHP, nongovernmental organizations [NGOs], and the private sector) connected to the FP database.* The information for this indicator is not generally available, however, and when it is available, it is not shared.

Specific objective 1.1: Ensure availability of family planning services in primary health care units at a rate of 100 percent for five years

EPIP 2015–2020 relied on three main activities: (a) implementing FP mobile clinics where there is no doctor or FP services; (b) training nurses on dispensing hormonal methods; and (c) creating mechanisms to redistribute doctors so as to cover all PHCUs providing FP services to ensure the presence of a female doctor. Funding was available for these activities.

By the end of 2018, FP services were available in 5,109 units out of Egypt's 5,414 PHCUs (94.4 percent). However, because of a severe shortage of doctors who could provide these services, the services were often unavailable.

A small number of mobile clinics—550 throughout Egypt—operated three days a week and visited three or four areas in one working day. About 1,200 mobile visits out of a targeted 1,500 were conducted to provide FP services. However, the mobile clinics also suffered from a shortage of doctors. Further, the target of 1,500 visits in total appeared insufficient to cover all the populations in the catchment areas of the PHCUs. This low coverage is because the mobile clinics covered 9–12 areas per week, or 468–624 annually—a stark difference from the number of PHCUs, suggesting that even the target of 1,500 would not meet actual needs.

The MOHP tried to cover the shortage of doctors by assigning them to more than one area per week and contracting with retired doctors (ages 60–65 years) to provide FP services as part of the "Continue, We Want You" initiative, which has the support of the World Bank in the governorates of Upper Egypt (from Fayoum to Aswan), Sharqia, Beheira, and Qalyoubia. But as of end-2018, there was no mechanism for redistributing doctors or ensuring the presence of a female doctor in PHCUs.

In the PHCUs, nurses were assigned to provide FP services and advice and, in theory, to dispense hormonal FP methods, but by end-2018, the necessary legal and administrative measures were not in place to train nurses to dispense these FP methods.

The following shows progress made on the specific objective 1.1's two indicators:

- *Percentage of PHCUs that provide FP services in total units*. By end-2018, services were available in 94.4 percent of units. But because of the severe shortage of doctors and the small number of visits to mobile clinics relative to the number of the PHCUs without doctors, actual availability throughout the year is expected to be less than this figure.
- *Percentage of villages and communities covered by FP services* (whether PHCUs or mobile clinics). The information for this indicator for all villages and *shiakhas* (subdistricts) was not available or not shared.

Specific objective 1.2: Ensure availability of family planning services in 100 percent of deprived and remote places at the end of five years

This objective consists of six main activities: (a) allocating land for building PHCUs; (b) building 50 PHCUs in the first two years in deprived and remote areas; (c) opening 17 civil society FP clinics annually; (d) providing technical support to NGOs; (e) carrying out 60,000 mobile clinic visits annually to deprived areas; and (f) conducting reproductive health caravans (1,000 annually). While funding was available for all activities, it was insufficient to allocate land for building new PHCUs.

As of the end of 2018, there was no information on the establishment of new PHCUs in deprived and remote areas. However, 64 new NGO clinics were opened to provide FP services between 2015 and 2018. The MOHP provided these NGOs with the updated quality standards guide, and a number of NGO doctors and nurses were trained by the FP sector.

The MOHP carried out 215,000 mobile clinic visits out of a targeted 240,000 during the assessment period (90 percent of target). By the end of 2018, the MOHP had conducted 2,700 reproductive health caravans, meeting 67.5 percent of its target of 4,000 health caravans. This number points to a delay in achieving the activities.

The following shows progress made on the specific objective 1.2 indicator:

- *The percentage of availability of FP services and primary health care services in remote and deprived areas throughout the year out of the total deprived areas*. The information for this indicator was not available or not shared.

Specific objective 1.3: Ensure availability of family planning services through the Health Insurance Organization, the Curative Care Organization, hospitals affiliated with other sectors, and public and central hospitals, at a rate of 100 percent in the first year

In achieving this specific objective, EPIP 2015–2020 relied on two main activities: (a) holding meetings to establish cooperation protocols with the Health Insurance Organization (HIO) and the Curative Care Organization (CCO); and (b) creating a reproductive health and FP department in the organizational structure of the HIO. Funding was available for the first activity but not for the second.

By end-2018, 32 clinics had been opened or reactivated, including 19 FP and reproductive health services clinics in university hospitals, four clinics in police hospitals, and nine outlets in HIO hospitals and CCO. However, the proposed reproductive health and FP department within the health insurance functional structure was not introduced.

The following shows progress made on the specific objective 1.3 indicator:

- *Percentage of HIO, CCO, and general and central hospitals that provide FP services in their totals.* Data for this indicator were not available or not shared.

Specific objective 1.4: Provide adequate quantities of equipment in 100 percent of clinics in all sectors, according to the standards

There were eight activities under this specific objective: (a) determining the annual and five-year needs of the FP methods to cover demand; (b) coordinating with agencies to obtain FP methods at competitive prices; (c) holding meetings with the Supreme Committee to ensure that FP methods are available; (d) purchasing the annual needs of the FP methods; (e) supplying universities, civil society, and private clinics with the FP methods; (f) building capabilities of pharmacists and store officials to manage FP methods; (g) conducting 10 training sessions annually for warehouse officials; and (h) developing and supplying the main stores and linking them electronically. The funding for these activities was mostly insufficient or unavailable.

The need for FP methods was estimated annually and was approved by the Supreme Committee to ensure availability of FP methods. The need estimates related only to the MOHP and its affiliates, which are supplied with subsidized FP methods based on availability. The needs of the private sector and civil society are not determined by the MOHP.

A special budget for the purchase of FP methods comes from the national general budget. Also, during the assessment period some support was provided for the purchase of FP methods, particularly long-acting ones (IUDs and hypodermic capsules) provided through donors such as UNFPA and the World Bank. There was also a tendency to increase the local manufacturing of FP methods such as pills and single injectables by the state-owned national Arab Company for Drug Industries and Medical Appliances to reduce costs.

The MOHP held multiple training courses for pharmacists and warehouse officials on stock management of FP methods. The MOHP supplied 152 stores in 15 governorates after 2015 with the necessary equipment, but the electronic capability of the stores had not been developed by end-2018.

The following shows progress made on the specific objective 1.4 indicator:

- *Percentage of available FP methods for all service delivery outlets during the year.* FP methods were provided to 100 percent of MOHP outlets based on availability. The FP methods were provided to some of the MOHP affiliates, but not to civil society organizations or the private sector.

Specific objective 1.5: Raise the skills and capabilities of service providers 100 percent according to standards annually in all service delivery outlets

This specific objective has eight activities that revolved around conducting trainings, carrying out supervisory visits, and motivating distinguished service providers and supervisory teams. However, funding was only available for training supervisory teams. Funding for other activities was either not available or insufficient.

Many training courses were held in the fields specified by the FP sector at the MOHP, except the training of nurses in the medical sector and health insurance. By the end of 2018, the NPC had not trained medical and nursing students in counseling skills.

Specific objective 1.5 has three indicators, but data on them were not available (that is, not shared or not measured):

- *Percentage of service providers who can implement the standards through observational evaluation in total trained service providers.*
- *Percentage of client satisfaction with health services provided.*
- *Percentage of medical and nursing school students trained in providing counseling and FP services.*

Specific objective 1.6: Reduce the gap between knowledge and practice to reduce unmet need within five years

This specific objective has eight activities focusing on raising awareness of the public, doctors, and NGOs of the importance of FP, and on carrying out home visits. Funding was available, however, for only four activities.

The MOHP conducted several media meetings. Public meetings and media seminars were carried out in all health units and gathering places outside the health units, such as youth centers, government departments, clubs, public libraries, schools, and universities. In the first two years of the strategy, the NPC carried out 38,972 media seminars and 1,133 awareness caravans in cooperation with the directorates of health affairs in the governorates, ministries, and various stakeholders.

A total of 700 rural "female pioneers" were contracted with support of the World Bank and the Small and Micro Enterprises Authority to reduce the workload and improve coverage of services provided by these frontline workers. These female pioneers were trained under the approved curricula in the FP sector. In 2015–18, 16 million home visits were conducted annually, fewer than the targeted 21.6 million (74 percent of the target).

Specific objective 1.6 has three indicators:

- *Percentage of unmet need for FP.* This indicator has not been measured since the 2014 EDHS. However, a study conducted by NPC in collaboration with the Faculty of Medicine of Ain Shams University in 2017 demonstrated high unmet need for FP in the following areas: Sharqia (20.8 percent), Ismailia (15.6 percent), Beheira (20.9 percent), Menia (23.1 percent), Assiut (15.2 percent), and Sohag (14.9 percent) (NPC and Ain Shams University 2017).
- *Percentage of health education, as shown by the share of workers passing the FP health message test.* Data on this indicator were not available, not shared, or not measured.
- *Percentage of women who know the importance of FP and basic information on reproductive health (of the total number of women surveyed).* Data on this indicator were not available, not shared, or not measured.

General objective 2: Amend legislation, laws, and regulations in line with constitutional rights and Egypt's ratified international obligations

For this general objective, EPIP 2015–2020 relied on four activities: (a) participating in the development of the health system in line with the population's needs; (b) holding meetings and workshops to review, amend, and complete the legislation; (c) holding workshops to look into legislation related to premarital testing; and (d) completing the system of legislation and mechanisms for providing preventive, curative, and psychological services for children ages 12–18 years. Funding for these activities was unavailable.

No information was documented that could provide any clues on whether any of these activities were conducted or not. However, there were some positive steps with related legislative actions, including amendments to the female genital mutilation law of 2016 and the child marriage law of 2018.

General objective 2 has three indicators, but for the first one, information was not available or not shared, and for the last two, data were not available, not shared, or not measured:

- *Assessment of the extent of compatibility of health-related laws with the human rights approach to reproductive health within the framework of international agreements.*
- *Percentage of spouses who underwent premarital testing with all its components (including for Hepatitis B virus, Hepatitis C virus, human immunodeficiency virus, and sickle-cell anemia).*
- *The number of units and clinics that provide preventive, curative, and psychological services for children ages 12–18 years.*

General objective 4: Provide safe maternity services and breastfeeding awareness for priority areas, especially rural and disadvantaged areas

This general objective has six activities that focus on FP services within the reproductive health care package and surveillance systems. Funding for all activities was insufficient, and there was no information on the progress of these activities.

General objective 4 has four indicators, but for the first two data were not available (that is, not shared or not measured) at the program level, and for the last two data were not available at any level:

- *Percentage of mothers in rural and deprived areas who exclusively breastfeed their children in the total number of mothers in the same area or governorate.* This indicator has not been measured at the national level since the 2014 EDHS.
- *Percentage of women who used postpartum care in their last childbirth in the total number of women.* This indicator has not been measured at the national level since the 2014 EDHS.
- *Number of governorates implementing the surveillance system for maternal deaths.*
- *Number of governorates implementing the surveillance system for newborns.*

A.2 ADOLESCENT AND YOUTH HEALTH

Engaging adolescents and youth is vital for controlling population growth. Developing their skills for the workplace has a clear and direct impact on their behaviors, attitudes, and beliefs, which in turn are reflected in their fertility preferences.

Under ENPS 2015–2030 and EPIP 2015–2020, this axis mainly focuses on intersectoral action and the partnership between various stakeholders, either as main implementing agencies or participating agencies, including ministries, the public sector, academia, and civil society.

The budget for this axis under the first scenario in EPIP 2015–2020 (see table 2.1 in the main report) is estimated at LE 3,116,196,460 annually for all activities (12.4 percent of the total budget for all activities) and LE 3,081,206,165 annually for priority activities (42.6 percent of the total budget for priority activities).

The axis has seven general objectives (see table 2.2 in the main report), but because the focus is on the first goal under EPIP 2015–2020—that is, to reduce population growth rates—this assessment concentrates on general objectives 2, 4, 5, 6, and 7.

General objective 2: Reduce the unemployment rate by 5 percent within five years, by 1 percent annually

This general objective has 11 activities, which can be summarized under the following four groups: (a) preparing a population map, (b) developing and modernizing operating offices, (c) holding training courses, and (d) providing a supportive environment for better job opportunities. Financial resources were not available or were insufficient for five activities. There was also no documented or shared information on the progress of these activities.

General objective 2 has four indicators, but data are not available, not shared, or not measured:

- *Percentage of unemployment in the total labor force in the 18–35 age group.*
- *Number of villages and* shiakhas *(subdistricts) with a single product.*
- *The rate of increase in youth lending over previous years.*
- *Number of youth entrepreneurship links.*

However, data on unemployment are available from other sources. Specifically, the unemployment rate among ages 15–24 years, as provided in the World Development Indicators database, fell by around 21.8 percent between 2015 and 2018 (figure A.1). However, this average hides a key gender disparity in Egypt's labor market: the drop was led by a decline in male unemployment in this age group, which fell by 40 percent, but there was an increase in the female unemployment rate of around 34.7 percent in the same period. Youth still suffer from high unemployment, and young women have less opportunity than young men to join the labor force. Further, the survey conducted by CAPMAS and Ain Shams University in 2017 revealed many differences in the youth unemployment rates among the six surveyed governorates, ranging from 12.5 percent in Sharqia to 2 percent in Ismailia (figure A.2) (NPC and Ain Shams University 2017).

General objective 4: Reduce the rate of child labor working in the labor market from 9 percent to 4 percent within five years

This general objective relied on four activities to decrease the rate of child labor through training, workshops, seminars, and legislation, as well as by establishing a monitoring mechanism. Funding was only available for workshops and seminars.

Though the progress on activities under this objective could not be monitored, efforts have been made to reduce the child labor rate. For example, the

FIGURE A.1

Trends in the youth unemployment rate, 15–24 years, 2015–18

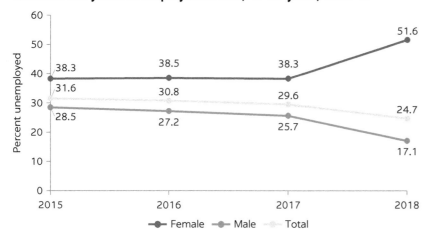

Source: World Development Indicators Database, https://datacatalog.worldbank.org/dataset /world-development-indicators.

FIGURE A.2

Youth unemployment rate in six governorates, 2017

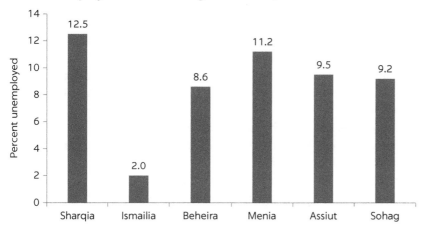

Source: NPC and Ain Shams University 2017.

Ministry of Manpower, with the International Labour Organization (ILO), organized training programs on occupational safety for health inspectors, child labor inspectors, and the vocational training department. The program trained 911 inspectors on the ILO's International Labor Standards between November 2013 and March 2018. Although this program is consistent with the activities in EPIP 2015–2020, it was not implemented within the framework of ENPS 2015–2030.

The National Council for Childhood and Motherhood launched the National Strategy for Childhood and Motherhood (2018–2030) in March 2018, which includes activities to combat child labor. However, there were no mechanisms by the end of 2018 to monitor child labor as planned in ENPS 2015–2030. In June 2018, the Ministry of Manpower also launched the National Action Plan for the Elimination of Child Labor in Egypt 2018–2025. In July 2018, the National Council for Childhood and Motherhood agreed with CAPMAS to conduct a national study on the prevalence of child labor, although this has still to be carried out.

General objective 4 has one indicator:

- *Child labor rate.*

According to the National Child Labour Survey, which was conducted by CAPMAS and the International Program for the Elimination of Child Labor (IPEC) in 2010, 1.6 million children ages 12–17 were working in Egypt, or 9.3 percent of the children in the country (IPEC and CAPMAS 2012). This already high rate is estimated to have increased to about 11 percent by 2014 (MOHP, El-Zanaty and Associates, and ICF International 2015). Although there are no more recent national figures, a 2017 survey conducted by NPC and Ain Shams University showed child labor among six governorates ranging from 1.7 percent in Ismailia, 2.8 percent in Beheira, 2.9 percent in Sohag, 3.0 percent in Menia, 5.4 percent in Assiut, to 7.7 percent in Sharqia (NPC and Ain Shams University 2017).

General objective 5: Increase the percentage of correct concepts on reproductive and sexual health among youth and adolescents (18–35 years) by 10 percent annually for a period of five years

This general objective consists of 12 activities addressing sexual and reproductive health (SRH) awareness among young people ages 18–35 years. It focuses on preparing comprehensive curricula, providing services, and training youth, as well as adding an educational component in medical curricula. Funding is largely insufficient or unavailable.

In 2016, the NPC launched a two-year outreach program with the United Nations Children's Fund (UNICEF) called the University Pioneer Initiative, to enable 100 students from 12 public universities to communicate with the surrounding community in the 86 areas identified by the NPC as the most in need of raising awareness. The universities were Zagazig, Benha, Tanta, Mansoura, Menoufia, Cairo, Ain Shams, Fayoum, Beni Suef, Menia, Assiut, and El-Wadi El-Gedid. Training of trainers was conducted for 48 university professors in the field of public health, who then trained 1,200 students.

In 2017, the second phase—the Egypt Youth Initiative—was launched. During this phase, 300 young people were selected to conduct community awareness in the governorates of the 12 universities. The Ministry of Youth and Sports cooperated with the NPC to train trainers and doctors on FP and SRH, but this partnership was interrupted as a result of limited financial and human resources.

Several other programs and initiatives were directed toward youth but lay outside the EPIP 2015–2020 framework of activities and are thus not discussed.

General objective 5 has two indicators, but progress cannot be monitored on either of them:

- *Frequency rate at youth-friendly clinics compared with previous years.*
- *Percentage of spouses who underwent premarital testing with all its components.*

General objective 6: Increase youth participation in developing policies and decisions regarding population policies in their communities, and monitoring their implementation, by 50 percent

This general objective has four activities that focus on training youth and engaging them in regional population councils. Funding was available for only two activities.

The NPC is, in theory, the body responsible for increasing youth participation in formulating and monitoring population policies in local communities. But in practice, it has not taken any steps to integrate youth in formulating, monitoring, or making decisions on population issues. For example, according to ENPS 2015–2030, a mechanism for youth representation in regional population councils should have been established by 2017, but as of the end of 2018, this had not materialized. The executive plan for EPIP 2015–2020 also stipulated that the NPC should organize workshops and civic education programs in youth centers to qualify a group of young people as ambassadors for dialogue, but it is the Ministry of Youth and Sports (MOYS) that plays this role, in a limited way.

According to the 2014 constitution, 25 percent of the seats in residents' local councils are reserved for youth. As a result, the Ministry of Social Solidarity, in partnership with the MOYS, the Ministry of Local Development, and 80 civil society organizations, embarked on the "Our Future is in Our Hands" initiative to build the capacities of youth to participate and assume leadership positions in the public sector in general and the local administration in particular. From 2015 to 2017, 37,925 young persons were trained in 27 governorates, and 3.8 million citizens were educated about the importance of youth integration. Beginning in 2015, the Egyptian government launched a series of initiatives to enhance youth participation in policy formulation and monitoring and in decision making. The first initiative was the "Presidential Program for Youth Leadership Qualification," and 1,000 young men and women had graduated from this program by October 2018. These two initiatives are, however, outside the EPIP 2015–2020 framework of activities.

General objective 6 has one indicator, but progress cannot be monitored on it:

- *Percentage of youth in the age group 18–35 years participating in regional population councils.*

General objective 7: Establish mechanisms for youth participation in addressing social issues, and increasing volunteer rates by 15 percent annually

This general objective has six activities to expand youth initiatives, support community development, and build capacity among NGOs and academia. Funding was only available to conduct capacity-building workshops and was either unavailable or insufficient for the other activities.

The MOYS supports 493 volunteer clubs within youth centers in 27 governorates. The role of these clubs is to involve young people in their communities by mobilizing them as volunteers and training them to become teachers in illiteracy classes, as well as organizing awareness seminars on community values and behaviors, fighting corruption, and discussing extremist ideologies. There is no evidence that these clubs hold seminars on issues related to population and SRH, or that they engage young people in dialogue on population issues.

General objective 7 has three indicators, but progress cannot be monitored on any of them:

- *The percentage of volunteers ages 18–35 years.*
- *Number of youth-led initiatives to address social issues related to reproductive health.*
- *Number of initiatives in which population and reproductive health messages were integrated by youth.*

A.3 EDUCATION

Education is one of the most important factors related to fertility. Education is strongly correlated with greater voice and agency, especially for women, which can translate into more power to control their own lives in terms of freedom to choose a spouse, decide family size, make decisions about when they want to have their first child, and adopt a culture of spacing between one child and the next.

This axis is mainly under the leadership of the Ministry of Education and Technical Education (MOETE) in coordination with the NPC, as well as other government sectors, civil society, and the private sector. The budget for this axis in EPIP 2015–2020 is estimated at LE 15,581,046,480 (62.2 percent of the total budget for all activities) and LE 3,614,327,620 (50 percent of the total budget for priority activities).

EPIP 2015–2020 has six general objectives for this axis (see table 2.2 in the main report). As this analysis focuses on population growth, only general objectives 1, 2, 3, 4, and 6 are discussed.

General objective 1: Integrate population issues into the educational process in its various types

This general objective has 15 activities, but funding was unavailable or insufficient for all of them. The activities include developing school curricula and building capacity of those in charge of the educational process (teachers and social workers) in all types and stages of education on population issues. Because of a paucity of information on progress achieved, the following are the only documented activities.

After the start of EPIP 2015–2020, the NPC formed a joint committee with MOETE to review textbooks in the Arabic language, social studies, and national education subjects with the aim of including population concepts before the start of the 2015/16 academic year. Yet given the lack of financial resources, the only result of the committee's work was to correct some demographic data and some paragraphs, and to include more pictures of girls in schoolbooks.

The MOETE created a "demographic educational bag," which is a number of stories and games related to population issues, in addition to an educational guide for students and those dealing with children; but once again, because of the lack of financial resources, the bag was neither printed nor distributed to schools.

The Equal Opportunities Unit has been created within MOETE and the Ministry of Culture. The unit carried out extracurricular activities to consolidate the concepts of the NPC, including population messages to educate against female genital mutilation and to halt early marriage, as well as to launch the NPC initiatives "I am against bullying" and "My daughter." However, financial resources were not sufficient to print the developed stories and distribute them.

The Ministry of Higher Education added population issues as part of the curricula of 41 educational institutions. Curricula were distributed over most of the governorates in the faculties of social service and the departments of social service in the faculties of arts, as well as in private intermediate and higher institutes and technological faculties.

The Public Authority for Adult Education requested technical support from the NPC to review, develop, and approve its population curriculum and the messages developed in 2009/10 in partnership with the NPC and MOHP, with financial support from the United States Agency for International Development (USAID). This curriculum is intended to train trainers and facilitators, as well as print guidebooks (the teacher book and the student book). The duration of the program is six months, with an average of four days per week and three hours per academic day. However, by end-2018, there was still no progress.

General objective 1 has three indicators, but progress to date cannot be monitored on any of them:

- *The percentage of students who know the risks of overpopulation, aspects of population characteristics, and changing perceptions of family shape and size.*
- *Percentage of teachers familiar with population issues and the ability to discuss them.*
- *Percentage of teachers who can play an advisory role in population and health issues.*

General objective 2: Increase the rate of enrollment in education from 93.4 to 100 percent

This general objective has seven activities aimed at increasing the chances of compulsory and community education enrollment by increasing the number of schools to fully accommodate children and dropouts. The funding for these activities was either unavailable or insufficient.

According to the MOETE strategy, the ministry launched a national project to build and operate language schools in partnership with the private sector in accordance with the provisions of Law 67 of 2010. The strategy also aimed at increasing the share of students enrolled in community schools, so the MOETE is working to increase the number of community schools (covering community schools, girl-friendly schools, and schools for children in difficult conditions).

General objective 2 has two indicators:

- *Percentage enrollment in compulsory education.* EPIP 2015–2020 aimed at increasing the enrollment rate in compulsory education, which requires increasing the number of schools, especially in primary education, to accommodate the increase in students. The overall net enrollment rate (figure A.3) has achieved the target for primary education, but the figure for preparatory (lower secondary) education is less than the target (85 percent) and is unacceptably low for secondary education (28 percent). The net enrollment rate is higher for girls than boys at all educational levels (MOETE 2020). The number of schools, classes, and students increased between 2015/16 and 2019/20 in the main pre-university education levels (table A.2). MOETE statistics show that the number of schools increased by 4,547 at all educational levels,

FIGURE A.3

Net enrollment rate, 2019/20

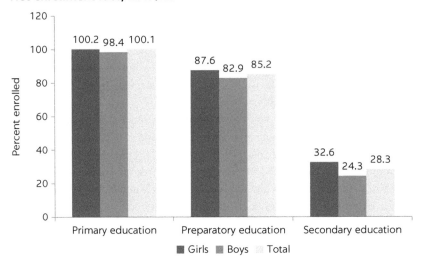

Source: MOETE 2020.

TABLE A.2 **Total number of schools, classes, and students, 2015/16 and 2019/20**

		2015/16	2019/20
Primary	Schools	18,085	19,059
	Classes	234,441	253,339
	Students	10,638,860	12,820,294
Preparatory	Schools	11,466	12,611
	Classes	109,189	112,374
	Students	4,630,636	5,238,908
General secondary	Schools	3,235	3,861
	Classes	39,856	44,499
	Students	1,576,336	1,819,497
	Density	40	41
Other secondary	Schools	2,150	2,472
	Classes	46,517	49,377
	Students	1,710,686	2,053,505

Source: MOETE 2020.

with an increase of 35,603 classes accommodating 3,637,473 more pupils from 2015/16 to 2019/20 (MOETE 2020). However, this increase was not enough to reduce class density (the number of students per class). While private schools managed to keep a steady class density of 32–34 students, there was an increase in class density in government schools from 43 in 2015/16 to 48 in 2019/20 (figure A.4). Class density showed an increasing trend in both rural and urban areas, with class density always higher in rural areas (figure A.5).

- *Percentage enrollment in community schools.* According to MOETE statistics, the number of community schools or classes decreased by 88 schools or classes alongside an increase of 18,753 students between 2015/16 and 2019/20, increasing class density from 23 in 2015/16 to 27 in 2019/20 (table A.3).

FIGURE A.4

Trends in class density by affiliation of schools, 2015/16–2019/20

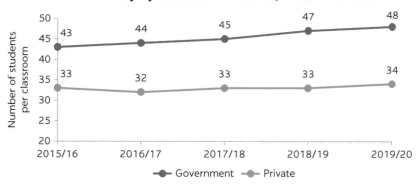

Source: MOETE 2020.

FIGURE A.5

Trends in class density by place of schools, 2015/16–2019/20

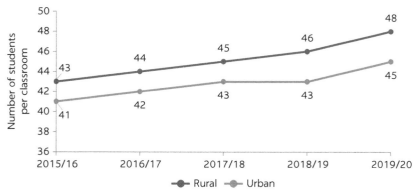

Source: MOETE 2020.

TABLE A.3 **Total number of community schools, classes, and students, 2015/16 and 2019/20**

	2015/16	2019/20
Schools or classes	5,083	4,995
Students	114,939	133,692
Density	23	27

Source: MOETE 2020.

General objective 3: Reduce the percentage of dropouts from education to 0 percent and provide them with a quality educational service as a second chance

This objective has six activities, including reviewing and amending legislation, reviewing the standards for measuring dropout rates, building capacities of those dealing with children exposed to dropping out, and ensuring availability of health care workers in schools to halt school dropouts. The activities also stipulate a feeding program and provision of educational scholarships to the poor. Financial resources were available for four of the six activities.

The only documented information is on the school feeding program. The MOETE reported that the number of students benefiting from the school feeding program at all levels of education in academic year 2017/18 was 11.2 million (54 percent), with financial expenditure of about LE 1 billion.

General objective 3 has one indicator:

- *Dropout rate.* The baseline for this indicator was taken from the results of the 2006 census, which showed a dropout rate of 2.6 percent for ages 6–18 years. The 2017 census showed a dropout rate of 7.3 percent for children ages 4 years and above (CAPMAS 2017). MOETE statistics for 2018/19 indicate a dropout rate of 0.25 percent for primary education and 2 percent for secondary education (MOETE 2020). The dropout rate was slightly higher for boys than girls at the two educational levels. Although there are differences in the age group used to calculate dropout rates across the various sources, not much progress has been made on this indicator. Further, the geographic inequalities in school dropouts are high, with a relative index of dissimilarity of 24.2 percent. According to the 2017 census (CAPMAS 2017), the governorates can be classified based on the risk of exposure and concentration of dropouts (see figures 3.10 and 3.11 in the main report) as follows:
  - In five governorates (Damietta, Gharbia, Qena, Aswan, and Matrouh) the risk and concentration of dropouts is high. This means that the education services are not reaching children in these governorates or are irresponsive to their needs.
  - In 10 governorates (Alexandria, Dakahlia, Qalyoubia, Menoufia, Beheira, Ismailia, Sohag, Luxor, Red Sea, and South Sinai) the risk of dropouts is high, but the concentration is less than expected. The education services seem to be reaching the children in these governorates.
  - In five governorates (Beni Suef, Fayoum, Menia, Assiut, and El-Wadi El-Gedid) the risk of dropouts is low, but the concentration is high as the observed distribution exceeds the expected population distribution for the same age group. This shows that children in these governorates are not at increased risk of school dropout, but the education services are lacking and irresponsive to their needs.
  - Seven governorates (Cairo, Port Said, Suez, Sharqia, Kafr El-Sheikh, Giza, and North Sinai) have school dropouts below the national average, and the observed distribution is less than expected. This means that children in these governorates are not at increased risk of school dropout, and the education services are responsive to their needs.

General objective 4: Reduce the illiteracy rate from 21.7 percent to 7.0 percent

This objective has seven activities, including establishing a literacy database for the age group 15–35 years, and activating the role of the branches of the General Authority for Literacy in the governorates to eradicate illiteracy among 3.5 million people. Financial resources were unavailable for most of the activities.

Several institutions have illiteracy databases, including the CAPMAS database, the Ministry of Social Solidarity Takamul and Karama program database, and the database for rural women leaders. However, these institutions do not share their databases with each other because of concerns about confidentiality.

The responsibility for adult literacy at the national level rests within the Public Authority for Adult Education, which cooperates with many institutions, ministries, NGOs, universities, and the Social Fund, as well as the Ministry of Religious Endowment, the Ministry of Local Development, the Ministry of Youth and Sports, the MOETE, and others. The Public Authority for Adult Education, in cooperation with the above ministries, has 10 educational curricula for trainers and students, but no information is available on progress.

General objective 4 has one indicator:

- *Illiteracy rate*. According to the 2017 census, the illiteracy rate is 25.8 percent for those ages 10 years and above; that is, no progress has been made on this indicator (CAPMAS 2017). This can be potentially attributed to the reduction in the number of community schools and classes (see table A.3). The illiteracy rate was higher among females than males except in Damietta, where it was about the same. The illiteracy rate exceeded the national average in nine governorates—Kafr El-Sheikh, Beheira, Beni Suef, Fayoum, Menia, Assiut, Sohag, Qena, and Matrouh (see figure 3.14 in the main report). There were no data to allow for assessing distributions.

General objective 6: Reaching religious leaders capable of updating religious discourse and addressing population issues

Given the influential role of religious leaders on the education of the nation and on the society in which they live, this general objective's activities include training and meeting with religious leaders to raise awareness about population issues, to provide them "training for trainers," and to advocate for reducing fertility. Financial resources were not available for three of the five activities.

According to its published list of training reports, the International Islamic Center for Population Studies and Research of Al-Azhar University[1] had conducted several training programs by the end of 2019. Most of these courses focused on women's health rather than population issues. The last training course, held in December 2019, was attended by 46 trainees from 14 governorates and had a general reproductive health focus (UNFPA 2019).

General objective 6 has one indicator, but progress on it cannot be monitored:

- *The rate of increase in the awareness of female imams of the importance of population issues following training.*

A.4 COMMUNICATION AND SOCIAL MEDIA

This axis has two main goals: to increase media coverage and to mobilize people. General objective 1 on media coverage (see table 2.2 in the main report) has four specific objectives.

Main implementing partners include the MOP (now the NPC), the Ministry of Culture, the State Information Service, the Radio and Television Union, Al-Azhar, the Ministry of Awkaf (Religious Endowments), the Church, the Ministry of Agriculture, and civil society.

The budget for this axis is estimated at LE 29,807,350 (0.1 percent of the total budget for all activities) and LE 67,532,410 (0.9 percent of the total budget for priority activities).

The analysis focuses on three specific objectives (1, 3, and 4) as they are related to the first goal of EPIP 2015–2020, to reduce population growth rates.

General objective 1: Increase media materials that include population issues in various media

This general objective has no overarching activities but includes four specific objectives with defined activities, three of which are discussed here (1.1, 1.3, and 1.4).

Specific objective 1.1: Benefiting from previously prepared informational materials

This specific objective has three activities that relate mainly to searching, compiling, reviewing, and redisseminating previous materials addressing the population issue. Funding was mostly unavailable or insufficient for these activities.

There was no concrete information to document the activities implemented under this objective, but there are scattered media materials referred to in unpublished reports. The available information documents that 26 advertisements and radio episodes included messages on the benefits of slowing population growth. The radio episodes, including those on FP, were converted into an animation video and disseminated on social media aired in the month of Ramadan for two seasons. The rough total of what was counted in the newspapers on population issues was 1,173 news items for 2018 (according to an NPC unpublished report). The Media Observatory of the National Council for Women (NCW) published 145 dialogues in various media outlets, and 225 news stories were covered by the press, magazines, websites, and on Facebook pages. The NCW issued 106 press releases aimed to improve the position of women. In addition, the Family Planning Media Group has a Facebook page, and an FP media channel has been launched on YouTube to display videos, messages, and alerts for the "My Health" channel episodes.

The Egyptian Youth Initiative printed marketing material on FP, including around 8,000 educational brochures, 500 health guides, and 240 posters. The MOHP produced posters on five subjects, and a women's guide with two brochures on FP was distributed to families and advocates during their training courses. Six thousand copies of a revised guide were printed, along with posters to promote the Egyptian Youth Initiative.

The Ministry of Religious Endowment issued several books, other publications, and a trainee's guide on the population challenge. However, messages were not specific to FP and increased fertility.

Specific objective 1.1 has one indicator:

- *The number of television and radio hours broadcasting information materials on population issues.* The total number of hours devoted to addressing population issues on television and radio through the end of 2018 was very low, at about 137 hours; that is, it averages 46 hours a year, or almost 4 hours a month. This was further split up as 77 television hours (56.2 percent) and 60 radio hours (43.8 percent). Population growth was dealt with from different aspects, but with a focus on issues of youth unemployment, housing, violence against women and girls, and street children.

Specific objective 1.3: Preparing specialized media cadres that adopt population issues

This specific objective has two activities, including holding a conference every two years and building capacities of media professionals on population issues. Funding for these activities was mainly unavailable or insufficient.

In 2018, UNFPA, with the European Union (EU) and the Ministry of Youth and Sports, celebrated National Population Day with a 5-kilometer run in Alexandria to boost visibility around the issue.

The NCW trained 20 people on how to prepare the population media messages. Media officials were trained in social communication on behavioral change with support from USAID. The NCW conducted training and awareness-raising meetings for media professionals on the role of the media in changing the negative image of women. The NCW drew up a media honor charter to address the image of women in the media and stop advertisements that are offensive to women. The NCW also analyzed the image of women in the Ramadan drama. About 300 male and female students from the Faculties of Media and the Faculties of Arts took training courses to analyze the results.

Specific objective 1.3 has one indicator:

- *The number of interviews given annually by the most-watched talk-show programs on overpopulation.* This indicator does not reflect activities, and no information is available to document progress.

Specific objective 1.4: Displaying media materials, tracking viewership rates, and analyzing results

This specific objective has four activities that include dissemination of messages and monitoring of viewership rates, capacity building for viewership monitoring rates, and review of laws to provide in-kind incentives to media channels. Funding was mostly unavailable or insufficient for the activities.

Specific objective 1.4 has one indicator, but no baseline was determined, and progress could not be monitored because of a lack of information:

- *The percentage of viewership of programs and media materials that affect the population issue.*

General objective 2: Increase mass mobilization to support the population issue

This general objective has 10 activities that focus on raising awareness about population challenges using different dissemination channels and building monitoring capacities. Funding was available for six out of 10 activities.

Several activities were carried out by the NPC, MOHP, MOETE, Ministry of Religious Endowment, Ministry of Agriculture, and NCW. However, these activities focused on FP and reproductive health issues, early age of marriage, and violence against women and girls.

General objective 2 has two indicators, but no baseline was specified, and no information was available to monitor progress for either:

- *Average number of mentions, number of channels that broadcast, and rate of increase each year.*
- *Average ideal number of children from the point of view of women and men in the age group 15–49 (nationally and by geographic area).*

A.5 EMPOWERMENT OF WOMEN

The empowerment of women affects fertility. It can help women improve the quality of their lives, avoid negative gender norms, and make decisions on the number of children they want.

The main implementing agencies include the NCW and some bodies such as the NPC, as well as several ministries and government agencies, as main or participating partners. Civil society was also a partner. The budget for this axis is estimated at LE 5,716,787,630 (22.8 percent of the total budget for all activities) and LE 8,682,380 (0.1 percent of the total budget for priority activities).

For this axis, EPIP 2015–2020 has 10 main objectives (see table 2.2 in the main report). Because the primary focus is on the EPIP 2015–2020 first goal, to reduce population growth rates, with a focus on fertility, this analysis considered objectives 1, 3, 5, and 10.

General objective 1: Increase the percentage of women's participation in the workforce from 23 percent to 35 percent

This general objective has three activities, which include building the capabilities of female workers in the government sector, publishing research and studies estimating the economic cost resulting from discrimination against women, and spreading the culture of the positive role of women in the labor market. However, funding for these activities was unavailable or insufficient.

The NCW made huge efforts in training and activities, but they were not linked to EPIP 2015–2020 activities. Several field campaigns targeted large numbers of women, but the results of the evaluations were not made available. The NPC's unpublished evaluation report points to a cost-benefit analysis of Egyptian FP in 2015 (Nassar and Fouad 2015), but the study was not linked to EPIP 2015–2020 research activities.

General objective 1 has one indicator:

- *Percentage of women's participation in the workforce.* The participation rate increased from 75.8 percent in 2015 to 78.6 percent in 2018 (figure A.6). Yet women's share of the labor force remained lower than men's in 2015–18.

FIGURE A.6

Percentage of working population (percentage of labor force) by sex, 2015–18

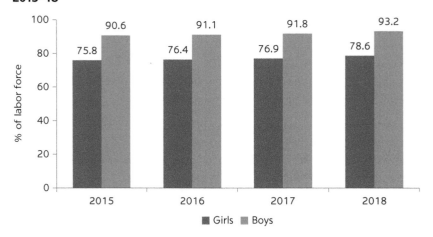

Source: CAPMAS 2020.

General objective 3: Inclusion of equal opportunity units in ministries' administrative structure, increasing their number from 26 units to 32, and increasing awareness toward equality

This general objective has three activities, including establishing equal opportunity units in the remaining ministries and including them in the administrative structure, as well as improving awareness of gender equality in all governorates.

There is no information on the achievement of these activities.

Objective 3 has one indicator:

- *Number of equal opportunity units in ministries.* The baseline was to increase the number of such units from 26 to 32. Yet, the Ministry of Local Development authorized the establishment of only 23 units.

General objective 5: Reducing the rate of female unemployment in rural areas from 20.2 percent to 15.0 percent

This general objective has three activities that can be summarized as developing villages and providing training opportunities to create an enabling environment for rural women to work. There was no information available to monitor progress on these activities.

General objective 5 has one indicator:

- *Rate of female unemployment in rural areas.* Data on this indicator were not available, however, and the overall unemployment rate was used as a proxy. The overall rate in 2015 was 24.2 percent for females and 9.4 percent for males, compared with 21.4 percent for females and 6.8 percent in males in 2018 (table 3.4 in the main report). Thus, the reduction in the female rate was much less (11.6 percent) than the male rate (27.7 percent). In 2018, the same pattern was seen in all Egyptian governorates. Further, in eight governorates (Cairo, Suez, Damietta, Giza, Assiut, Aswan, Red Sea, and North Sinai), unemployment for both females and males was higher than the national average for both sexes; in seven governorates (Port Said, Dakahlia, Beheira, Ismailia, Qena, Luxor, and Matrouh), female unemployment was higher than the national average for females; and in three governorates (Alexandria, Qalyoubia, and Gharbia), male unemployment was higher than the national average for males. The distributions of female and male unemployment (compared with female and male labor force distributions, respectively) confirm that for both females and males (figures 3.12 and 3.13 in the main report), unemployment is concentrated in governorates where the rates are above the national average. Unemployment is clearly a shared challenge for both women and men in many governorates, and efforts to address it are not responding to people's needs (Sanad, Kalil, and Beddah 2019).

General objective 10: Reducing early age at marriage by 25 percent within five years

This general objective has five activities, including raising awareness and building an environment that works against early age of marriage among females. Funding was available for two activities only. Documents to illustrate progress on implanting these activities were not available.

FIGURE A.7

Percentage of marriages at ages 15–17 years by sex and urban-rural residence

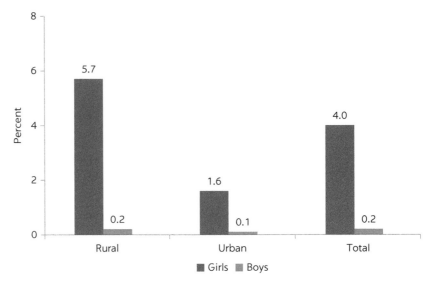

Source: CAPMAS 2017.

General objective 10 has one indicator:

- *Percentage of women 20–24 years who are married before age 18.* Data on this indicator are not available, however. In the 2014 EDHS, all age groups shared in the recent rise in fertility rates except women ages 40–49 years (MOHP, El-Zanaty and Associates, and ICF International 2015). The increase was highest among women in the 20–24 age group; fertility rose by 26 percent in this age group between the 2008 EDHS and the 2014 EDHS. Further, CAPMAS statistics in 2020 revealed that the average age at marriage did not change between 2015 and 2018, staying at 24 years for females and 30 years for males (CAPMAS 2020). However, the 2017 census showed that 4 percent of girls ages 15–17 and 0.1 percent of males in the same age group were married (CAPMAS 2017). Early age of marriage for both females and males was higher in rural than urban areas (figure A.7).

NOTES

1. The International Islamic Center for Population Studies and Research, https://alazhar-iicpsr.org/population.php?id=75. In Arabic.

REFERENCES

CAPMAS (Central Agency for Public Mobilization and Statistics). 2017. "Egypt Population, Housing, and Establishments Census 2017." Central Agency for Public Mobilization and Statistics, Cairo. In Arabic. https://www.capmas.gov.eg/party/party.html.

CAPMAS (Central Agency for Public Mobilization and Statistics). 2020. "Statistical Yearbook." December. Cairo: Central Agency for Public Mobilization and Statistics. http://www.capmas.gov.eg/.

Dawood, Ahmed, and Abla Abdel Latif. 2019. "Population Policy in Egypt: An Analysis of the Constituents for Success and the Optimal Institutional Form, a Comparative Study." Working Paper 203, Egyptian Center for Economic Studies, Cairo. http://www.eces.org.eg /cms/NewsUploads/Pdf/2019_12_8-15_45_41Working%20Paper%20203. pdf. In Arabic.

IPEC (International Program for the Elimination of Child Labor) and CAPMAS (Central Agency for Public Mobilization and Statistics). 2012. *Working Children in Egypt: Results of the 2010 National Child Labour Survey*. Cairo: International Labour Organization (ILO). https://www.ilo.org/ipecinfo/product/download.do?type=document&id=21017.

MOETE (Ministry of Education and Technical Education). 2020. "Statistical Yearbook 2019/2020." MOETE, Cairo. http://emis.gov.eg/Site%20Content/book/019-020/main _book2020.html. In Arabic.

MOHP (Ministry of Health and Population), El-Zanaty and Associates, and ICF International. 2015. *Egypt Demographic and Health Survey, 2014*. Cairo: MOHP. https://dhsprogram.com /publications/publication-fr302-dhs-final-reports.cfm.

Nassar, Heba, and Jasmin Fouad. 2015. "Family Planning in Egypt Is a Financial Investment: Benefit-Cost Analysis of Egypt Family Planning Program, 2014–2050." Cairo: Center for Economic and Financial Research and Studies, Cairo University. https://egypt.unfpa.org /sites/default/files/pub-pdf/99fe2139-fed0-4239-a81a-4dbcede71886.pdf.

NPC (National Population Council) and Ain Shams University. 2017. "Demographic and Health Indicators in Some Governorates in the Arab Republic of Egypt." NPC in collaboration with the Community and Environment Department, Faculty of Medicine, Ain Shams University. In Arabic.

Sanad, Zakaria F., Nora Abd El-Hadi Kalil, and Eman S. El-Rahman Beddah. 2019. "Infertility and Related Risk Factors among Women Attending Rural Family Health Facilities in Menoufia Governorate." *Menoufia Medical Journal* 32 (4): 1365–70. http://www.mmj.eg.net /text.asp?2019/32/4/1365/274250.

UNFPA (United Nations Population Fund). 2019. "Activity Report Implementing Partner: IICPSR Activity's Title: Conducting Educational Seminars in Cairo for RL Including RL Students." International Islamic Center for Population Studies and Research (IICPSR), Al-Azhar University/UNFPA, Cairo. http://alazhar-iicpsr.org/azhariicpsr/uploads /Activity%20Report%20E%2021-12-2019.pdf.

Estimating Population Outcomes for a Declining TFR Scenario through 2020

Effective planning on population policy to achieve the population dividend requires in-depth demographic analysis and mathematical models to project and simulate different population structures over time for alternative scenarios resulting from different policy interventions. So, to quantify the potential savings and economic impacts for the Arab Republic of Egypt, we constructed several models using alternative scenarios to project the population trends and trajectories using Spectrum software (version 5.89) with different assumptions about the total fertility rate (TFR). Spectrum software uses the DemProj software model, which forecasts population for a country by age and sex based on assumptions about the initial population size and structure, fertility, mortality, and migration. The default scenario for the model is generated using the latest historical and projection data from the World Population Prospects of the Population Division of the United Nations (UN).

The aim of this exercise was to model population structures as if Egypt's TFR had continued the rate of its 1970–2000 decline into the trend that occurred after 2000. The model shows what the population distribution by age and sex would likely have looked like, and what would have been the probable differences with regard to the historical data observed in 2000–20.

The default scenario is defined as the projected population using the historical population in 2000 with the estimated actual TFRs for Egypt from the UN for 2000–20. The default is then compared with a hypothetical scenario in which, after 2000, the TFRs continued to decline at a rate modeled on TFRs observed during 1970–2000. The alternative TFRs for 2000–20 were produced using a time-series statistical model computed using an exponential smoothing method (table B.1).

The modeled rate of the continued fertility decline scenario was about 2.7 percent. The modeled hypothetical fertility rates are summarized in table B.2, which served as the input for the model. The fertility rates of the default scenario were preloaded by the software using historical data from the UN. The rest of the population parameters for the continued decline scenario were the same as in the default scenario, which were based on estimated historical data for the years between 2000 and 2020. Both the default population projected from 2000 using historical population parameters and the population modeled from 2000 using the alternative fertility rates were produced by the DemProj software model.

TABLE B.1 **Statistical model for producing alternative TFRs in 2009–20**

MODEL			QUALITY METRICS					SMOOTHING COEFFICIENTS		
LEVEL	TREND	SEASON	RMSE	MAE	MASE	MAPE	AIC	ALPHA	BETA	GAMMA
Multiplicative	Multiplicative	None	0.06112	0.04686	0.55	1.0%	−208	0.500	0.500	0.000

INITIAL			CHANGE FROM INITIAL	SEASONAL EFFECT		CONTRIBUTION	
2009			2009–21	High	Low	Trend	Season
2.98399	±	0.07173	−0.18643	None		100.0%	0.0%

Source: Original calculations using the DemProj software model.
Note: AIC = Akaike information criterion; MAE = mean absolute error; MAPE = mean absolute percentage error; MASE = mean absolute scaled error; RMSE = root mean squared error.

TABLE B.2 TFR, population size, dependency ratio, and working-age share of population under the actual outcome and continued decline scenario, 2000–20

YEAR	TFR ACTUAL OUTCOME	TFR CONTINUED DECLINE SCENARIO	TFR % DIFFERENCE	POPULATION SIZE ACTUAL OUTCOME	POPULATION SIZE CONTINUED DECLINE SCENARIO	POPULATION SIZE % DIFFERENCE	DEPENDENCY RATIO ACTUAL OUTCOME	DEPENDENCY RATIO CONTINUED DECLINE SCENARIO	DEPENDENCY RATIO % DIFFERENCE	WORKING-AGE SHARE OF POPULATION ACTUAL OUTCOME	WORKING-AGE SHARE OF POPULATION CONTINUED DECLINE SCENARIO	WORKING-AGE SHARE OF POPULATION % DIFFERENCE
2000	3.39	3.39	0.0	68,778,528	68,778,528	0.0	0.72	0.72	0	0.58	0.58	0
2001	3.29	3.30	0.3	70,077,976	70,084,664	0.0	0.70	0.70	0	0.59	0.59	0
2002	3.21	3.21	0.0	71,382,824	71,393,024	0.0	0.68	0.68	0	0.60	0.60	0
2003	3.15	3.13	−0.6	72,700,440	72,698,896	0.0	0.66	0.66	0	0.60	0.60	0
2004	3.11	3.04	−2.3	74,034,568	73,997,520	−0.1	0.65	0.64	0	0.61	0.61	0
2005	3.08	2.96	−3.9	75,383,728	75,283,880	−0.1	0.63	0.63	0	0.61	0.61	0
2006	3.05	2.88	−5.6	76,751,984	76,557,888	−0.3	0.62	0.62	−1	0.62	0.62	0
2007	3.03	2.80	−7.6	78,145,400	77,819,832	−0.4	0.61	0.60	−1	0.62	0.62	0
2008	3.02	2.73	−9.6	79,572,544	79,070,520	−0.6	0.60	0.59	−2	0.62	0.63	1
2009	3.06	2.65	−13.4	81,066,216	80,311,088	−0.9	0.60	0.58	−2	0.63	0.63	1
2010	3.17	2.58	−18.6	82,666,608	81,542,848	−1.4	0.60	0.58	−4	0.63	0.63	1
2011	3.30	2.51	−23.9	84,386,608	82,762,472	−1.9	0.60	0.57	−5	0.63	0.64	2
2012	3.41	2.44	−28.4	86,212,304	83,965,896	−2.6	0.60	0.56	−7	0.62	0.64	3
2013	3.45	2.38	−31.0	88,103,664	85,149,416	−3.4	0.61	0.55	−9	0.62	0.64	3
2014	3.44	2.31	−32.8	90,025,816	86,309,848	−4.1	0.61	0.55	−11	0.62	0.65	4
2015	3.42	2.25	−34.2	91,969,008	87,446,384	−4.9	0.62	0.54	−13	0.62	0.65	5
2016	3.39	2.19	−35.4	93,923,608	88,555,256	−5.7	0.62	0.53	−15	0.62	0.65	6
2017	3.36	2.13	−36.6	95,881,648	89,632,080	−6.5	0.63	0.52	−17	0.61	0.66	7
2018	3.33	2.07	−37.8	97,838,376	90,673,944	−7.3	0.63	0.51	−19	0.61	0.66	8
2019	3.30	2.02	−38.8	99,787,208	91,676,624	−8.1	0.64	0.50	−21	0.61	0.66	9
2020	3.26	1.96	−39.9	101,719,608	92,636,184	−8.9	0.64	0.50	−23	0.61	0.67	10

Source: Original calculations based on UN World Population Prospects data and Spectrum DemProj model.
Note: TFR = total fertility rate.

Estimating Forgone Savings in Public Expenditure due to Population Increase

A key approach to understanding the cost of high fertility is to assess the loss in potential savings that could have occurred as a result of fertility decline. This appendix details the methodology used to estimate such forgone savings in public expenditures during 2008–20 on health, housing, and education (three sectors) in the Arab Republic of Egypt. The approach considered costs in a retrospective manner under two scenarios: the actual outcome scenario and the continued fertility decline scenario.

Total forgone savings in public expenditure were calculated as the difference between total real public expenditure and total real retrospective expenditure and as a percentage of total public expenditure. The retrospective projections of the increase in per capita real expenditure were calculated assuming that the population size could have been reduced, and hence that per capita expenditure would have been higher, given the same expenditure level.

For all data, we relied on official Egyptian sources such as the Ministry of Finance, Information and Decision Support Center (IDSC), and the Central Agency for Public Mobilization and Statistics.

TABLE C.1 **Costs and forgone savings of health, 2007/08–2019/20**

| | INPUT DATA | | | | | | CALCULATED FIGURES | | | | | |
| | TOTAL POPULATION, MILLIONS | | | | | | REAL RETROSPECTIVE PROJECTIONS OF PUBLIC EXPENDITURE ON HEALTH | | FORGONE SAVINGS IN PUBLIC EXPENDITURE ON HEALTH | | | |
YEAR	ACTUAL OUTCOME (1)	CONTINUED FERTILITY DECLINE SCENARIO (2)	ACTUAL PUBLIC EXPENDITURE ON HEALTH (CURRENT PRICES, LE MILLIONS) (3)	GDP DEFLATOR: 2017 = 100 (4)[a]	REAL ACTUAL PUBLIC EXPENDITURE ON HEALTH (CONSTANT PRICES, LE MILLIONS) (5 = 100* (3/4))	REAL PER CAPITA ACTUAL PUBLIC EXPENDITURE ON HEALTH (CONSTANT PRICES, LE) (6 = 1000* (5/1))	CONSTANT PRICES, LE MILLIONS (7 = 2*6)	PER CAPITA ACTUAL (CONSTANT PRICES, LE) (8 = 1000* (5/2))	CONSTANT PRICES, LE MILLIONS (9 = 57)	% OF REAL ACTUAL PUBLIC EXPENDITURE ON HEALTH, LE MILLIONS) % (10 = 9/5)	CURRENT PRICES, LE MILLIONS (11 = 100* (9*4))	RETROSPECTIVE PROJECTIONS OF INCREASE IN REAL PER CAPITA PUBLIC EXPENDITURE ON HEALTH, % (12 = 100* (8-6/6))
2007/08	79.57	79.07	13,161	35.3	37,283	468.54	37,047.85	471.52	235.43	0.63	83.11	0.64
2008/09	81.07	80.31	13,495	39.2	34,426	424.67	34,105.43	428.66	320.59	0.93	125.67	0.94
2009/10	82.67	81.54	17,342	43.2	40,144	485.61	39,597.62	492.30	658.90	1.36	284.6	1.38
2010/11	84.39	82.76	20,038	48.2	41,573	492.64	40,772.30	502.31	800.31	1.93	385.75	1.96
2011/12	86.21	83.97	22,492	57.6	39,049	452.94	38,031.27	465.05	1,017.34	2.61	585.99	2.68
2012/13	88.10	85.15	26,128	62.6	41,738	473.74	40,338.33	490.17	1,399.69	3.35	876.21	3.47
2013/14	90.03	86.31	30,759	69.6	44,194	490.90	42,369.70	512.04	1,824.27	4.13	1,269.69	4.31
2014/15	91.97	87.45	37,224	76.6	48,595	528.39	46,205.61	555.72	2,389.70	4.92	1,830.51	5.17
2015/16	93.92	88.56	45,061	81.3	55,426	590.11	52,257.43	625.89	3,168.15	5.72	2,575.71	6.06
2016/17	95.88	89.63	54,123	100.0	54,123	564.48	50,595.08	603.84	3,527.92	6.52	3,527.92	6.97
2017/18	97.84	90.67	60,833	121.4	50,110	512.17	46,440.35	552.63	3,669.20	7.32	4,454.41	7.90
2018/19	99.79	91.68	73,064	138.0	52,945	530.58	48,641.73	577.52	4,303.20	8.13	5,938.41	8.85
2019/20	101.72	92.64	73,062	156.8	46,596	458.08	42,434.57	503.00	4,161.09	8.93	6,524.59	9.81
Cumulative			**586,200**				**558,837**		**27,363**		**28,414**	

Sources: Original calculations based on, for column (1), UN World Population Prospects data and Spectrum DemProj model; for column (2) for 2007/08–2018/19, https://www.mof.gov.eg/; and for column (3) for 2019/20, planned budget, https://www.mof.gov.eg/.

Note: Cumulative forgone savings in public expenditure on [this sector] in 2008–20 is calculated as $\sum_{t=2008}^{t=2020} S_t$. Forgone savings in public expenditure on [this sector] in year t (S_t) = Real actual public expenditure on [this sector] – Real retrospective projections of public expenditure on [this sector] t for year t, where $t = 2008–20$.

a. World Bank estimation of GDP deflator, 2017 = 100.

TABLE C.2 Costs and forgone savings of housing, 2007/08–2019/20

| | INPUT DATA | | | | | CALCULATED FIGURES | | | | | | |
| | TOTAL POPULATION, MILLIONS | | ACTUAL PUBLIC EXPENDITURE ON HOUSING (CURRENT PRICES, LE MILLIONS) | GDP DEFLATOR: 2017 = 100 | REAL ACTUAL PUBLIC EXPENDITURE ON HOUSING (CONSTANT PRICES, LE MILLIONS) | REAL PER CAPITA ACTUAL PUBLIC EXPENDITURE ON HOUSING (CONSTANT LE) | REAL RETROSPECTIVE PROJECTIONS OF PUBLIC EXPENDITURE ON HOUSING | | FORGONE SAVINGS IN PUBLIC EXPENDITURE ON HOUSING | | | RETROSPECTIVE PROJECTIONS OF INCREASE IN REAL PER CAPITA PUBLIC EXPENDITURE ON HOUSING, % |
YEAR	ACTUAL OUTCOME (1)	CONTINUED FERTILITY DECLINE SCENARIO (2)	(3)	(4)a	(5 = 100* (3/4))	(6 = 1000* (5/11))	CONSTANT PRICES, LE MILLIONS (7 = 2*6)	PER CAPITA ACTUAL (CONSTANT PRICES, LE) (8 = 1000* (5/2))	CONSTANT PRICES, LE MILLIONS (9 = 5-7)	% OF REAL ACTUAL PUBLIC EXPENDITURE ON HOUSING (CONSTANT PRICES, LE MILLIONS) % (10 = 9/5)	CURRENT PRICES, LE MILLIONS (11 = 100* (9*4))	(12 = 100* (8-6/6))
2007/08	79.57	79.07	13,865	35.3	39,278	493.60	39,029.59	496.74	248.03	0.63	87.55	0.64
2008/09	81.07	80.31	14,294	39.2	36,464	449.81	36,124.72	454.04	339.57	0.93	133.11	0.94
2009/10	82.67	81.54	20,342	43.2	47,088	569.61	46,447.63	577.46	640.33	1.36	276.62	1.38
2010/11	84.39	82.76	12,800	48.2	26,556	314.69	26,044.79	320.87	511.23	1.93	246.41	1.96
2011/12	86.21	83.97	11,495	57.6	19,957	231.48	19,436.66	237.68	519.93	2.61	299.48	2.68
2012/13	88.10	85.15	11,912	62.6	19,029	215.98	18,390.62	223.47	638.13	3.35	399.47	3.47
2013/14	90.03	86.31	17,363	69.6	24,947	277.11	23,917.07	289.04	1,029.77	4.13	716.72	4.31
2014/15	91.97	87.45	20,437	76.6	26,680	290.10	25,368.15	305.10	1,312.01	4.92	1,005.00	5.17
2015/16	93.92	88.56	24,922	81.3	30,654	326.37	28,902.15	346.16	1,752.22	5.72	1,424.55	6.06
2016/17	95.88	89.63	43,027	100.0	43,027	448.75	40,222.35	480.04	2,804.65	6.52	2,804.65	6.97
2017/18	97.84	90.67	42,229	121.4	34,785	355.54	32,237.92	383.63	2,547.09	7.32	3,092.16	7.90
2018/19	99.79	91.68	48,232	138.0	34,951	350.25	32,110.04	381.24	2,840.69	8.13	3,920.15	8.85
2019/20	101.72	92.64	63,387	156.8	40,425	397.42	36,815.31	436.39	3,610.07	8.93	5,660.60	9.81
Cumulative					423,841		405,047		18,794		20,066	

Sources: Original calculations based on, for column (1), UN World Population Prospects data and Spectrum DemProj model; for column (2) for 2007/08–2018/19, https://www.mof.gov.eg/; and for column (3) for 2019/20, planned budget, https://www.mof.gov.eg/.

Note: Cumulative forgone savings in public expenditure on [this sector] in 2008–20 is calculated as $\sum_{t=2008}^{t=2020} S_t$. Forgone savings in public expenditure on [this sector] in year t (S_t) = Real actual public expenditure on [this sector] – Real retrospective projections of public expenditure on [this sector] t for year t, where t = 2008–20.

a. World Bank estimation of GDP deflator, 2017 = 100.

TABLE C.3 **Costs and forgone savings of education, 2007/08–2019/20**

| | TOTAL POPULATION, MILLIONS | | INPUT DATA | | | CALCULATED FIGURES | | | | | | |
| | | | | | | | REAL RETROSPECTIVE PROJECTIONS OF PUBLIC EXPENDITURE ON EDUCATION | | FORGONE SAVINGS IN PUBLIC EXPENDITURE ON EDUCATION | | | |
YEAR	ACTUAL OUTCOME (1)	CONTINUED FERTILITY DECLINE SCENARIO (2)	ACTUAL PUBLIC EXPENDITURE ON EDUCATION (CURRENT PRICES, LE MILLIONS) (3)	GDP DEFLATOR: 2017 = 100 (4)[a]	REAL ACTUAL PUBLIC EXPENDITURE ON EDUCATION (CONSTANT PRICES, LE MILLIONS) (5 = 100* (3/4))	REAL PER CAPITA ACTUAL PUBLIC EXPENDITURE ON EDUCATION (CONSTANT LE) (6 = 1000* (5/1))	CONSTANT PRICES, LE MILLIONS (7 = 2*6)	PER CAPITA ACTUAL (CONSTANT PRICES LE) (8 = 1000* (5/2))	CONSTANT PRICES, LE MILLIONS (9 = 5-7)	% OF REAL ACTUAL PUBLIC EXPENDITURE ON EDUCATION (CONSTANT PRICES, LE MILLIONS) % (10 = 9/5)	CURRENT PRICES, LE MILLIONS (11 = 100* (9*4))	RETROSPECTIVE PROJECTIONS OF INCREASE IN REAL PER CAPITA PUBLIC EXPENDITURE ON EDUCATION, % (12 = 100* (8-6/6))
2007/08	33.33	33.34	33,678	35.3	95,405	2,862.44	95,433.72	2,861.58	−28.62	−0.03	−10.10	−0.03
2008/09	33.51	33.47	36,047	39.2	91,957	2,744.15	91,846.87	2,747.43	109.77	0.12	43.03	0.12
2009/10	33.66	33.58	44,946	43.2	104,042	3,090.96	103,794.39	3,098.32	247.28	0.24	106.82	0.24
2010/11	33.87	33.68	47,017	48.2	97,546	2,880.00	96,998.44	2,896.25	547.20	0.56	263.75	0.56
2011/12	34.08	33.75	56,409	57.6	97,932	2,873.60	96,984.00	2,901.70	948.29	0.97	546.21	0.98
2012/13	34.32	33.82	66,180	62.6	105,719	3,080.39	104,178.66	3,125.93	1,540.19	1.46	964.16	1.48
2013/14	34.63	33.88	84,066	69.6	120,784	3,487.86	118,168.59	3,565.07	2,615.89	2.17	1,820.66	2.21
2014/15	35.06	33.95	92,286	76.6	120,478	3,436.33	116,663.48	3,548.68	3,814.33	3.17	2,921.78	3.27
2015/16	35.63	34.02	96,545	81.3	118,752	3,332.91	113,385.55	3,490.64	5,365.98	4.52	4,362.54	4.73
2016/17	36.34	34.10	103,683	100.0	103,683	2,853.14	97,291.97	3,040.56	6,391.03	6.16	6,391.03	6.57
2017/18	37.11	34.17	109,188	121.4	89,941	2,423.62	82,815.24	2,632.15	7,125.45	7.92	8,650.30	8.60
2018/19	37.91	34.20	122,945	138.0	89,091	2,350.05	80,371.88	2,604.99	8,718.70	9.79	12,031.81	10.85
2019/20	38.71	34.21	132,038	156.8	84,208	2,175.35	74,418.82	2,461.50	9,789.09	11.62	15,349.29	13.15
Cumulative					**1,319,538**		**1,272,352**		**47,185**		**53,441**	

Source: Original calculations based on, for column (1), UN World Population Prospects data and Spectrum DemProj model; for column (2) for 2007/08–2018/19, https://www.mof.gov.eg/; and for column (3) for 2019/20, Planned Budget, https://www.mof.gov.eg/.

Note: Cumulative forgone savings in public expenditure on [this sector] in 2008–20 is calculated as $\sum_{t=2008}^{t=2020} St$. Forgone savings in public expenditure on [this sector] in year t (St) = Real actual public expenditure on [this sector] – Real retrospective projections of public expenditure on [this sector] t for year t, where t = 2008–20.

a. World Bank estimation of GDP deflator, 2017 = 100.

TABLE C.4 **Forgone savings in public expenditure on health, housing, and education, 2007/08–2019/20, LE millions**

YEAR	CONSTANT 2017 PRICES				CURRENT PRICES			
	HEALTH	HOUSING	EDUCATION	ALL 3 SECTORS	HEALTH	HOUSING	EDUCATION	ALL 3 SECTORS
2007/08	235.43	248.03	−28.62	454.84	83.11	87.55	−10.10	160.56
2008/09	320.59	339.57	109.77	769.93	125.67	133.11	43.03	301.81
2009/10	658.90	640.33	247.28	1,546.51	284.6	276.62	106.82	668.04
2010/11	800.31	511.23	547.20	1,858.74	385.75	246.41	263.75	895.91
2011/12	1,017.34	519.93	948.29	2,485.56	585.99	299.48	546.21	1,431.68
2012/13	1,399.69	638.13	1,540.19	3,578.01	876.21	399.47	964.16	2,239.84
2013/14	1,824.27	1,029.77	2,615.89	5,469.93	1,269.69	716.72	1,820.66	3,807.07
2014/15	2,389.70	1,312.01	3,814.33	7,516.04	1,830.51	1,005.00	2,921.78	5,757.29
2015/16	3,168.15	1,752.22	5,365.98	10,286.35	2,575.71	1,424.55	4,362.54	8,362.8
2016/17	3,527.92	2,804.65	6,391.03	12,723.6	3,527.92	2,804.65	6,391.03	12,723.6
2017/18	3,669.20	2,547.09	7,125.45	13,341.74	4,454.41	3,092.16	8,650.30	16,196.87
2018/19	4,303.20	2,840.69	8,718.70	15,862.59	5,938.41	3,920.15	12,031.81	21,890.37
2019/20	4,161.09	3,610.07	9,789.09	17,560.25	6,524.59	5,660.60	15,349.29	27,534.48
Cumulative	**27,478**	**18,794**	**47,185**	**93,457**	**28,463**	**20,066**	**53,441**	**101,970**

Sources: Original calculations based on UN World Population Prospects data and Spectrum DemProj model; for 2007/08–2018/19, on actual expenditures, https://www.mof.gov.eg/; and for 2019/20, on planned budget, https://www.mof.gov.eg/.

APPENDIX D

Methodology for Estimating Opportunity Costs for the Economy as a Whole

This analysis uses the data compiled by Cruz and Ahmed (2018), which consists of demographic data, country-specific geographic and governance data, and economic data. Their data set consists of quinquennial data for 180 countries for 1950–2010 across all global regions. Data sources include the UN World Population Prospects and the Penn World Table. Additionally, to quantify the opportunity cost of the reversal in the Arab Republic of Egypt's fertility decline for GDP and savings, population projections produced were also used. These data included detailed projections by age group in 2000–20 under two scenarios: the default scenario and a scenario that depicts the population structure resulting from a continuation of the fertility rate decline after 2010.

Theoretically, an increase in the share of the working-age population leads to higher GDP per capita growth, but showing this empirically is problematic because of potential endogeneity biases. Addressing these issues is particularly critical because changes in income per capita also affect fertility and migration decisions, in addition to health and thus mortality, further affecting the age structure of the economy. To deal with time-invariant unobservable factors that could simultaneously affect income and working-age population share, a panel fixed-effects estimation is used. Three specifications are tested: S1 uses no controls; S2 controls for human capital proxied by years of education, and initial GDP per capita controls for convergence; and S3 additionally controls for institutions, geography, population, and health.

$$g_y = \beta_0 + \beta_1 X + \beta_2 g_{ADR} + \beta_3 \left(g_{ADR} * EGY\right) + \varepsilon \qquad (1)$$

$$g_s = \beta_0 + \beta_1 X + \beta_2 g_{wpop} + \beta_3 \left(g_{wpop} * EGY\right) + \varepsilon \qquad (2)$$

Equations 1 and 2 show the basic relationship being modeled, where g_y and g_s are the growth rates of income and savings, respectively. X is a vector of control variables, and g_{ADR} and g_{wpop} are the growth rates of the dependency ratio and working-age share of population, respectively. EGY is a binary variable for Egypt.

After getting the regression results (tables D.1 and D.2), coefficients of interest that show the impact of a change in the demographic variables of interest on the economic variables of interest are taken with the projections to estimate the opportunity cost. In particular, β_2 and β_3 in equation 1 are added to estimate the impact of a 1 percentage point increase in the dependency ratio on the growth rate of GDP per capita (table D.1). Using 2020 population projections under the hypothetical scenario of a continued decline in fertility, the difference in the dependency ratio in 2019 is taken and multiplied by the sum of β_2 and β_3 to estimate the hypothetical growth rate associated with the hypothetical scenario. This growth rate is then used to estimate GDP per capita and forgone GDP. The same steps are applied for the savings rate.

TABLE D.1 **GDP regression results**

VARIABLES	S1	S2	S3
Total dependency ratio	−0.08**	−0.06*	−0.06*
	(0.04)	(0.03)	(0.03)
Total dependency ratio Egypt	0.11**	−0.19**	−0.31***
	(0.05)	(0.09)	(0.08)
Linear combination (Global effect + effect with indicator variable for Egypt)[a]	0.03	−0.25	−0.37
Constant	2.78***	26.31***	30.61***
	(0.28)	(5.37)	(4.68)
Observations	1,615	1,266	1,169

Note: Standard errors clustered at the country level are reported in parentheses.
*$p < .1$, **$p < .05$, ***$p < .01$.
Additional control variables include Institutions (British colony, French colony, Noncolony); Geography (Landlocked, Latitude), Population size (Population size in the initial period 1950, population size in the final period 2010), and Health (Incidence of Malaria in 1994).
a. The linear combination is not part of the regression output. It is added to show the sum, which is used in the calculations and projections. Taking the third specification, S3, a 1 percentage point increase in the dependency ratio decreases GDP per capita growth by approximately 0.37 percentage points.

TABLE D.2 **Gross domestic savings regression results**

VARIABLES	S1	S2	S3
Working-age population share	0.22	0.64**	0.65**
	(0.31)	(0.32)	(0.33)
Working-age population share Egypt	−−0.11	0.78**	0.79**
	(0.31)	(0.34)	(0.37)
Linear combination (Global effect + effect with indicator variable for Egypt)[a]	0.22	1.42	1.44
Constant	0.27	9.76***	9.85***
	(0.17)	(1.63)	(1.70)
Observations	1,520	1,197	1,196

Note: Standard errors clustered at the country level are reported in parentheses.
*$p < .1$, **$p < .05$, ***$p < .01$.
Additional control variables include Initial GDP, Years of schooling, and Regions.
a. The linear combination is not part of the regression output. It is added to show the sum, which is used in the calculations and projections.

REFERENCE

Cruz, Marcio, and S. Amer Ahmed. 2018. "On the Impact of Demographic Change on Economic Growth and Poverty." *World Development* 105: 95–106. https://ideas.repec.org/a/eee/wdevel /v105y2018icp95-106.html.

A Retrospective Analysis of Job Opportunities, 2007/08–2019/20

This appendix analyzes the amount of total public investment needed to create new job opportunities. Table E.1 shows real public investment at LE 796.4 billion in current prices versus LE 507.9 billion in constant prices in 2019/20 (2017 = 100). The cost of a job opportunity shows a trend toward "jobless growth," that is, growth with the same or lower levels of employment, because the increase in employment fluctuated and in several years was very small (in 2010/11 and from 2017/18) (table E.2).

The change in employment (actual outcome or continued decline scenario) shows a small fluctuating increase in new job opportunities in the period, assuming that the employment rate is the same in both scenarios, and ranges between 39 percent and 43 percent (table E.2).

To our surprise, the figures below show that only in the last three years, 2017/18–2019/20, is there a decline in the job opportunities required. These figures rely on official sources for new employment every year. Official figures show very high investment levels, in particular after 2015, and relatively low increases in employment.

Total real potential savings in total public investment needed to create new jobs is also small and reaches only LE 0.116 million (constant 2017 prices) in 2019/20, or LE 0.399 million in total over the last three years (figure E.1 and table E.3).[1] Figures E.1 and E.2 show forgone savings in total and public investments needed to create new job opportunities, in constant 2017 prices.

TABLE E.1 **Actual and real actual investment to create employment (total, public), 2007/08–2019/20**

YEAR	TOTAL ACTUAL INVESTMENT (CURRENT PRICES, LE BILLIONS) (1)	ACTUAL PUBLIC INVESTMENT (CURRENT PRICES, LE BILLIONS) (2)	GDP DEFLATOR: 2017 = 100 (3)[a]	REAL TOTAL ACTUAL INVESTMENT (CONSTANT 2017 PRICES, LE BILLIONS) (4)	REAL PUBLIC ACTUAL INVESTMENT (CONSTANT 2017 PRICES, LE BILLIONS) (5)	NEW JOBS (MILLIONS) CREATED $_t$ = EMPLOYMENT$_t$ − EMPLOYMENT$_{t-1}$ (6)	REAL PER JOB ACTUAL INVESTMENT (LE THOUSANDS, 2017 PRICES) (7)	REAL PER JOB ACTUAL PUBLIC INVESTMENT (LE THOUSANDS, 2017 PRICES) (8)
2007/08	199.53	65.43	35.30	565.25	185.37	0.39	1,438.31	471.67
2008/09	197.14	83.64	39.20	502.90	213.36	0.47	1,076.88	456.87
2009/10	231.83	105.13	43.20	536.64	243.35	0.85	628.38	284.95
2010/11	229.07	87.37	48.20	475.24	181.26	−0.48[b]	—	—
2011/12	246.07	92.57	57.60	427.20	160.71	0.25	1,708.81	642.83
2012/13	241.61	95.91	62.60	385.96	153.21	0.38	1,023.77	406.40
2013/14	265.09	110.49	69.60	380.88	158.75	0.33	1,168.34	486.97
2014/15	333.71	147.81	76.60	435.65	192.96	0.48	907.61	402.01
2015/16	392.04	181.44	81.30	482.21	223.17	0.55	873.57	404.30
2016/17	514.31	300.81	100.00	514.31	300.81	0.68	761.94	445.64
2017/18	721.13	470.43	121.40	594.01	387.50	0.02	39,600.64	25,833.48
2018/19	922.50	438.30	138.00	668.48	317.61	0.10	6,553.71	3,113.81
2019/20	796.40	473.80	156.80	507.91	302.17	0.10	4,960.04	2,950.86

Source: Original calculations based on https://www.idsc.gov.eg/IDSC/DMS/List.aspx for columns (1) and (2).

Note: Cumulative forgone savings in public investment required to create employment = $\sum_{t=2008}^{m=2020} St$.

Forgone savings in public investment required to create employment in year t (St) = Total real actual public investment required to create employment t − Total real retrospective projections of public investment required to create employment for year t, where t = 2007/08–2019/20.

Total real actual public investment to create employment t = Total real actual investment to create employment t * Percentage of public investment of total investment.

Total real retrospective projections of public investment required to create employment t = Total real retrospective projections of investment required to create employment t * Percentage of public investment in total investment.

New job opportunities t = Employment ^{t} − Employment $_{t-1}$.

Employment 2020 is not available; calculated as (Employment 2019 * Employment growth rate 2018/19). — = not available.

a. World Bank estimation of GDP deflator, 2017 = 100.

b. 2011 saw negative employment growth owing to exceptional political circumstances; thus 2011 is excluded from the analysis.

TABLE E.2 Change in employment (actual outcome and continued decline scenario), 2006/07–2019/20 (assuming the same employment rate as % of total population, 15+)

YEAR	EMPLOYMENT 15+ (MILLIONS - IDSC) (1)	POPULATION 15+ (MILLIONS, DEFAULT) (2)	EMPLOYMENT RATE (% OF POPULATION 15+) (3)a	NEW JOB OPPORTUNITIES (MILLIONS, DEFAULT) (4)b	POPULATION 15+ (MILLIONS, CONTINUED DECLINE) (5)	EMPLOYMENT 15+ (MILLIONS, CONTINUED DECLINE)—ASSUMING EMPLOYMENT RATE IS THE SAME (6)	NEW JOB OPPORTUNITIES (MILLIONS, CONTINUED DECLINE) (7)	NEW JOB OPPORTUNITIES (MILLIONS, DEFAULT) (8)	CHANGE IN NEW JOB OPPORTUNITIES REQUIRED (MILLIONS) (9)
2006/07	22.115	52.294	0.42	—	52.294	22.115	—	0.393	0
2007/08	22.508	53.448	0.42	0.393	53.448	22.508	0.393	0.467	0
2008/09	22.975	54.594	0.42	0.467	54.594	22.975	0.467	0.854	0
2009/10	23.829	55.739	0.43	0.854	55.739	23.829	0.854	−0.483	0
2010/11	23.346	56.890	0.41	−0.483	56.890	23.346	−0.483	0.25	0
2011/12	23.596	58.049	0.41	0.25	58.049	23.596	0.25	0.377	0
2012/13	23.973	59.215	0.40	0.377	59.215	23.973	0.377	0.326	0
2013/14	24.299	60.385	0.40	0.326	60.385	24.299	0.326	0.48	0
2014/15	24.779	61.557	0.40	0.48	61.557	24.779	0.48	0.552	−0.003
2015/16	25.331	62.706	0.40	0.552	62.713	25.334	0.555	0.675	−0.001
2016/17	26.006	63.866	0.41	0.675	63.876	26.010	0.676	0.015	0.005
2017/18	26.021	65.045	0.40	0.015	65.044	26.020	0.01	0.102	0.013
2018/19	26.123	66.252	0.39	0.102	66.215	26.109	0.089	0.1024	0.0234
2019/20	26.226	67.485	0.39	0.1024	67.386	26.188	0.079	0.393	0

Source: Original calculations based, on for column (1), https://www.idsc.gov.eg/IDSC/DMS/List.aspx; for column (2), UN World Population Prospects (population 15+).

Note: — = not available.

a. (1)/(2).

b. Calculated using column (1): New job opportunities in year t = Employment$_t$ − Employment$_{t-1}$.

TABLE E.3 **Total real possible savings in total public investment needed to create new job opportunities, 2017/18–2019/20**

YEAR	CHANGE IN NEW JOB OPPORTUNITIES REQUIRED (MILLIONS) (1)	REAL PER JOB ACTUAL INVESTMENT (LE THOUSANDS, CONSTANT 2017 PRICES) (2)	TOTAL REAL POSSIBLE SAVINGS IN TOTAL PUBLIC INVESTMENT NEEDED TO CREATE NEW JOB OPPORTUNITIES (2017/18–2019/20), CONSTANT 2017 PRICES, LE MILLIONS (3)
2017/18	0.005	39,600.64	0.198
2018/19	0.013	6,553.71	0.085
2019/20	0.0234	4,960.04	0.116
Total	0.0414		0.399

Sources: Original calculations based on https://www.idsc.gov.eg/IDSC/DMS/List.aspx; for 2017/18–2019/20, https://www.mof.gov.eg/; and for 2019/20, planned budget, https://www.mof.gov.eg/.

FIGURE E.1

Forgone savings in total investment needed to create new job opportunities, 2017/18–2019/20 (constant 2017 prices)

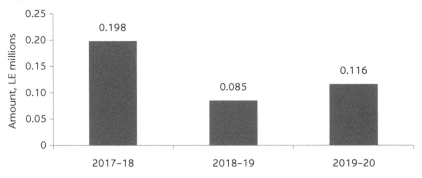

Source: Original calculations based on https://www.idsc.gov.eg/IDSC/DMS/List.aspx (in Arabic).

FIGURE E.2

Forgone savings in public investment needed to create new job opportunities, 2017/18–2019/20 (constant 2017 prices)

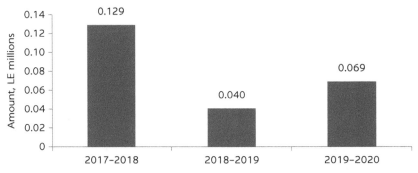

Source: Original calculations based on https://www.idsc.gov.eg/IDSC/DMS/List.aspx (in Arabic).

NOTE

1. These calculations rely on the figures in the official sources for new employment and investment values published every year. Official figures show very high investment levels, in particular after 2015, and relatively low increases in employment levels.

APPENDIX F

Population Projections, 2020–30

TABLE F.1 **TFR, population size, and dependency ratio, 2020–30**

YEAR	TFR			POPULATION SIZE			DEPENDENCY RATIO		
	DEFAULT	MODERATE DECLINE SCENARIO	ACCELERATED DECLINE SCENARIO	DEFAULT	MODERATE DECLINE SCENARIO	ACCELERATED DECLINE SCENARIO	DEFAULT	MODERATE DECLINE SCENARIO	ACCELERATED DECLINE SCENARIO
2020	3.26	3.26	3.26	102,416,696	102,416,696	102,416,696	0.648	0.648	0.648
2021	3.21	3.18	3.14	104,330,176	104,304,648	104,273,392	0.650	0.649	0.649
2022	3.17	3.10	3.02	106,220,696	106,143,520	106,052,008	0.651	0.649	0.648
2023	3.13	3.03	2.91	108,089,520	107,931,464	107,748,880	0.651	0.648	0.645
2024	3.10	2.95	2.79	109,938,968	109,667,760	109,360,912	0.649	0.645	0.640
2025	3.06	2.88	2.68	111,771,176	111,353,056	110,887,944	0.645	0.638	0.632
2026	3.03	2.80	2.56	113,589,920	112,989,320	112,331,032	0.637	0.629	0.619
2027	2.99	2.73	2.45	115,399,672	114,578,912	113,691,576	0.628	0.616	0.604
2028	2.96	2.65	2.33	117,204,568	116,123,528	114,970,528	0.617	0.602	0.586
2029	2.93	2.58	2.22	119,009,760	117,625,616	116,169,384	0.607	0.588	0.569
2030	2.90	2.50	2.10	120,822,416	119,089,200	117,291,384	0.597	0.574	0.550

Source: UN World Population Prospects data (for the default scenario), and original simulations (for the moderate and accelerated decline scenarios).

Projected Real Public Expenditure on Health, Housing, and Education, 2018/19–2029/30 (2017 = 100) and Projected Potential Savings

TABLE G.1 **Growth rates in per capita expenditure in health, housing, and education**

YEAR	REAL PER CAPITA ACTUAL HEALTH EXPENDITURE (CONSTANT LE)	REAL PER CAPITA ACTUAL HOUSING EXPENDITURE (CONSTANT LE)	REAL PER CAPITA ACTUAL EDUCATION EXPENDITURE (CONSTANT LE)
2007/08	469	494	2,862
2008/09	425	450	2,744
2009/10	486	570	3,091
2010/11	493	315	2,880
2011/12	453	231	2,874
2012/13	474	216	3,080
2013/14	491	277	3,488
2014/15	528	290	3,436
2015/16	590	326	3,333
2016/17	564	449	2,853
2017/18	512	356	2,424
2018/19	531	350	2,350
2019/20	458	397	2,175
Average growth (%)	2.25	8.39	4.91

Health column note: "Included in growth rate calculation" (spanning 2012/13–2016/17). Housing column note: "Included in growth rate calculation" (spanning 2014/15–2016/17). Education column note: "Included in growth rate calculation" (spanning 2010/11–2014/15).

Source: Original estimates based on, for 2007/08–2018/19, https://www.mof.gov.eg/; for 2019/20, planned budget.

TABLE G.2 **Projected real public expenditure on health, 2018/19–2029/30 (2017 = 100) and projected potential savings**

YEAR	REAL PER CAPITA PUBLIC EXPENDITURE ON HEALTH (LE)	PROJECTED REQUIRED REAL PUBLIC EXPENDITURE (LE MILLIONS)				PROJECTED POTENTIAL SAVINGS (LE MILLIONS)	
		DEFAULT	MODERATE DECLINE SCENARIO	ACCELERATED DECLINE SCENARIO		MODERATE DECLINE SCENARIO	ACCELERATED DECLINE SCENARIO
2018/19	530.58	n.a.	n.a.	n.a.		n.a.	n.a.
2019/20	542.52	55,563.75	55,563.75	55,563.75		0.00	0.00
2020/21	554.72	57,876.29	57,862.13	57,844.79		14.16	31.50
2021/22	567.21	60,251.77	60,207.99	60,156.08		43.78	95.69
2022/23	579.97	62,692.30	62,600.62	62,494.72		91.67	197.57
2023/24	593.02	65,200.69	65,039.84	64,857.86		160.84	342.82
2024/25	606.36	67,779.80	67,526.24	67,244.19		253.55	535.61
2025/26	620.00	70,433.65	70,061.23	69,653.05		372.41	780.60
2026/27	633.95	73,166.94	72,646.55	72,083.95		520.39	1,082.99
2027/28	648.22	75,984.46	75,283.61	74,536.12		700.85	1,448.34
2028/29	662.80	78,891.96	77,974.41	77,009.07		917.55	1,882.89
2029/30		81,896.93	80,722.10	79,503.49	Cumulative potential savings (2020–30)	1,174.82	2,393.44
Annual average growth rate (%)		3.96	3.81	3.65		4,250.03	8,791.44

Sources: For 2018/19, actual expenditures, and 2019/20, planned budget, https://www.mof.gov.eg/; all other years, World Bank estimates.
Note: The actual annual growth rate of the real per capita public expenditure on health during 2005–19 was 2.25 percent, which was used to calculate the growth rate of per capita expenditure starting from the actual real per capita public expenditure on health for 2018/19 through 2029/30 (see table G.1). n.a. = not applicable.

TABLE G.3 **Projected real public expenditure on housing, 2018/19–2029/30 (2017 = 100) and projected potential savings**

YEAR	REAL PER CAPITA PUBLIC HOUSING EXPENDITURE (LE)	PROJECTED REQUIRED REAL PUBLIC EXPENDITURE (LE MILLIONS)				PROJECTED POTENTIAL SAVINGS (LE MILLIONS)	
		DEFAULT	MODERATE DECLINE SCENARIO	ACCELERATED DECLINE SCENARIO		MODERATE DECLINE SCENARIO	ACCELERATED DECLINE SCENARIO
2018/19	350.25	n.a.	n.a.	n.a.		n.a.	n.a.
2019/20	379.64	38,881.50	38,881.50	38,881.50		0.00	0.00
2020/21	411.50	42,931.52	42,921.02	42,908.16		10.50	23.37
2021/22	446.03	47,377.22	47,342.80	47,301.98		34.42	75.24
2022/23	483.45	52,256.24	52,179.82	52,091.55		76.41	164.68
2023/24	524.02	57,610.32	57,468.20	57,307.41		142.12	302.91
2024/25	567.99	63,485.21	63,247.72	62,983.54		237.49	501.67
2025/26	615.65	69,932.11	69,562.35	69,157.07		369.76	775.04
2026/27	667.32	77,007.94	76,460.24	75,868.11		547.71	1,139.84
2027/28	723.31	84,775.35	83,993.42	83,159.44		781.93	1,615.91
2028/29	784.01	93,304.32	92,219.14	91,077.45		1,085.18	2,226.87
2029/30	849.79	10,2674.07	10,1201.19	99,673.42	Cumulative potential savings (2020–30)	1,472.88	3,000.65
Annual growth rate (%)		10.20	10.04	9.87		4,758.40	9,826.17

Sources: For 2018/19, actual expenditures, and 2019/20, planned budget, https://www.mof.gov.eg/; all other years, World Bank estimates.
Note: The actual annual growth rate of the real per capita public expenditure on housing during 2013–19 was 8.4 percent, which was used to calculate the growth rate of per capita expenditure starting from the actual real per capita public expenditure on housing for 2018/19 through 2029/30 (see table G.1). n.a. = not applicable.

TABLE G.4 **Projected real public expenditure on education, 2018/19–2029/30 (2017 = 100) and projected potential savings**

| YEAR | REAL PER CAPITA PUBLIC EDUCATION EXPENDITURE (LE) | REQUIRED REAL PUBLIC EXPENDITURE ON EDUCATION (LE MILLIONS) | | | | PROJECTED POTENTIAL SAVINGS (LE MILLIONS) | |
		DEFAULT	MODERATE DECLINE SCENARIO	ACCELERATED DECLINE SCENARIO		MODERATE DECLINE SCENARIO	ACCELERATED DECLINE SCENARIO
2018/19	2,350.06	n.a.	n.a.	n.a.		n.a.	n.a.
2019/20	2,465.52	96,717.53	96,717.53	96,717.53		0.00	0.00
2020/21	2,586.66	103,682.30	103,682.30	103,682.30		0.00	0.00
2021/22	2,713.75	111,069.26	111,069.26	111,069.26		0.00	0.00
2022/23	2,847.08	118,905.37	118,905.37	118,905.37		0.00	0.00
2023/24	2,986.97	127,221.42	127,221.42	127,221.42		0.00	0.00
2024/25	3,133.72	136,035.35	136,035.35	136,035.35		0.00	0.00
2025/26	3,287.69	145,274.35	145,190.85	145,088.61		83.49	185.73
2026/27	3,449.22	155,018.78	154,753.76	154,439.53		265.01	579.25
2027/28	3,618.69	165,247.96	164,678.26	164,020.11		569.70	1,227.84
2028/29	3,796.48	175,954.02	174,928.02	173,767.15		1,026.01	2,186.88
2029/30	3,983.01	187,153.43	185,493.38	183,646.71	Cumulative potential savings	1,660.05	3,506.72
Annual growth rate (%)		6.82	6.73	6.62		3,604.26	7,686.42

Sources: For 2018/19, actual expenditures, and 2019/20, planned budget, https://www.mof.gov.eg/; all other years, World Bank estimates.
Note: The actual annual growth rate of the real per capita public expenditure on education during 2009–14 was 4.91 percent, which was used to calculate the growth rate of per capita expenditure starting from the actual real per capita public expenditure on education for 2018/19 through 2029/30 (see table G.1). n.a. = not applicable.

Applying Model Estimates to Quantify the Potential Gain in Income by 2030 under Two Fertility Scenarios

The population projections are used to estimate the difference in the dependency ratio and the difference in population annually between 2020 and 2030. Regression coefficients are used to estimate the impact of changes in the dependency ratio on GDP per capita growth rates, which are then used to estimate GDP per capita and respective GDP values through multiplying by the projected population sizes.

The coefficients of interest (see table D.1) are further used with the projections through 2030 to estimate the potential gain in income, using projected changes in per capita income under different fertility scenarios. Similar to estimating the opportunity cost through 2020, β_2 and β_3 in equation 1 in appendix D are added to estimate the impact of a 1 percentage point change in the dependency ratio on the growth rate of GDP per capita. Differences in the dependency ratio for each year are calculated and multiplied by the sum of β_2 and β_3, yielding the annual GDP per capita growth rate under the hypothetical scenarios. These growth rates are then used to estimate GDP per capita for each year under each hypothetical scenario, as well as under a constant growth scenario. GDP per capita is then multiplied by the population under each scenario to yield projected GDP for each year. The total potential gain is then summed over the years, yielding the cumulative potential gain.

Different specifications are used to show the impact of different policy effects and to ensure robustness. Six different estimations are done using two fertility scenarios and three different growth rates for baseline results. Projections are done to estimate the potential gain under a fertility rate decline to 2.5 and a fertility rate decline to 2.1. To ensure results are not driven by the high growth rate in GDP per capita, which was based on the 2019 value of 3.5 percent as reported in the World Development Indicators database, each of the estimations is repeated using a 2.5 percent growth rate and a 2.0 percent growth rate. Only the results yielded using the 3.5 and 3.0 percent growth rates are shown.

TABLE H.1 **Detailed GDP projections with 3.5 percent constant growth and a TFR of 2.5**

YEAR	DEFAULT DEPENDENCY RATIO	DEPENDENCY RATIO WITH FERTILITY DECLINE	DIFFERENCE IN GROWTH RATE ATTRIBUTED TO DEPENDENCY RATIO	GROWTH RATE + DIFFERENCE	GDP PER CAPITA WITH CONSTANT GROWTH (LE)	GDP PER CAPITA WITH POPULATION EFFECTS (LE)	GDP WITH CONSTANT GROWTH (LE)	GDP WITH POPULATION EFFECTS (LE)	DIFFERENCE (LE)
2020	0.65	0.65	0.00	1.035	39,771	39,771	4,073,192,429,829	4,073,192,429,829	0
2021	0.65	0.65	0.00	1.035	41,163	41,163	4,294,518,288,248	4,293,467,485,239	−1,050,803,009
2022	0.65	0.65	0.00	1.035	42,603	42,603	4,525,369,120,599	4,522,081,156,009	−3,287,964,591
2023	0.65	0.65	0.00	1.035	44,095	44,095	4,766,162,050,292	4,759,192,637,263	−6,969,413,029
2024	0.65	0.64	0.37	1.039	45,801	45,638	5,017,382,628,116	5,022,897,556,359	5,514,928,243
2025	0.64	0.64	0.00	1.035	47,404	47,235	5,279,535,762,734	5,278,588,872,665	−946,890,068
2026	0.64	0.63	0.37	1.039	49,239	48,888	5,553,235,088,968	5,563,437,635,298	10,202,546,330
2027	0.63	0.62	0.37	1.039	51,144	50,600	5,839,170,945,618	5,860,041,002,645	20,870,057,027
2028	0.62	0.60	0.74	1.042	53,313	52,371	6,138,065,287,957	6,190,854,330,987	52,789,043,030
2029	0.61	0.59	0.74	1.042	55,573	54,203	6,450,745,294,088	6,536,822,268,686	86,076,974,598
2030	0.60	0.57	1.11	1.046	58,135	56,101	6,778,212,505,701	6,923,255,288,213	145,042,782,513
									308,241,261,043

Cumulative potential gain in GDP with a fertility decline from 2.9 to 2.5.

Sources: Original calculations; World Development Indicators database.

TABLE H.2 **Detailed GDP projections with 3.5 percent constant growth and a TFR of 2.1**

YEAR	DEFAULT DEPENDENCY RATIO	DEPENDENCY RATIO WITH FERTILITY DECLINE	DIFFERENCE IN GROWTH RATE ATTRIBUTED TO DEPENDENCY RATIO	GROWTH RATE + DIFFERENCE	GDP PER CAPITA WITH CONSTANT GROWTH (LE)	GDP PER CAPITA WITH POPULATION EFFECTS (LE)	GDP WITH CONSTANT GROWTH (LE)	GDP WITH POPULATION EFFECTS (LE)	DIFFERENCE (LE)
2020	0.65	0.65	0.00	1.035	39,771	39,771	4,073,192,429,829	4,073,192,429,829	0
2021	0.65	0.65	0.00	1.035	41,163	41,163	4,294,518,288,248	4,292,180,901,925	−2,337,386,323
2022	0.65	0.65	0.00	1.035	42,603	42,603	4,525,369,120,599	4,518,182,428,222	−7,186,692,377
2023	0.65	0.65	0.00	1.035	44,095	44,095	4,766,162,050,292	4,751,141,672,361	−15,020,377,931
2024	0.65	0.64	0.37	1.039	45,638	45,801	5,017,382,628,116	5,008,843,598,574	−8,539,029,542
2025	0.64	0.63	0.37	1.039	47,235	47,574	5,279,535,762,734	5,275,332,165,509	−4,203,597,225
2026	0.64	0.62	0.74	1.042	48,888	49,591	5,553,235,088,968	5,570,569,934,648	17,334,845,679
2027	0.63	0.60	1.11	1.046	50,600	51,877	5,839,170,945,618	5,897,953,862,205	58,782,916,587
2028	0.62	0.59	1.11	1.046	52,371	54,268	6,138,065,287,957	6,239,256,097,115	101,190,809,157
2029	0.61	0.57	1.48	1.050	54,203	56,971	6,450,745,294,088	6,618,270,920,558	167,525,626,470
2030	0.60	0.55	1.85	1.054	56,101	60,019	6,778,212,505,701	7,039,689,521,837	261,477,016,136

Cumulative potential gain in GDP with a fertility decline from 2.9 to 2.1   569,024,130,633

Sources: Original calculations; World Development Indicators database.

TABLE H.3 Detailed GDP projections with 2.5 percent constant growth and a TFR of 2.5

YEAR	DEFAULT DEPENDENCY RATIO	DEPENDENCY RATIO WITH FERTILITY DECLINE	DIFFERENCE IN GROWTH RATE ATTRIBUTED TO DEPENDENCY RATIO	GROWTH RATE + DIFFERENCE	GDP PER CAPITA WITH CONSTANT GROWTH (LE)	GDP PER CAPITA WITH POPULATION EFFECTS (LE)	GDP WITH CONSTANT GROWTH (LE)	GDP WITH POPULATION EFFECTS (LE)	DIFFERENCE (LE)
2020	0.65	0.65	0.00	1	39,387	39,387	4,033,837,913,599	4,033,837,913,599	0
2021	0.65	0.65	0.00	1	40,371	40,371	4,211,933,325,483	4,210,902,729,752	−1,030,595,730
2022	0.65	0.65	0.00	1	41,380	41,380	4,395,462,263,687	4,392,268,684,578	−3,193,579,109
2023	0.65	0.65	0.00	1	42,415	42,415	4,584,614,955,042	4,577,911,012,779	−6,703,942,263
2024	0.65	0.64	0.37	1	43,475	43,632	4,779,635,738,558	4,785,055,631,397	5,419,892,840
2025	0.64	0.64	0.00	1	44,562	44,723	4,980,773,923,892	4,980,053,681,030	−720,242,862
2026	0.64	0.63	0.37	1	45,676	46,007	5,188,366,760,512	5,198,260,249,003	9,893,488,491
2027	0.63	0.62	0.37	1	46,818	47,327	5,402,805,265,980	5,422,681,005,848	19,875,739,867
2028	0.62	0.60	0.74	1	47,989	48,860	5,624,489,934,573	5,673,846,485,340	49,356,550,766
2029	0.61	0.59	0.74	1	49,188	50,444	5,853,896,643,063	5,933,449,712,416	79,553,069,353
2030	0.60	0.57	1.11	1	50,418	52,265	6,091,634,701,346	6,224,140,773,312	132,506,071,966
Cumulative potential gain in GDP with a fertility decline from 2.9 to 2.5.									284,956,453,319

Sources: Original calculations; World Development Indicators database.

TABLE H.4 **Detailed GDP projections with 2.5 percent constant growth and a TFR of 2.1**

YEAR	DEFAULT DEPENDENCY RATIO	DEPENDENCY RATIO WITH FERTILITY DECLINE	DIFFERENCE IN GROWTH RATE ATTRIBUTED TO DEPENDENCY RATIO	GROWTH RATE + DIFFERENCE	GDP PER CAPITA WITH CONSTANT GROWTH (LE)	GDP PER CAPITA WITH POPULATION EFFECTS (LE)	GDP WITH CONSTANT GROWTH (LE)	GDP WITH POPULATION EFFECTS (LE)	DIFFERENCE (LE)
2020	0.65	0.65	0.000	1.0250	39,387	39,387	4,033,837,913,599	4,033,837,913,599	0
2021	0.65	0.65	0.000	1.0250	40,371	40,371	4,211,933,325,483	4,209,640,887,848	−2,292,437,635
2022	0.65	0.65	0.000	1.0250	41,380	41,380	4,395,462,263,687	4,388,481,875,060	−6,980,388,627
2023	0.65	0.65	0.000	1.0250	42,415	42,415	4,584,614,955,042	4,570,166,715,857	−14,448,239,184
2024	0.65	0.64	0.370	1.0287	43,475	43,632	4,779,635,738,558	4,771,667,150,130	−7,968,588,427
2025	0.64	0.63	0.370	1.0287	44,562	44,885	4,980,773,923,892	4,977,154,122,988	−3,619,800,904
2026	0.64	0.62	0.740	1.0324	45,676	46,339	5,188,366,760,512	5,205,284,878,325	16,918,117,813
2027	0.63	0.60	1.110	1.0361	46,818	48,012	5,402,805,265,980	5,458,517,594,126	55,712,328,146
2028	0.62	0.59	1.110	1.0361	47,989	49,745	5,624,489,934,573	5,719,191,351,127	94,701,416,554
2029	0.61	0.57	1.480	1.0398	49,188	51,725	5,853,896,643,063	6,008,825,624,431	154,928,981,368
2030	0.60	0.55	1.850	1.0435	50,418	53,975	6,091,634,701,346	6,330,769,170,734	239,134,469,388

Cumulative potential gain in GDP with a fertility decline from 2.9 to 2.1.   526,085,858,490

Sources: Original calculations; World Development Indicators database.